Hardy Gingers

Hardy Gingers

including
Hedychium, *Roscoea*, and *Zingiber*

T. M. E. Branney

Foreword by Tony Schilling

Timber Press
Portland • London

ROYAL HORTICULTURAL SOCIETY

Published in association with the Royal Horticultural Society in 2005 by
Timber Press, Inc.

The Haseltine Building
133 S.W. Second Avenue, Suite 450
Portland, Oregon 97204-3527
www.timberpress.com

2 The Quadrant
135 Salusbury Road
London NW6 6RJ
www.timberpress.co.uk

Design by Dick Malt
ISBN 978-1-60469-173-3

The Library of Congress has cataloged the hardcover edition as follows:

Branney, T. M. E. (Tim M. E.)
  Hardy gingers : including Hedychium, Roscoea, and Zingiber / T.M.E.
Branney ; foreword by Tony Schilling.
     p. cm. – (Royal Horticultural Society plant collector guide)
  Includes bibliographical references and index.
  ISBN 0-88192-677-9 (hardback)
  1. Ginger. I. Title. II. Series.
  SB304.G5B73 2005
  633.8'3–dc22   2004017198

A catalogue record for this book is also available from the British Library.

Contents

Foreword

When I was invited to write this foreword to Tim Branney's guide to hardy gingers, I readily agreed as I am, and have been for fifty years, an incurable fan of this fascinating group of plants.

This long overdue book is both comprehensive in content and exceptionally well researched. The text has both depth and breadth. It is also scholarly, erudite, educational, and anecdotal.

The author states that gingers were all but gone from Western cultivation by the mid-twentieth century and asserts that their current popularity can probably be traced to the introduction of *Hedychium densiflorum* 'Assam Orange'. By testing this particular ginger for hardiness at Wakehurst Place (and later exhibiting it at a Royal Horticulture Society show), I was apparently responsible for opening the floodgates which caused entries in the *RHS Plant Finder* to rise from zero in 1981 to eighty-six in 2003–04.

My interests in this group of plants accelerated dramatically in 1965 when I was sent to Nepal from Kew to advise on the development of a national botanical garden on the edge of the Kathmandu Valley. Within my two-year contract I was able to plant hunt as well as advise, and it was during that time that I was fortunate to discover and introduce such botanical treasures as *Hedychium* 'Tara' and *H. densiflorum* 'Stephen'—named for my daughter and son, respectively. My collection of *H. thyrsiforme* was another fortuitous event as it apparently represented a reintroduction of this distinctive species which, although originally brought into our gardens in 1802, had over the years been lost to cultivation.

During my many years at Wakehurst Place I encouraged others to share my passion for things zingiberaceous. Because of this I can state with modest pleasure that 'Tara' and 'Stephen' (plus others) now flourish in far-flung corners of the globe including the Royal Botanic Gardens Melbourne (Victoria, Australia), the University of British Columbia Botanical Garden

(Vancouver), and Hawaii. It is a well-known fact that the best way to establish a plant and ensure it a permanent niche in cultivation is to share it with others. More than twenty years ago when I wrote that gingers were "overlooked and underappreciated", little did I believe that a revival of interest would occur so relatively quickly or to such a degree. Nevertheless, here we are today at the beginning of the twenty-first century with access to hundreds of ornamental gingers; thanks largely to the enthusiasm of North American and Japanese hybridists, the numbers continue to grow apace.

I first admired flowering plants of *Roscoea purpurea* and *Hedychium gardnerianum* while serving as a horticultural student at the Cambridge University Botanic Garden. Little did I realize at that time that I would one day see and collect them for myself in the monsoon forests of Nepal. Sheets of *Roscoea* as common as bluebells in a Sussex woodland, the gardenia-like heavy evening scent of *H. coronarium* in a Kathmandu palace garden, the greater cardamon (*Amomum subulatum*) luxuriating within the shade of Nepalese alders and alpinias in the tropical humidity of beautiful Bali were all experiences to savour. I even managed on one occasion to collect seeds of *Costus speciosus* from the back of a female Indian elephant (courtesy of her trunk!) in the Nepalese Terai. As Tim Branney so aptly states, "Every plant has its own story to tell".

Tony Schilling, V.M.H.

Acknowledgements

I would particularly like to thank Edward Needham for a vividly memorable day spent in his magnificent garden, discussing and photographing his plants while musing on their origins and relationships to one another. Thanks also to Eddie Mole for showing me around his NCCPG collection of *Hedychium* at Bristol Zoological Gardens, and to Lyn Spencer-Mills for sharing her thoughts and experiences of that same genus.

Thanks to Tony Avent (Plant Delights Nursery, Raleigh, North Carolina), Linda B. Gay (Mercer Arboretum and Botanic Gardens, Humble, Texas), and Robert Lee Riffle (Houston, Texas) for use of their photos, and to Nigel Rowland (Long-Acre Plants, Charlton Musgrove, Somerset) for his guidance on new forms of *Roscoea*.

Special thanks go to Tony Schilling for his support and, in kindly writing his foreword, lending an air of experience and authority to my book.

Finally, thanks must go to my commissioning editor, Anna Mumford, for her patience and encouragement, and to my editor, Linda J. Willms, for her great enthusiasm, efficiency, and networking skills.

Introduction to Gingers

Mention the word "ginger" to most Western non-gardeners, and even a number who do regularly cultivate their plots, and the familiar culinary root ginger, *Zingiber officinale*, is immediately summoned up as the one and only representative of the family *Zingiberaceae*. Yet the *Zingiberaceae* and the closely related *Costaceae*, which together comprise the gingers, form one of the largest groups of flowering plants in the world, with approximately 1400 species, and counting.

The word "ginger" is an Anglicized version of the Latin "zinziber", although that name itself has a disputed origin. Some believe it to be derived from the Sanskrit "shrngavera", meaning "horn-body", a reference to the hornlike appearance of the rhizomes of the culinary ginger. Others see it as deriving from the Malayan word "inchi-ver", "inchi" meaning "root". In either case, the origins of the name and its associations go deep into human history. There are an astounding 118 different words for the plant we know as culinary ginger, in languages as diverse as Icelandic, Hebrew, Swahili, and Malay, a testament to the cultural importance of the plant the world over.

Indeed, as a group the gingers have a powerful and long-standing relationship with mankind. *Zingiber officinale* has been cultivated for at least 2000 years and is included in Roman texts on cookery and farming from the second century BC. It has long been a prized spice. A ginger with an even longer history of use as a spice is turmeric, derived from the rhizomes of *Curcuma longa*, and with recorded use dating back nearly 4000 years to the Indian Vedic culture. But these two species are merely the best known of a truly vast array of medicinal, herbal, folkloric, and edible uses to which the family has been put. These uses would (and hopefully one day will) constitute a book in themselves.

In this present volume our primary concern lies elsewhere, for gingers are also an exceedingly ornamental group of plants, ranging from the small, ground-hugging species of *Kaempferia* with their often gorgeously patterned foliage, to the alpine *Roscoea*, the richly evocative *Hedychium*, the towering *Alpinia*, and the tropical *Etlingera*. Many gingers have flamboyant, intricately constructed, and sometimes beautifully perfumed flowers that come in a comprehensive rainbow of colours. Some even follow their floral display with startling seedpods of scarlet and tangerine, and many gingers can be appreciated for their lush foliage.

Most gingers originate in the tropics and thus are strictly the domain of the hot-house gardener, but a significant number come from temperate zones or high altitudes in the Himalayas and China. Still others have a natural growth habit that can be adapted to allow them to be cultivated in temperate gardens. It is these hardy or adaptable plants that form the subject of this book.

Gingers were once the height of gardening fashion. No respectable Victorian glasshouse would have been without at least a modest collection. Their fall from grace was both swift and ignominious, as the increasing cost of heating spelled the end of most tropical plant collections. Gingers were shunted out of many of the glasshouses that remained in favour of smaller, more constantly floriferous (I would be temped to say less aristocratic) subjects. The recent rise in interest in tropical-style planting in both Europe and North America has brought the hardy gingers into the full glare of horticultural fashion as never before. Many nurseries have sprung up to cater for this demand, offering an exciting range of beautiful plants.

But fashions in horticulture, as in other walks of life, are notoriously fickle masters, and I fervently hope that, having grabbed the stage, the gingers are now here to stay. The key to their long-term horticultural future surely lies in their diversity. Certainly, many gingers do make fantastic accents in tropical-style plantings, but others can look equally impressive and be equally successful in traditional English borders, and still others in woodland gardens, or rock gardens, or among shrubs, or beneath trees or even in water gardens.

In writing this book I have become hugely aware that the story of gingers is also the story of people. This story begins with the plants' earliest uses as spices and in ceremonial and medicinal contexts, and goes through to the founding of the family *Scitamineae* by Carl Linnaeus in 1764, from which was born the *Zingiberaceae* courtesy of John Lindley in 1835, to the dedication of William Roscoe, who was responsible for classifying and introducing many species in the 1800s. Today the story continues with the introductions and enthusiasm of Tony Schilling in the 1970s and 1980s, the modern-day hybridization programmes of Tom Wood, together with the passion of nurserymen like Tim Chapman who seek to introduce thrilling new species and push the boundaries of what is growable, and the research of W. John Kress and others who seek to reveal the relationships between the gingers. Every plant in this book has its own story to tell, but those stories can only be learned because of the people associated with them.

Chapter 1
Botany

Classification

Gingers are members of the order *Zingiberales*, where they are close relatives of familiar plants in the genera *Musa* (bananas), *Heliconia*, *Canna*, and *Maranta*. The gingers are contained within the superfamily *Zingiberariae*, which is comprised of two families, the *Zingiberaceae* and the *Costaceae*. Until the creation of this superfamily by W. John Kress in 1990, all ginger species were considered part of the family *Zingiberaceae*; however, most botanists now agree that the genera *Costus, Dimerocostus, Monocostus,* and *Tapeinochilos* constitute a separate family known as the *Costaceae*.

Order *Zingiberales*
    Family *Musaceae*
    Family *Strelitziaceae*
    Family *Lowiaceae*
    Family *Heliconiaceae*
    Superfamily *Zingiberariae*: Family *Zingiberaceae*, Family *Costaceae*
    Superfamily *Cannariae*: Family *Marantaceae*, Family *Cannaceae*

Family *Zingiberaceae*

The *Zingiberaceae* are a family of approximately 1300 species divided among 50 genera. They are found throughout the tropical and subtropical world, with their primary populations and species diversity centred on southern and Southeast Asia.

Along with *Cannaceae* and *Marantaceae*, all members of the *Zingiberaceae* and the *Costaceae* are monandrian plants, meaning that each flower possesses only one true stamen, the remaining stamens having developed into the (generally) petal-like lateral staminodes. This arrangement marks the gingers as being more advanced in an evolutionary sense than the related five-stamen families (*Musaceae, Lowiaceae, Heliconiaceae, Strelitziaceae*) from which they have diverged.

W. John Kress, Linda Prince, and Kyle Williams published a new classification for the family *Zingiberaceae* in 2002 in the *American Journal of Botany*. Based upon recent phylogenetic research coupled with morphological and chemotaxonomic analysis, their classification offers the most accurate and refined arrangement of the relationships within the family. The genera are listed here, broadly in order of their closeness to one another:

Subfamily: *Siphonochiloideae*
  Tribe: *Siphonochileae*
    Genus: *Siphonochilus*
Subfamily: *Tamijioideae*
  Tribe: *Tamijioideae*
    Genus: *Tamijia*
Subfamily: *Alpinioideae*
  Tribe: *Alpinieae*
    Genera: *Aulotandra, Afromomum, Renealmia, Elettaria, Leptosolena, Geostachys, Geocharis, Cypostigma, Amomum, Paramomum, Elettariopsis, Alpinia, Plagiostachys, Vanoverberghia, Etlingera, Hornstedtia, Siliquamomum*
  Tribe: *Riedelieae*
    Genera: *Burbidgea, Pleuranthodium, Riedelia, Siamanthus*
Subfamily: *Zingiberoideae*
  Tribe: *Zingibereae*
    Genera: *Curcuma, Smithatris, Hitchenia, Stahlianthus, Paracautleya, Laosanthus, Camptandra, Pyrgophyllum, Hedychium, Rhynchanthus, Pommereschea, Stadiochilus, Nanochilus, Cautleya, Roscoea, Haniffera, Boesenbergia, Curcumorpha, Kaempferia, Haplochorema, Zingiber, Distichochlamys, Scaphochlamys, Cornukaempferia, Parakaempferia, Caulokaempferia.*
  Tribe: *Globbeae*
    Genera: *Globba* (incorporating *Mantisia*), *Gagnepainia, Hemiorchis*

Family *Costaceae*

The *Costaceae* comprise approximately 120 species in four genera that are primarily native to the tropical regions of South America (where they replace the *Zingiberaceae*), Africa, and Southeast Asia. Botanically they are separated from the *Zingiberaceae* in three ways. First, the *Costaceae* have leaves that are held in a spiral upon the stem, where in *Zingiberaceae* the leaves are always held distichously—in two vertical rows on opposing sides of the stem. Second, in *Costaceae* all the staminodes (modified stamens) are fused into the labellum, where in *Zingiberaceae* only the inner staminodes are fused into the labellum, with the outer pair remaining visible, often as petal-like structures. Finally, the *Costaceae* lack the aromatic essential oils that are present in all of the *Zingiberaceae*. A fourth supposed distinction, involving the arrangement of the leaf sheaths, has proven to be inconsistent and unreliable.

In 1995 the findings of research undertaken (at the National Museum of Natural History of the Smithsonian Institute) to establish the relationships of the four genera within the newly recognized family of *Costaceae* were published. After examination of material from both living and preserved plants, using methods of phylogenetic analysis, the following cladistic arrangement was discovered:

Basal genus: *Tepeinochilos*
    Main clade: *Costus, Dimerocostus, Monocostus*
      Terminal clade: *Dimerocostus, Monocostus*

This research showed that the two-chambered (bilocular) ovary (deemed an important character in the classification of the genera) has evolved independently in the genus *Tapeinochilos* and in the terminal clade genera of *Dimerocostus* and *Monocostus*. This is the first serious examination of the relationships within the *Costaceae* and I eagerly await the outcome of a project being undertaken by Chelsea D. Specht, which promises to be a full look into the systematics and evolution of the *Costaceae*.

Morphology

The gingers are a fairly diverse group of plants, but certain defining features unite them. An awareness of those aspects common to all will allow better appreciation of the plants, as well as aiding identification. Many different terms, some botanical, others more literal, have been used to describe the structures of the gingers, and further details are given under each genus description.

Rhizomes

All gingers grow from fleshy rhizomes, which are underground stems that have been modified for food storage. The shape and size of the rhizome varies considerably between genera, from the tough, forearm-thick structures of the largest *Hedychium* species to the slender, twiglike rhizomes of *Hemiorchis*. Several gingers have adapted to epiphytic growth, a trait further encouraged by the fact than many have rhizomes more-or-less at ground level, with branches often emerging above ground. When this happens the branches invariably colour deep green or brown, where their underground elements are typically white or pale fawn.

The rhizomes have a number of dormant growth buds along their surface. The buds nearest the surface will form the upright leafy shoots, while the lower buds will branch to form new rhizomes. Gingers with a spreading growth habit tend to branch regularly, and their rhizomes form into a sympodium, meaning "branched foot". Under ideal growth conditions such species can colonize an area (large or small) to the exclusion of most other plants, as the rhizomes interlock at ground level to prevent external competition.

The roots of gingers issue forth from the rhizomes, and some members of the family *Zingiberaceae* develop tubers towards the ends of these roots. The tubers are invariably located much deeper into the ground (particularly so in genus *Siphonochilus*), and represent an additional food storage system that is removed from the surface hazards of climate and predation.

The rhizomes of the *Costaceae* are not aromatic, but those of most members of the *Zingiberaceae* are, to one degree or another, noticeably "gingery", or sometimes "lemony" in odour. Some are also brightly coloured orange or yellow when cut.

Stems and Leaves

The apparent "stems" on most ginger plants in the *Zingiberaceae* are not stems at all, Instead, they are elongated sheaths from which the leaves appear. These sheaths form an interlinking structure known as a pseudostem. It is the pseudostem that creates the height of most members of the family. The true stems are generally very short and entirely basal.

The modified leaves at the base of the pseudostem often consist of nothing but a sheath, and are adapted to maintain the strength of the structure above them. Further up the pseudostems, the true leaves (that is, those with blades) occur, and these are arranged distichously (in two vertical rows on opposite sides of the stem). Each leaf sheath ends in a membranous outgrowth known as a ligule from which the petiole (leaf stalk) emerges to bear the leaf blade itself. Some species do not have any petiole to speak of and the blade is attached directly to the sheath.

The leaves of gingers in the family *Zingiberaceae* are often lanceolate, as for example in *Roscoea*, but can also be ovate or nearly circular, as in *Kaempferia*. In most leaves the midvein is very prominent and sometimes differently coloured to the main blade. In *Curcuma* species all the leaf veins are raised and create a ribbed effect across the leaf surface. The leaf edges of all members of the *Zingiberaceae* are unbroken, although some have undulating margins. Gingers may have glabrous (hairless) foliage or have stems and leaves with slight or occasionally dense pubescence. Variegated leaves are relatively rare in the family, although some cultivars have leaves marked with white or cream. More frequent are those plants with red, bronze, or silvery pigments, either on the stems or arranged in interveinal patterns across the leaf surface.

The *Costaceae* differ from the *Zingiberaceae* in that they produce true stems, rather than pseudostems, and their leaves are, as previously mentioned, arranged in a characteristic spiral along the length of those stems. The stems often form loose spirals too, and are characteristically kinked at random points along their length. Also, unlike the *Zingiberaceae*, the *Costaceae* often have branched stems with the branches emerging through the base of the leaf sheaths. The leaves are generally elliptic to ovate and may also be glabrous or pubescent, always with unbroken margins.

Flowers

While the *Costaceae* have relatively homogenous flowers, the *Zingiberaceae*, at first glance, have a considerable range of floral diversity. Closer examination, however, shows the diversity to be variations on the same floral structure. The inflorescence takes the form of a spike and may be produced either terminally (at the top of the pseudostems that bear the leaves) or, as is often the case, radically (on a flowering stalk that grows from a separate bud on the rhizome, and which emerges independently, either before or after the leafy stem). Those plants that produce their inflorescence terminally have an extended flowering stalk, known as a peduncle, which bears a series of ovate bracts. Each bract holds a "partial inflorescence" which can comprise one to several individual flowers. Gingers that flower radically either bear their inflorescences on peduncles, or, in the case of many *Amomum* and some *Zingiber* species, open entirely at ground level from the uppermost portion of the rhizome. Occasionally species can produce inflorescences both terminally and radically, generally in two separate flowering seasons. Some *Curcuma* species bear an inflorescence that bursts through the base of the leaf sheaths, to emerge parallel to the pseudostems.

From a horticultural perspective the bracts can vary considerably. In *Kaempferia* species they are reduced, brown or green, and play no ornamental role, but in *Curcuma* and *Zingiber* they are typically brightly coloured and form the showiest part of the inflorescence. In all cases the bracts are arranged around a main flowering stem, or rachis, generally in a spiral fashion, often overlapping and tightly clasped to one another. In many *Zingiber* and some *Hedychium* species, the bracts amalgamate into a solid pinecone shape. In *Roscoea* they are often partially concealed, and in *Curcuma* and other *Zingiber* species they form pouches in which the flowers are seated.

Aside from the flowers of *Siphonochilus* species, the individual flowers of gingers are bisexual, with the male and female organs located together at the tip of the stamen. The calyx is thin and tubular, and splits on one side to allow the corolla to emerge. The corolla has a tubular "stem" and three lobes that open to form the true petals, with the upper (dorsal) lobe typically larger than the lower pair. Again, in some gingers, such as *Hedychium* species, the lobes are dwarfed by the rest of the flower and play no ornamental role, whereas in *Roscoea* and very differently in *Kaempferia rotunda*, they represent a large portion of the flower.

As the flower emerges the corolla lobes split open to reveal the labellum (lip) and the staminodes. In many gingers these structures appear to be the "petals" of the flower. They are in fact both formed from hugely modified stamens: the labellum is a fused amalgamation of the three central stamens, and the staminodes are a further lateral pair of stamens. For most gingers the labellum is the largest, showiest, and most colourful part of the flower. Frequently it is patterned with intricate veining and bright spotting to aid pollinators towards the reproductive organs. The labellum may consist of a single lobe, or it may be notched or deeply cleft to its base, creating the impression of two separate lobes, as in *Kaempferia*. In the family *Costaceae* the labellum often has three shallow lobes. The margin of the labellum in both the *Zingiberaceae* and the *Costaceae* may be crinkled, crisped, or look like tissue paper.

The staminodes of some members of the *Zingiberaceae* are petal-like. One example is the *Globba* flower. In other members of the *Zingiberaceae*, primarily in the tribes *Alpinieae* and *Zingibereae*, the staminodes are absent or reduced to small teeth. In the *Costaceae* all of the five peripheral stamens are amalgamated into the showy labellum.

The single remaining stamen (not included in the labellum or lateral staminodes) may be slender and held on a hugely exerted filament, as in many *Hedychium* species, or thick and shorter than the labellum, as in *Zingiber*. In all cases the two-pouched (biloculed) anther is held at the end of the filament and generally releases pollen by means of two slits. In *Globba* the anther is often surrounded by distinctive appendages, while in other genera including *Zingiber* and *Kaempferia* the anther forms a thick central crest. The style is very thin and extends the length of the filament and along a groove between the anther locules to terminate in the stigma, which, in the *Costaceae*, often has appendages.

Little is known about the pollinators of most ginger flowers. Some *Costus* species have tubular flowers that hummingbirds are known to pollinate, and many *Hedychium* species are most powerfully fragrant in the evening, with moths having been observed as regular visitors. As with so many aspects of these plants much research remains to be done, particularly on plants growing in their native habitats.

Seeds

All gingers bear their seed within a capsule that may be dry and papery or thick and waxy. In the *Costaceae* there are either two or three distinct seed-bearing valves within the fruit. In the *Zingiberaceae* the chambers are less distinct and more amorphous.

The fruit of most gingers is smooth or slightly ridged externally, and typically green and inconspicuous until ripe. The capsules open either by splitting in three vertical sections (two sections in the biloculed members of the *Costaceae*) or merely by irregularly breaking up. The interior of *Hedychium* seed capsules is characteristically vivid orange, with the seeds held in a fleshy aril (a pulpy appendage that develops near the ovule). The seeds may be numerous or few, and are black, dark brown, or occasionally green. The aril can be brightly coloured red, orange, or white, and is also full of nutrients. In such species the entire arrangement is clearly designed as a major attractant for animals who might act as agents of dispersal for the seeds.

The precise methods of seed dispersal have rarely been documented. Recent studies with *Globba* revealed that numerous species of ants visited the capsules and transported seed back to their nests, although the brightly coloured arils and capsule interiors of other species have certainly evolved in tandem with larger animals.

Chapter 2
Ecology

Distribution

The *Zingiberaceae* are a widespread and ecologically highly successful family. While research into the natural habits and evolutionary relationships in the family is still in its infancy, the present ginger species are believed to be among the most recently evolved and sophisticated of flowering plants. Their ability to adapt, and (potentially) the speed with which such adaptations have occurred, may be a part of their success.

As a group, the *Costaceae* and the *Zingiberaceae* are found naturally in every tropical and subtropical region of the world, with the exception of North Africa. Their largest centre of diversity is undoubtedly Southeast Asia, from where many new species and indeed new genera are currently emerging. In their book *Gingers of Peninsular Malaysia and Singapore* (1999), Kai Larsen and his co-authors state, "We are convinced that less than 90% of the (*Zingiberaceae*) species in Southeast Asia have been discovered". Considering there are 600 species already known to be native to the region, this statement gives some indication of the wealth of diversity that the family has there. Large numbers of currently recognized species are native to Thailand and Malaysia, in particular, but the family extends west, across the humid tropics of southern Asia until it meets the more arid regions of Afghanistan.

Another major centre of species diversity lies to the north, around the northern and southern Himalayan foothills, with 216 species from 20 genera also found in southern China, as far north as Sichuan province. The gingers also extend south, through Indonesia and the Philippines, with small numbers native to New Guinea and Australia, and others endemic to the islands of the South Pacific.

While they are not as diverse in Africa as they are in Asia, the

Zingiberaceae are represented across most of sub-Saharan Africa, with the large genus *Afromomum* particularly prevalent, and a lone species of *Hedychium* endemic to Madagascar. The New World is the domain of the *Costaceae*. In fact, this family is the sole ginger representative in the Americas, with a territory that extends from Brazil through all of northern South America and Central America as far north as Mexico. In Asia, the *Costaceae* are represented by both *Costus* and *Tepeinochilos*.

Human activities have, of course, spread the gingers even further than their original natural boundaries. Japan, Florida, Hawaii, the Atlantic islands of the Azores and Madeira, the Caribbean Islands, and North Africa all have naturalized populations of *Zingiberaceae*.

Natural Habitats and Climates

The gingers occupy a large natural territory and have evolved to fit a variety of ecological niches. Many species are present in lowland tropical and sub-tropical forests in moist, often shady conditions, frequently growing near natural watercourses. The smallest species occupy banks and the leaf-litter of the forest floor. Brighter locations in secondary forest or sites at the margins of cultivated land are the favoured habitats of many medium-sized species, and the taller members of the family often form part of the dense subcanopy vegetation. Although the tallest and most luxuriant gingers are native to tropical humid lowlands, probably larger numbers of species are native to higher elevation cloud forests above 1500 m (4900 feet).

In each of their humid forest habitats some species have evolved to grow epiphytically, on rocks, or more usually on the forks of tree branches and old trunks. This type of habit is not a common one for any of the gingers, however, and those species that are largely epiphytic tend also to be relatively scarce.

Many of the Himalayan and Chinese gingers are woodland plants also, but at much higher elevations, often growing in a layer of humus over limestone. Some of these gingers specialize in bright shade within gorges and river valleys; others occupy deeper shade beneath galleries of trees. *Roscoea* species occur at the highest elevations of all the gingers, and many were originally plants of grassland and open scrub. In most locations, such habitats are now primarily given over to arable cultivation or are grazed by domestic animals. Gingers from such regions tend to be concentrated into pockets between the agriculture, congregated on banks and roadsides, and are often highly successful and rapid colonizers (some regarded as indicator species) of disturbed ground where they may grow so densely as to force out all other plant competition.

The hardiest gingers come from either these Sino-Himalayan zones or the northern part of Southeast Asia, a region centred on northern Thailand but encompassing Cambodia, Vietnam, Laos, and Myanmar (formerly Burma). The terrain here is very different to that of the perpetually moist tropics and is dominated by the cycles of the monsoons. Most of the flora is deciduous, and the typical habitat is open, bright forest with well-spaced trees above mixed grasses. These ecosystems are extremely wet in the rainy season, but also become extremely parched, with little or no rainfall for up to five months of the year when the forests are occasionally swept by fire. The gingers that have evolved among these seasonally dry forests have an annual dormant period. This dormancy is brought on by drought in the wild and is also triggered by falling temperatures in temperate locations, allowing the plants to tolerate sometimes severe cold in cultivation.

The African gingers are also deciduous and native to a variety of forested ecosystems, from cloud forests inhabited by mountain gorillas to open Tondo bush (land dominated by herbaceous species of *Afromomum*) and Mopane woodlands (forest dominated by the mopane tree, *Colophospermum mopane*). The gingers that may be cultivated as hardy plants, such as *Siphonochilus* species, are native to the transitional belts between the African tropical and subtropical zones. In many respects these habitats mirror the dry forests of Southeast Asia with alternating seasons of extreme drought punctuated by periods of high rainfall.

Chapter 3
Cultivation

History of Cultivation

Many gingers were introduced into Western cultivation in the 1800s when plant-hunters were scouring Asia for new introductions for their various sponsors. *Hedychium* species, in particular, were extremely fashionable subjects during Victorian times, but were invariably maintained in heated glasshouses. As is detailed elsewhere in this book, the gingers were all but gone from Western cultivation by the mid-1900s, with only one or two *Roscoea* species being grown as alpine rarities. The origins of the current popularity of gingers as garden plants can probably be traced to the introduction of one specific plant.

Hedychium densiflorum 'Assam Orange' was originally collected (as KW 13875) in 1938 in India by Frank Kingdon-Ward. Material was transferred to cultivation, but initially, at least, it was grown entirely under glass. In the early 1970s the then-unnamed cultivar was finally planted outdoors, in a sunny, south-facing border at Wakehurst Place in Sussex. It proved to be fully hardy there, and in 1974 was named 'Assam Orange' and given a Royal Horticultural Society Award of Merit. This event marked a major turning point: gardeners realized that, when cultivated correctly, *Hedychium* and other gingers that had been supposed entirely tropical subjects, were, in fact, tolerant of (in some cases) severe cold. The floodgates were finally, if slowly, opened. Over the coming decades hundreds of different gingers were trialled across the United Kingdom and the United States, eventually leading to the great diversity of ornamental gingers that are available to the twenty-first-century gardener.

Definition of Hardiness

Since the word "hardy" appears in the title of this book, it is clearly important to consider what that word means in this context. All the species described in chapter 8 have been successfully overwintered to at least a few degrees below freezing. Most are far more cold tolerant still. Hardiness, however, is a more complicated matter than merely considering the minimum temperature at which a plant will survive.

Hardy gingers are widely grown in both the United Kingdom and the United States, and I attempt to address both regions when describing the plants. But although the minimum winter temperatures in, say, Cornwall and Florida may be broadly similar, the ability of given plants to thrive in those areas depends at least as much on the length of the growing season. In the United States, with its continental climate, the seasons are much more clearly defined than they are in the United Kingdom, and in the southerly states late or even midspring temperatures are generally sufficient to trigger most gingers to emerge from dormancy. The plants typically then grow, without encountering significant drops in temperature, often until November, giving them a season that corresponds in length to their growing season in the wild. Of course the more northerly states have shorter growing seasons, and the patterns of climate within each state are also hugely variable, but the basic principle of a steady and predictable growth period remains.

The maritime climate of the United Kingdom produces a very different growing environment. The southernmost tip of the mainland lies at a latitude of 50° north, roughly the same as southern Newfoundland, a region not noted for its subtropical gardens. The United Kingdom is (at least until global warming turns it into an adjunct of Scandinavia) bathed by the warm waters of the Gulf Stream, which prevent severe winter temperatures and maintain Cornwall and much of the west coast of Britain and Ireland at temperatures generally above freezing year-round. The Gulf Stream does not, however, affect sunlight hours or the seasonal irregularities for which Britain is famed.

From the perspective of a ginger grower in the United Kingdom, two issues related to the seasons must be addressed. The first is that most species require a consistent and sustained rise in temperatures for twenty to thirty days to trigger their emergence from winter dormancy. In the United Kingdom such a period often does not occur outdoors until early summer.

The second feature of the British seasons is that they are affected by weather systems arriving from all four directions. This means that atypical surges or drops in temperature can occur at just about any time of the year, with the resulting problems for plants attuned to clear seasonal demarcations.

The end result within these two different climates is that plants grown in the southern United States have a considerably longer active growing season (six or seven months) and are thus much better able to withstand low winter temperatures. Plants grown in the United Kingdom have a much shorter growing season (as short as three or four months for some species), are significantly less hardy as a result, and thus are more susceptible to damage in winter. The sometimes sudden drops in temperature in late autumn can also damage plants that are in active growth. This is not to say that all the species and varieties listed in the book cannot be grown successful in the United Kingdom; in reality, almost all of them can, and are, but specimens are frequently smaller than their American counterparts, and some gingers do not readily flower outdoors in the United Kingdom, again, because of the shorter growing season.

This shorter growth season can be combatted or at least ameliorated if gardeners are prepared to be proactive in their cultivation techniques. To achieve better, longer growth and larger plants with more reliable flowering in those varieties that emerge late from dormancy, gardeners may strive to create a longer growing season for the plants. Broadly speaking this may be achieved in one of two ways, either by triggering growth earlier than would be the case in the open garden, or by extending the growing season through winter. In both cases the plants will need to be potted up and moved to an appropriately warmer environment. With many gingers, the temperature difference need not be all that great, and the additional warmth of an unheated greenhouse can allow a plant to emerge a vital few weeks earlier. Where heating is available, dormancy may be controlled much more fully, and plants brought into growth in, say, April for positioning in the open garden by late May. The same treatment can be applied at the other end of the growing season and can be particularly effective in allowing plants that are late to form their inflorescences to flower effectively rather than aborting their blooms.

One further aspect to consider is that of light levels. The growth patterns of gingers are responsive to light, as well as heat, although certainly to a lesser extent. The brighter spring days tend to be more conducive to good growth than the generally duller, and shorter days of autumn. Where only one option is available, triggering growth early is generally preferable to continuing it artificially into winter.

Cultivation in the Garden

Most deciduous species of ginger emerge late from dormancy, typically in May, although some may not appear until late June. Almost all the hardy species have a natural growth cycle attuned to their native monsoon climates, with new shoots appearing to coincide with the arrival of heavy rains and retreating when the inter-monsoonal dry or cold seasons arrive. When plants are first positioned in the garden it is important to remember their potentially long dormancy. They should not be sited where they will be overwhelmed or lost among other garden inhabitants with different patterns of growth.

Each genus has its own requirements for the specific garden location in which its species will do best, and these are covered in more detail in their respective sections. All hardy gingers, however, have broadly similar soil needs, which are, once again, dictated by their native habitats. Whether from Southeast Asia or the Sino-Himalayan regions, all deciduous gingers are in active growth during rainy seasons and become dormant in dry seasons. In the West, their active growth is during our relatively dry summer, and their dormancy during our wet winter, in other words, the opposite of their natural environments. Some gingers are far more tolerant of this difference than others, but all require a free-draining medium to minimize the chances of rhizome rot when the plants are not in active growth. Moisture content is equally important through summer, and all species must be kept well watered when rain is not forthcoming, with larger species requiring copious amounts of water to grow strongly.

Many gingers produce considerable quantities of leafy growth each season and can rapidly deplete their soil, so nutrition levels are also vital. The ground should be well prepared prior to planting, with well-rotted manure as well as grit, bark, or leaf mould to allow for good drainage. Once in growth the plants benefit from feeding, either by regular application of a liquid fertilizer, or through an annual mulch of well-rotted manure. Clumping species may need to be lifted and divided every two or three years to maintain their vigour and to allow the soil to be refreshed and bulked up.

Overwintering

Winter treatments of the genera differ, from those that have no special winter needs (*Roscoea, Cautleya*, many *Hedychium*) to those that must be kept in near dryness (*Siphonochilus*). Most gingers fall somewhere between the two extremes and should be given an annual application of a dry mulch in autumn, before the onset of frosts. Suitable materials include straw, chopped bracken, and chipped (not composted) bark. These should be placed around and over the rhizome area to a depth of 15 cm (6 inches). The mulch will serve to protect against extreme cold and also help to absorb and deflect excess wet.

A number of species, such as *Costus cuspidatus*, are reasonably hardy but cannot tolerate any great degree of winter wet when the plants are not in active growth. Such species could be accommodated in pots, allowing them to be transferred to an environment where water levels can be monitored, although this can also make them more susceptible to both desiccation, as the pots dry out, and cold damage, since the pot walls provide little protection from frosts.

A more satisfactory approach, which also gives a greater leeway for weather and temperature conditions, is merely to cover the plants with an impermeable shelter once they approach dormancy. Mark the positions of plants while they are in growth, then, once they have finished growth and are beginning to die back (typically by late autumn), dry mulch the plants for insulation and cover them. The cover should allow for air flow and transmission of moisture and should allow the plant to completely die back naturally. Cutting back the plant may seriously deplete its growth potential for the following season. Suitable materials for cover include, for instance, a pane of glass seated upon four bricks, or an open ended cloche. Always bear in mind that the aim is not to let the soil dry out (which could be equally damaging) but rather simply to prevent the possibility of the rhizomes sitting in water.

Cultivation in Containers

As has been established, some gingers benefit from being moved into different temperatures and environments at various times of the year, but even if this were not true, any good collection will necessarily contain a percentage of specimens that are grown in pots. Pots offer the advantage of portability where the needs of the plant dictate it. Furthermore, almost all other gingers may also be grown satisfactorily as container subjects. These may be placed on patios or seating areas where their flowers and fragrances can be closely appreciated, or positioned in the garden as focal points or among larger beds of companion plants. In either instance, the keys to successful container culture are the same as with plants in the open garden, namely, attention to drainage, moisture levels, and nutrition. Any plant grown in a pot certainly requires more care and attention than it would when planted in the soil, but gingers can make excellent subjects so long as they are never neglected.

Choice of pot size is crucial, as the larger gingers can rapidly fill smaller containers and also make them unstable with their large vertical growth. Careful consideration should be given to the ultimate size of the chosen subject, bearing in mind that any species that naturally attains a height of 120 cm (48 inches) or so in the open ground is likely to reach only half its typical size when grown in a pot.

The growing medium should be well drained, to prevent waterlogging and potential rotting of the rhizome, but must contain sufficient nutrition to allow for good, sustained growth. Professional ginger growers often use soil-based John Innes style composts, with up to 50% additional grit, to promote free drainage. An alternative medium, with an even lower risk of waterlogging, is a bark or leaf-mould based compost, with added chopped (not composted) bark to assist in drainage, together with slow-release fertilizer granules to compensate for the otherwise low nutrition of the bark. All container-grown gingers should ideally also be fed monthly or fortnightly with a balanced liquid fertilizer.

Pests and Diseases

It is often said that one of the great appeals of cultivating gingers is that they are pest- and disease-free. Although this statement is not entirely accurate, gingers are certainly troubled by far fewer problems than are most groups of ornamental plants and, for all practical purposes, are indeed disease-free. Most pests of gingers are of the leaf-eating or sap-sucking variety. Aphids attack the new shoots of many species, although they rarely favour the fully developed leaves and do not generally cause serious problems of leaf distortion. Slugs and snails occasionally dine upon freshly unfurled ginger leaves, especially those of *Curcuma*, *Kaempferia*, and *Roscoea*, partly because their foliage is closest to the ground. Mealybugs and red spider mites are regularly reported on gingers grown under glass, but they are almost never a problem with plants in the open garden. Good hygiene and air circulation, plus early removal of the pests and any badly affected foliage, will minimize any outbreak of mealybugs and mites.

Larger pests of gingers in some locales are grasshoppers. Although these insects do not target gingers any more than other garden plants, they can cause moderate, if temporary, damage in areas with heavy infestations. Squirrels are an occasional problem, with local populations sometimes developing a taste for the developing shoots of gingers. *Costus*, *Hedychium*, and *Zingiber* are all favoured, with *Globba* and *Kaempferia* also occasionally eaten. Fortunately, neither grasshoppers nor squirrels are likely to cause serious problems for plants grown in Great Britain.

The most frequently seen ginger pests are the caterpillars of several species of moth. Once again, the damage inflicted by such pests is only cosmetic, but a heavy infestation can shred the foliage of many species in an alarmingly short period of time. Removal or treatment of the insects as soon as the damage is first noticed will prevent a problem escalating. It may also prevent a re-occurrence of the problem the following season if the insects' life cycle can be broken.

Chapter 4

Propagation

By Seed

In the United Kingdom only *Roscoea*, *Cautleya*, and the higher elevation *Hedychium* species regularly produce seed when grown outdoors. Many more gingers produce fruit in the southern United States where the growing season is longer. *Hedychium* species in particular, are reliable and prolific in this respect. The larger seed merchants also offer some species, although accurate identification and viability can be a problem.

Seed of any member of the *Zingiberaceae* and *Costaceae* should ideally be sown as soon as it is harvested. The seed of many species has a relatively short viability, and germination success drops rapidly the longer the seed is stored. Seed collected in autumn and early winter will not germinate naturally until the next spring, but is still best sown immediately.

Seed may be sown in pots or trays, depending on the numbers available. A free-draining, moisture-retentive mix is most important. If you will have time to dedicate to the care of the germinated seedlings, then the ideal medium for germination is pure perlite. Sterilize the perlite with boiling water, then cover the seed with approximately its own depth of perlite. Seal the pots or trays tightly with polythene to retain the high moisture levels but allow the passage of light, and then place them into the protected environment of a greenhouse, cold frame, or other similar structure.

In cooler locations the seeds of many gingers require additional heat to germinate successfully and will need to be kept at around 21 to 24ºC (70 to 75ºF). Such seeds can be given heat immediately after sowing, that is, in autumn or winter. Alternately, heating can be left until spring; the advantage of waiting until spring before applying heat is that the naturally increasing light and warmth levels will make the resulting seedlings much easier to care for without further artificial heat and light.

Where seed must be stored it should be done so in a cold (frost-free), dry environment. Before stored seed (including that purchased from seed merchants) is sown, it should be thoroughly rehydrated by soaking it in water at room temperature for twenty-four hours. Even so, viability will be reduced compared to that of seed sown fresh, and germination may take much longer and be sporadic.

Seedlings germinated in perlite will have little access to nutrients and will need to be potted into a free-draining compost once they are large enough to handle. Those seedlings germinated in a compost mix can remain in situ for several months if necessary. In either situation, the young plants benefit greatly from fortnightly applications of dilute feed. When so treated, some of the smaller species can be induced to reach flowering size within their first season.

By Division

All gingers grow from subterranean rhizomes, and by far the best way of propagating most species, particularly where only small numbers of further plants are required, is by dividing the rhizome. Some genera, including *Boesenbergia*, *Kaempferia*, *Roscoea*, and some *Curcuma* naturally divide themselves. Well-grown plants of these genera produce single rhizomes with multiple growth points which evolve into two or more independent plants by the end of the growing season. Plants such as these may be separated at any time during their dormancy, as there is generally no damage to their tissue, and no cutting of the rhizome surface is required.

The small rhizomes of *Roscoea* become detached, although they are still positioned directly beside one another and often appear to be fused, with the tuberous roots interlocked to some extent. These plants should be washed free of all soil, and the rhizomes gently teased apart, to prevent damage to rhizomes or tubers. Plants divided in this way require no further special treatment and may be returned to their intended destinations and planted out as normal.

The tuberous roots of *Kaempferia* and *Roscoea* are just that—tuberous roots—and the plants cannot be reproduced by removal of the tubers on their own. Although they are the plants' major underground storage organs, the tubers do not have growth points and care should be taken not to damage the sometimes brittle and tenuous junctions between the rhizome and its tuberous roots.

Many gingers have a thick, fleshy rhizome that bears a number of adventitious buds across its surface. In genera such as *Hedychium* and *Zingiber* this rhizome will extend (sometimes considerably) with each season but not evolve into separate plants. Such species may be easily divided in spring, preferably just before the onset of growth. On small specimens the rhizome should be lifted and washed free of soil for close inspection of the best point of division. Larger plants may have a considerable mass of root attached, and these need not always be cleaned so thoroughly, although it is vital to establish exactly how the rhizome has grown, and where the shoots are. Many *Hedychium* species, in particular, can produce contorted, heavily branched rhizomes, and unless the full extent of the structure is examined it is all too easy to divide in the wrong place.

Each division should have a minimum of two, and preferably three, growth points, plus a reasonable number of roots. Cut the rhizomes with a sterile, sharp knife. Do not break them or snap them by hand, as this invariably leads to far greater tissue damage and a larger wound surface area. Where different division points are possible, choose the narrowest part of the rhizome, again to minimize the surface area of the wound. After dividing the rhizome, treat both cut surfaces with a fungicidal agent, such as sulphur, to minimize the chance of rotting. Do not attempt this kind of division in winter, or while the plants are fully dormant, since there is a far greater chance of rot occurring. Instead, use plants just entering active growth as they will be able to heal and grow away far more readily.

Unless they are very large sections (in which case they can be planted straight into their intended position) gingers that have been divided by cutting should initially be potted up, using a well-drained, nutritious, and moisture-retentive compost, and the pot placed in a warm location. Do not bury the rhizome too deeply, and if new leafy growth is visible, then do not bury the growing tips. With smaller divisions, place the rhizome near the surface, or even at the surface, to encourage growth. Watch the compost carefully so that it does not dry out, since the rhizome is far less protected than it would be when buried deeper into the medium. Once strong new growth is evident, plant the new divisions in their chosen locations, this time positioned more deeply into the soil.

By Cuttings

Surprisingly, perhaps, some gingers may also be reproduced from cuttings. Success has been reported from cuttings of *Globba* and *Hedychium*, but the genus most usually involved is *Zingiber*. The uppermost portion of the pseudostem is used; it may be anywhere from 15 to 45 cm (6–18 inches) or so in length, depending upon the variety, and should bear one or two leaves. Pseudostems that have a developing inflorescence are not suitable for use, but once the pseudostems have become rigid, cuttings may be attempted.

Most *Costus* species can also be reproduced from cuttings, which is rather more expected, since that genus produces true canelike stems rather than pseudostems. For best results, use elongated portions of the upper stem measuring 30–35 cm (12–14 inches) long. Remove any lower leaves, leaving only the uppermost pair intact. Spray or dip the cuttings into a soluble fungicide mix. Then plant them in a very free-draining, moisture-retentive compost to provide the optimum rooting results. Plant the cuttings deeply into the medium, with a minimum of three leaf nodes buried. Alternatively, place the entire stem horizontally, either submerged into the medium and lightly covered with about 1 cm (1/2 inch) of compost, or laying on the surface and "pinned" down with wire or small stones. Whichever method is used, heat and total humidity are essential for successful rooting, and the cuttings should be covered in transparent polythene and kept out of direct sunlight at a minimum temperature of about 24°C (75°F). When successful, cuttings will generally root within three or four weeks, and the resulting plants may be potted up individually after a further four to six weeks.

By Plantlets

Some members of the *Zingiberaceae* are naturally viviparous, with small plantlets forming from the inflorescence. Foremost among these are *Globba* species, many of which produce large crops of bulbils at the base of the inflorescence in place of the lower flowers. The tropical *Alpinia purpurata* and the hardy *Hedychium greenii* also both produce plantlets that develop from the fading inflorescence. If left intact these plantlets will develop small aerial roots before eventually falling to the ground as the inflorescence decays and disintegrates.

Whether as bulbils or plantlets, these youngsters may be potted up in a nutrient-rich, free-draining mixture and treated like seedlings or rooted cuttings. Since such offspring occur in the autumn, they will not have the same degree of hardiness as their parents; thus, they should be protected and kept frost-free in winter. Once they have emerged from dormancy, the young plants should be well fed. They will rapidly grow large enough to be placed in their permanent positions in the garden that same season.

By Micropropagation

Micropropagation, also known as tissue culture, is the process of generating large numbers of genetically identical plants from a portion of one or two stock plants. The young plants (known as explants) resemble tiny rooted cuttings and may be generated from a wide range of host material, including leaf and root tips, shoots, and even flowering stems. The host material used contains undifferentiated meristematic cells, whose final function is determined by both environmental and hormonal signals. When harvested this tissue generates callus material that can be repeatedly divided to produce more and more cells. Groups of these cells are taken and cultured in a sterile, nutrient-rich, and hormone-rich medium that promotes the production of growth shoots, which are in turn rooted and become the explants.

Micropropagation is often referred to as an art as much as a science and certainly is not the domain of most gardeners. Some plants do not readily lend themselves to being reproduced in this manner, but gingers have proven to be willing subjects for the most part. An increasing number of them are being micropropagated in Europe, Asia, and the United States. Many *Curcuma*, *Globba*, *Hedychium*, *Kaempferia* species are now micropropagated in huge numbers, leading to their increasing availability and reduced cost to the enthusiast.

Another notable application of the technology involves the African species *Siphonochilus aethiopicus*, a plant whose value as a traditional medicine led to the virtual extinction of all wild populations. This species is now being reintroduced back into the wild and is also readily available in cultivation, thanks to micropropagation programmes instigated in South Africa.

Chapter 5
Culinary and Medicinal Uses

The family *Zingiberaceae* contains a number of volatile and essential oils including terpenoids and phenylpropanoids. The obvious aromatic nature of most parts of most species has led to the plants being used by mankind for a vast array of purposes throughout almost all of recorded human history. On top of this, various culinary gingers have been further utilized for their medicinal qualities. These uses are not merely the preserve of ancient traditional folklore, and modern trials are revealing new applications for the plants every year.

Several *Alpinia* species are utilized by humans. Aboriginal peoples have long favoured the blue-fruited Australian clumping cane, *A. caerulea*, both for its edible fruit and rhizome tips and for its leaves, which are traditionally used as a bed on which to lay meat while it is cooked in an earth oven.

Alpinia galanga, known as the greater galangale or simply galangale, is a very popular spice throughout Southeast Asia and particularly in the cuisine of Thailand. It is also known and used in Malaysia, Indonesia, Cambodia, Vietnam, and southern China and is an occasional supplement in the Chinese five spice powder. While little encountered in the West these days, the galangale was a valuable and much used spice in the early Middle Ages. The rhizome is used both fresh and dried and is employed as a remedy for indigestion, colic, dysentery, food poisoning, problems of the spleen, and even to alleviate stomach cancer. An infusion of the leaves is also used as a stimulant and to combat rheumatism.

The leaves of *Alpinia zerumbet* were used traditionally as a wrapper for food, where they acted as both a preservative and a flavouring agent. A Brazilian research company affiliated with Federal University of Ceará has determined that the species contains compounds known as kavatoids, and the company markets a medicinal compound made up of the ground leaves for use in combating stress and hypertension.

Among the hardy *Amomum* species, two are edible. The immature inflorescence of *A. dealbatum* is eaten in curries, and the seed of the species used as a form of cardamom. The fruit of a number of gingers from several genera are used to produce different forms of this important spice. *Amomum subulatum* is cultivated in large quantity in Nepal and Sikkim, where its partially ripened seed pods are harvested and dried to form black cardamom, a valued spice with a smoky flavour that is employed in a wide range of Indian dishes.

Boesenbergia rotunda is not as widely seen, but the swollen tuberous roots, known as Chinese keys or fingerroot, are popular in Thailand, both in raw and cooked forms, to flavour a variety of dishes. The pickled tubers are a delicacy in Thailand and Indonesia, and the young shoots and fresh leaves of the species are also occasionally consumed. Despite its common name, *B. rotunda* is not eaten in China itself, but does have medicinal applications there; both the small rhizome and the tuberous roots are applied as a cure for stomach ailments as well as a general tonic particularly following childbirth. The species is also used to assist with coughs and diarrhoea, as a skin liniment, and for the treatment of rheumatism and muscular pains.

The genus *Curcuma* is one of the most important of the *Zingiberaceae* in terms of human applications. *Curcuma amada* has been the subject of several medical studies to assess its value as an anti-inflammatory agent. The same species is also grown as a crop in India, where it is known as the mango ginger, and where its fragrant rhizomes are used in curries in both fresh and dried form. *Curcuma amada* is also currently under assessment as a potential contraceptive.

Curcuma aromatica has been found to have powerful antibiotic properties. Chinese medicinal practitioners also promote this plant as a method of reducing and preventing cancers.

The species with the most applications is *Curcuma longa*. It is used to produce the spice turmeric, and its alternative name of Indian saffron gives an indication as to its other properties. Turmeric has been used for at least as long as root ginger (*Zingiber officinale*) and is an important agricultural crop in modern India, where it is a vital constituent of all curry powders and is added to almost every savoury dish. The rhizome also yields a very strong dye, derived from its primary dark yellow pigment, curcumin. The dye has been much confused with saffron (the word "kurkum", from which "curcuma" is derived, originally meant "saffron") and is used to colour the distinctive orange-yellow robes of Buddhist monks.

As a colourant, turmeric is used in the manufacture of cosmetics, confectionary, and cattle food. It also plays a part in several Indian religious ceremonies. Soaking unglazed white paper in a tincture of the rhizome and then drying it produces turmeric paper, used as a test for alkaloids and boric acid. Turmeric's medicinal applications are numerous also. Traditionally it has been used as a remedy for diarrhoea and rheumatism, and to relieve coughs, tuberculosis, and jaundice. Recent clinical studies have found it to be effective in reducing blood lipids, improving blood circulation to the heart, lowering blood pressure, removing gallstones, reducing inflammation, and alleviating pain. Most significant of all, however, are the results of studies at the University of California that established a link between turmeric and the prevention and slow-down of Alzheimer's disease. Previous studies had found that the neurodegenerative disease affects just one percent of the population over the age of sixty-five in rural India, and it seems that the regular consumption of the spice is the agent responsible. The plant may also have an application as a spermicidal agent.

Curcuma zedoaria, commonly known as zedoary, is another important *Curcuma* with an ancient medicinal history in China and Japan where the plant is used as a carminative and stomachic. Zedoary essential oil has some utility in the perfume and liquor industries, and the bitter-tasting rhizome is used in the preparation of some curry powders and is eaten as a vegetable in Thailand.

Cardamom, referred to as the queen of spices, is obtained from the dried seedpods of the tropical species *Elettaria cardamomum*. It is the third most valuable spice (only saffron and vanilla are more expensive) and is used across Asia and in the West for flavouring curries and for seasoning sweet pastries. The seeds are chewed as a breath freshener in India and are a flavouring additive to Arabian coffee. They also yield an oil that is widely used in perfumes, confectionaries, and liqueurs.

Globba is one of the least used genera of the *Zingiberaceae*. Some species are occasionally seen as traditional medicines. The spicy inflorescence bulbils can be eaten as a vegetable.

Another of the lesser-used genera is *Hedychium*, whose main relationship to mankind has always been as an ornamental. The flowers of *H. coccineum* have been used as a talisman of good fortune and health, and those of *H. coronarium*, the butterfly ginger, are occasionally steamed and eaten as a vegetable in Thailand. *Hedychium coronarium* and *H. gardnerianum* are both introduced alien species much used in Hawaii for the creation of traditional welcome garlands and other floral displays. The essential oil derived from the rhizome of *H. coronarium* has also found a limited application as a mild tranquilizer and antibiotic. This species, along with *H. flavum*, has a long-standing history of use in the Ayurvedic medicinal system for the prevention of cataracts.

Hedychium spicatum is undoubtedly the most widely utilized species in the genus. The powdered rhizome produces a flavouring found in many Asian commercial preparations of chewing tobacco. The flavouring is also used as incense. The essential oil of this species is widely available and is used for aromatherapy and the production of perfumes. It has also been found to have tranquilizing, analgesic, and anti-inflammatory properties.

The mildly spicy leaves of *Kaempferia galanga*, the lesser galangale, play an important part in Malaysian and Indonesian cooking. This species is widely grown across southern Asia for its rhizomes, which are sliced and dried, or grated and used fresh, to flavour savoury dishes. *Kaempferia galanga* is also cultivated in India where the rhizomes are steam distilled to produce an essential oil and in New Guinea where it has a history as an hallucinogen. Finally, traditional Asian medicines use the rhizome as an expectorant and carminative. Recent studies have revealed that *K. pulchra* yields two pimarane diterpenes that have an anti-inflammatory action when applied topically. *Kaempferia rotunda* has multiple applications. The tubers are used to treat abdominal illness and gastric complaints, the small rhizome has been found to relieve stomachache and is utilized in the production of cosmetics, and the crushed leaves are applied as a body lotion.

The southern African species *Siphonochilus aethiopicus* was brought to the brink of extinction, largely as a result of overexploitation of wild populations for traditional medicine, where it is one of the most coveted native plants. South Africans have cultivated this plant for many years for its highly aromatic elongated roots and tubers which have various applications. The Zulu peoples chew the rhizomes and roots fresh to treat asthma, hysteria, and colds, and administer a preparation to horses to ward off illness. They also utilize the plant as a protection against lightning and snakes. The species is valued by the Swati (Swazi) people as a treatment for malaria and a painkiller during menstruation.

The genus *Zingiber* may safely be described as the most utilized member of the *Zingiberaceae*. The properties of *Z. montanum* have only recently been investigated, but a preparation of the rhizomes has been found to relieve cough and asthma, and when powdered the rhizome has antidiarrhoeal properties. The essential oil of the plant was found in 1996 to have antibacterial and antifungal properties, and the species is also used as an antidote to snake venom.

While *Zingiber officinale* is certainly the best-known species in the genus, *Z. cassumnar* probably ranks as the ginger with the greatest number of applications, all of them medicinal, and most of them recently discovered. The rhizome is used in traditional medicine primarily to prevent nausea and also to cure headaches. Numerous clinical trials conducted since the 1980s have revealed an extraordinary range of properties and effectiveness in curing aches and pains, inflammations, joint problems, muscle spasms, sprains and strains, torn muscles and ligaments, asthma, catarrh, chronic colds, colic, constipation, diarrhoea, fevers, flatulence, heartburn, immune problems, influenza, respiratory problems, and indeed nausea. In addition, two studies conducted in the late 1990s demonstrated that a curcuminoid derived from *Z. cassumnar* operates as an anti-tumour agent and protects cells suffering from oxidative stress. The potential commercial applications for a plant with proven ability to fight both cancers and the aging process are immense, but yet more studies have shown *Z. cassumnar* to be effective as a fungicide, antihistamine, and insecticide. Truly this is a wonder plant.

Zingiber mioga seems rather humble in comparison to its sister species, but the plant is used to combat both malaria and intestinal parasites. Although not native to Japan *Z. mioga* has long been cultivated there as a crop plant and the tender new growing shoots are widely eaten in as a vegetable in both fresh and preserved form. Another species with limited uses is *Z. rubens*. Its pulped rhizomes are a cure for dizziness, and its seedpods are occasionally seen as a spice in Indian cooking.

Zingiber officinale, the root ginger, barely requires an introduction, but has been cultivated across Asia for millennia for its culinary and medicinal properties. Ginger is regarded as probably humankind's first and oldest spice—another ginger (turmeric) may have been used earlier, but primarily as a dye. Charak, an ancient Indian sage of medicine, wrote: "Every good quality is found in ginger". The plant was the most valuable spice in Roman times and so it continues, with the species in demand internationally as never before. In Europe the primary application is to flavour ginger beer, ginger wine, and various biscuits and confectionaries. *Zingiber officinale* is a substantial crop plant in Jamaica for the production of its preserved (crystallized) young rhizomes, and those same rhizomes are, of course, synonymous with virtually all Asian cuisines. The medicinal properties of the plant are also well established. *King's American Dispensatory* guide of 1898 (the 18th edition, by Felter and Lloyd) stated:

Action, Medical Uses, and Dosage. Ginger is stimulant, rubefacient, errhine, and sialagogue. When chewed it occasions an increased flow of saliva, and when swallowed it acts as a stimulating tonic, stomachic, and carminative . . . . It is much used to disguise other drugs . . . . It has been used in combination with astringents or other agents, in *diarrhoea* and *dysentery* . . . in *cholera morbus* and *cholera infantum* . . . . It is eminently useful in *habitual flatulency, atonic dyspepsia, hysteria,* and enfeebled and relaxed habits, especially of old and gouty individuals; and is excellent to relieve *nausea, pains and cramps of the stomach and bowels* . . . . Ginger is occasionally of value in *fevers* . . . is popular and efficient as a remedy for breaking up colds, forms an excellent poultice to *indolent ulcers*; and has been used as a sialagogue to relieve *paralytic affections of the tongue, toothache,* and *relaxed uvula.* Ginger . . . has relieved violent *headache.*

Current applications are as a stimulant in cases of bad circulation and cramps, as a promoter of perspiration in the treatment of fever, and as a gargle for sore throats. It is also the basis of many treatments for muscle and ligament sprains. The sesquiterpenes in *Z. officinale* have been found to have specific effects against cold viruses. Ginger also regulates blood cholesterol levels.

Zingiber spectabile has some minor applications; the leaves are pounded and an infusion made to bathe infected eyelids, and the rhizome is occasionally utilized as a spice. *Zingiber zerumbet* is commonly known as the shampoo ginger. Water trapped in the pouched bracts mixes with the sap of the inflorescence to form a thick oozing juice that has long been used as a natural hair wash and is now also a constituent of commercial shampoos manufactured by both Freemans and Paul Mitchell. The young rhizomes are eaten as a vegetable, have been found to have anti-inflammatory properties, and are useful in combating abdominal pain and bladder diseases. Perhaps most significantly the rhizome has also yielded the drug zerumbone, which is a proven anticarcinogenic agent.

Members of the family *Costaceae* have, generally speaking, found far fewer ethnobotanical applications than the *Zingiberaceae*, since the *Costaceae* do not contain the aromatic oils of the *Zingiberaceae*. A recent study using extracts of the leaves and stem of *Costus lasius* has demonstrated that the species is partially successful in neutralizing snake venom and could potentially be used as an antivenom constituent.

Costus scaber has similar properties and is traditionally used by Trinidadian hunters, both on themselves and their hunting dogs, as a cure for snakebite, scorpion sting, and canine mange. The rhizome of *Costus speciosus* has found a wider range of applications. Not only is its ground into a paste for use in treating skin boils, but it also serves as an expectorant, contraceptive, laxative, diuretic, stimulant, and aphrodisiac. The stem of the species is used in a poultice to treat fever and small pox, and the whole plant is crushed and used for washing hair.

The ground rhizome of the Himalayan species *Costus angustifolia* is taken orally to cure headaches and abdominal pain. It is also used to create "East Indian arrowroot", a substitute for the true arrowroot, which is derived from the ginger relative, *Maranta arundinacea.*

Chapter 6

Cut Flower Uses

The explosion in the popularity of tropical-style plants and gardening has been accompanied by an equal surge in demand for exotic cut flowers. Alongside *Heliconia*, *Anthurium*, and *Strelitzia*, several gingers are now being grown as commercial cut-flower crops.

Foremost among these is *Curcuma*; many cultivars and hybrids of this genus have been evaluated for use as either cut flowers or as short-term house or container plants. Curcumas have ephemeral true flowers but showy and long-lasting floral bracts in a variety of white, pink, and purple shades. *Curcuma amada* and *C. angustifolia* are occasionally grown as small-scale flower crops, and the cut stems have a life of around 10 days, but the main species used is the Siam tulip, *C. alismatifolia*. Many cultivars of this species have been selected, particularly in Thailand, and an array of different colours forms, from deep pink to pure white, are grown and offered. In addition to exporting the flowers, Thailand now annually distributes millions of bahts worth of rhizomes of the plant (known locally as "patum-ma") to be grown on in Europe, Japan, and the United States for ultimate use as cut flowers. *Curcuma alismatifolia* is also cropped in South America and is currently under evaluation as a commercial cut-flower crop in a number of other countries, including Israel.

Like *Curcuma*, *Zingiber* has equally ephemeral flowers but large, colourful, and beautifully shaped inflorescences comprised of many showy bracts. *Zingiber neglectum*, the jewel pagoda, is the epitome of exoticism, and one of the two main species grown for cut flowers. The individual stems of this ginger last for fourteen days or more. *Zingiber neglectum* and *Z. spectabile* are grown as small-scale crops, and many different colour forms of the shampoo ginger, *Z. zerumbet*, are grown commercially in Asia and the Americas.

With the benefit of its beautiful perfume, the white butterfly ginger,

Hedychium coronarium, is used as a cut flower in many tropical countries. It has limited commercial appeal due to its relatively short stem life, and the problems of packaging and transporting the delicate flowers, but the prolific nature of its growth allows stems to be regularly cut and used. Gardeners, of course, are not bound by issues of storage and transportation, and many hedychiums, in particular the fragrant varieties, may be enjoyed in vases where they will typically last for a week or more.

While it is in no sense a hardy plant, mention must be made of *Etlingera elatior*, the torch ginger. It too is grown as a cut-flower crop year-round in Thailand and South America, and a number of cultivars were developed specifically for the trade. *Etlingera* inflorescences are heavy and their bracts are easily bruised, causing problems with long-distance transportation, so the spectacular stems can rarely be exported great distances. The other main species of tropical ginger grown for cut flowers are *Costus barbatus*, with its waxy spires of long-lasting scarlet bracts, and more commonly the cone ginger, *Alpinia purpurata*, of which a number of cultivars have also been selected specifically for the trade.

Rather surprisingly, and despite their rather delicate looking inflorescences, *Globba* species make very good cut flowers, with the waxy stems lasting for a remarkable four weeks or more. *Globba winitii* (and other species masquerading under its name) has recently become hugely popular in Southeast Asia, and large numbers of many cultivars are now being crop grown there to service the local demand.

Unfortunately, in Southeast Asia, where the trade in exotic cut flowers is the strongest, tens of thousands of plants are taken from the wild each year for use in the trade. Such collecting has particularly affected the globbas, decimating many wild populations. Considering how amenable these plants are to cultivation in Southeast Asia, it is tragic to see their names on the lists of vulnerable and endangered species, a situation that has been created since the 1990s. It also seems highly likely that species are being wiped out before they have even been named and described. It is therefore vital that consumers not aggravate the problem. All consumers should be vigilant as to the sources of both plants and flowers offered for sale, particularly within Southeast Asia itself.

Chapter 7
Landscaping Uses

The diverse nature of the gingers allows different species to be used in various garden situations. Their recent rise to prominence has been prompted by the passion for tropical, or perhaps more accurately, tropical-looking gardens, and few plants better lend themselves to such a situation than do the gingers. *Hedychium* is the genus most frequently used for tropical-style gardens in the United Kingdom and in the United States. The handsome foliage and exotically perfumed flowers are essential elements to any such planting scheme. A wide range of other genera may be equally valuable to such a scheme, and where gardens offer areas of both sun and shade, the range extends considerably. A complete tropical-style ginger collection might include *Alpinia* and *Curcuma* in the brightest and warmest areas with *Globba*, *Kaempferia*, and *Zingiber* in the protection of moist shade.

Visually, many of the large-leafed gingers look particularly effective when positioned beside contrasting, small or cut-leafed plants such as *Dicksonia* (tree-ferns) as well as many of the more architectural smaller ferns, such as *Cyrtomium*, *Matteuccia*, *Osmunda*, and *Polystichum*. Taller plants, such as the delicate-leafed, shade-loving mountain bamboos *Thamnocalamus* and the more sun-loving *Phyllostachys* can also be incorporated, accompanied by palms, cannas, aroids such as *Colocasia* and *Alocasia*, and *Musa basjoo* (the hardy Japanese banana) to complete the full tropical look.

Tropical-style gardens may be the first type of garden that many gardeners associate with gingers, but they are merely the beginning of the possible options. Few plants look better than when given a naturalistic setting in which to display themselves, and the gingers are certainly no exception. While it may require too much climate-control to mimic the Thai forest conditions (alternately dripping wet and parched dry) to which some of the hardy species are native, it is realistic to re-create the Sino-Himalayan landscape in a temperate garden. Of course there is already a long standing British tradition of Sino-Himalayan gardening, and many magnificent large estates are packed with plants brought back by the Victorians, some even with gingers.

Taking inspiration from the wild but reducing it to a manageable scale, the Sino-Himalayan garden begins with a canopy of small trees (larger ones where space allows) including perhaps *Magnolia* and *Acer*. Beneath these should be a shrubby realm that in the wild is typified by *Rhododendron* and bamboo. Alongside these would come the gingers, of which *Alpinia*, *Curcuma*, *Hedychium*, and *Roscoea* are suitable along with several of the smaller species of *Kaempferia* and *Zingiber*. The low level and groundcover flora of this region is among the richest and most diverse in the world, so the hardy gardener may well find themselves spoilt for choice. Companion genera such as *Arisaema*, *Asarum* (the unrelated, so-called wild gingers), *Epimedium*, *Lilium*, *Polygonatum*, *Primula*, and *Smilacina* associate well with gingers and will help to enhance the desired effect.

Continuing the theme of taking inspiration from the wild, many gingers naturally grow in association with water. Virtually all of the species love humid conditions and will invariably produce better and bigger foliage the more moist the atmosphere that surrounds them. Hedychiums in particular often have severely arching (pseudo)stems, which, in plants growing on the steep banks of rivers and streams, cascade straight downwards, with the flower spikes being held erect at the stem tip. In cultivation gingers are seldom grown in direct association with water, but they can look extremely effective and particularly naturalistic when placed either at the side of a pond or waterway, or tumbling down the bank of a stream.

Hedychium greenii and *Alpinia aquatica* are naturally found growing in waterlogged and boggy soil, and both may be grown as marginal aquatics. *Hedychium coronarium* is reportedly successful as a marginal, and having seen the habits of certain other wild *Hedychium* species (with rhizomes growing through running water) I am reasonably certain that others from that genus would thrive as seasonal aquatics, in much the same way that *Canna* are also occasionally used.

At the other end of the gardening spectrum come the alpine and rock garden possibilities, habitats that, in ginger terms, are largely the preserve of *Roscoea*. Until very recently the Royal Botanic Gardens, Kew, had a vast alpine garden display mounted upon many hundreds of tons of rock. The Asiatic section of the garden was dominated by many varieties of *Roscoea*, growing in pockets of soil in exposed positions in full or partial sun. While this genus is often thought of as consisting of woodland plants, most roscoeas naturally colonize scree slopes and bare, rocky ground, where they are open to the full force of the elements.

Some gingers are specifically adapted to life in the deep shade created by overhanging trees. Shady gardens are frequently perceived as problem gardens, but the vast diversity of ground-dwelling forest plants, including many of the most interesting and ornamental temperate plants, call this environment home. Anyone lucky enough to have a shade garden may take full advantage of these gems. Among the gingers, *Kaempferia* species are the first choice, their beautiful foliage perfect for a sheltered shady spot. *Amomum* and *Boesenbergia* species also grow well in shade, as do most *Costus* and many *Zingiber* species. In warmer gardens in the southern United States, the high-elevation *Hedychium* species will only succeed in full or nearly full shade, and many others are reasonably shade tolerant, although flowering may be impaired.

An extension of the shady garden is the woodland garden. Whether created by design or inherited from nature, the sheltered woodland understorey will provide ideal conditions and a more stable microclimate for many gingers whose large foliage might become scorched or wind damaged in more exposed locations. Given a balance of open, bright clearings and margins and darker, shady nooks, all of the gingers described in this book may be accommodated in fine style in a woodland setting.

Moving away from the naturalistic, and towards the traditional style of English gardening, the herbaceous border is an excellent place for *Curcuma* and *Hedychium* in particular. Writing in 1993 Tony Schilling expressed his hope that one day "the Himalayan gingers (will) become as common as bearded irises in the sunny fertile borders of British gardens". That day is certainly not yet with us, but more gardeners are beginning to experiment with the possibilities. Hardy gingers can contribute their floral colours to "hot" beds, alongside the likes of *Crocosmia*, *Dahlia*, and *Hemerocallis*, providing late-season flowering that often continues until the first frosts. They may equally well be used as foliar focal and punctuation points between fine-leafed subjects, or blended into colour-themed beds with other white-, yellow-, or pink-flowered plants, for instance. The exquisitely perfumed varieties of *Hedychium* should also form an integral part of any fragrant garden. Once again, different species and varieties will offer themselves for locations in full sun and in partial shade. An additional advantage of growing gingers in an herbaceous border is the protection afforded the rhizomes by their neighbouring plants. Where evergreen subjects (be they shrubs or grasses) are used as companion planting, they can act as insulation, and underground temperatures may be significantly higher than in a more open and exposed bed.

One of the earliest outdoor uses for the gingers was as a seasonal bedding plant in large-scale municipal plantings. While such short-term and labour-intensive practices are far from the current horticultural vogue, a smaller-scale adaptation is seen in individual groups of plants used as specimens or in mass plantings. A richly prepared soil, in a warm sunny position without any other plant competition, will see specimens of many of the larger gingers increase hugely in size, both at the rhizome and in leaf, as access to nutrients is increased. Groups of three or five plants may be sited in small beds, as lawn specimens, or at the margins of a shrubbery. Where space allows, larger numbers of rhizomes may be placed in substantial drifts to give a massed foliar and later floral effect, perhaps creating a frame or foreground to a wider landscape or contrasting grouping. Such massed plantings may also be interplanted with spring- or late winter-flowering bulbs to give a prolonged season of interest, the foliage of the bulbs dying down as the ginger growth emerges.

Chapter 8
A–Z of Hardy Gingers

Alpinia

With more than 230 species, *Alpinia* is the largest genus in the *Zingiberaceae*. The biggest concentration of species centres in Southeast Asia, but western outposts of distribution occur in India and extend south into Australasia and the islands of the South Pacific. Most alpinias are entirely tropical plants, but a few are candidates for cultivation in the temperate garden.

Aside from the genus *Amomum* and the single hardy species of *Pleuranthodium*, *Alpinia* is the only member of the recently created subfamily *Alpinioideae* and the tribe *Alpinieae* that contains any remotely hardy species. All of the remaining hardy species and genera are contained within the subfamily *Zingiberoideae*. As a result, *Alpinia* species are notably different from most of the other ginger species described in this chapter.

The genus *Alpinia* was created in 1810 by William Roxburgh and was named to honour the sixteenth-century Italian botanist Prospero Alpinio. Alpinias are generally medium or large plants endemic to shady forests. They are characterized at a tribal level by the absence of developed lateral staminodes and at a generic level by the inflorescence produced at the end of the leafy stem rather than on a separate flowering stem. This inflorescence comprises a dense raceme of flowers in which the lateral staminodes have been drastically reduced in size and play no ornamental role. From a gardener's point of view the labellum is the entire focus of the flower. The labellum is generally large and very showy, almost always brightly coloured, and often heavily lined with a darker, contrasting colour that acts as a display and guide for pollinators. The single stamen, with its fused anther and stigma, is seated directly above the labellum, to deposit and collect pollen from the backs of pollinating insects. The flowers of many *Alpinia* species look very similar to those of some orchid species, such as *Serapias*, the tongue orchids. The flowers, which are also often referred to as being shell-like in appearance, typically open from waxy, rounded buds.

While several *Alpinia* species are indisputably hardy, all but one of these flowers only on the previous year's shoots, the exception being *A. galanga*. Since most plants will become deciduous with a few degrees of frost, this inevitably means that most *Alpinia*, regardless of their rhizome hardiness, will not flower in temperate gardens. This does not prevent them from growing successfully and even vigorously, and several are worth cultivating purely for their handsome, spicily aromatic, and often pubescent foliage. But, except where noted, to produce their often-beautiful flowers, alpinias need to be overwintered as close to frost-free as possible. To achieve this they may be grown in pots, either permanently or seasonally, allowing them to be moved to a greenhouse or conservatory in winter, or they can be left in situ and provided with full protection using appropriate insulating materials.

Generally, alpinias are resentful of strong sunlight and should be grown in a sheltered position in semi-shade where they can be provided with copious food and water while in active growth. Despite their tropical heritage those species that will tolerate colder temperatures tend to be plucky and vigorous customers, often interesting in foliage, and remarkable in flower, and certainly well worth attempting.

Alpinia aquatica

Minimum temperature: -10°C (15°F)
Height: to 210 cm (83 inches)

Among the earliest gingers to be named, this species was originally described as *Heritiera aquatica* by Anders Jahan Retzius in 1791, before William Roscoe transferred the plant to the new genus *Alpinia* just 16 years later. Possibly unique among gingers, *A. aquatica* is a true marginal aquatic species native to Southeast Asia, where the plants typically grow at the edges of ponds and streams. In hardy cultivation it may be successfully grown either as a seasonal water marginal, in a bog garden, or simply in a typical moist ginger soil or compost medium. Horticulturally, it is not a particularly noteworthy species: it produces slender stems; narrow, upwards-facing, lanceolate foliage; and racemes of small flowers with a pink-lined white labellum. Plants grown outside in temperate gardens are unlikely to exceed 120 cm (48 inches) in height.

Alpinia calcarata

Minimum temperature: -10ºC (15ºF)
Height: to 180 cm (71 inches)

Named by William Roscoe in 1807, this species is a native of the forests of Guangdong province in eastern China and has populations in India, Sri Lanka, and Myanmar. It is a vigorous and easily grown hardy species that produces a dense network of stems, each clothed by gently arching, narrowly lanceolate leaves, 30 cm (12 inches) long and 5 cm (2 inches) wide. The overall impression of the foliage resembles that of a small, broad-leafed bamboo. The 10-cm (4-inch) tall inflorescence is produced in late spring, solely on the previous year's growth, and comprises a loose panicle that bears small flowers. The pale orange-red labellum is 3 cm (1¼ inches) long by 2 cm (¾ inch) wide and is intricately and conspicuously lined with dark red. As with similar species, plants grown outside in frost-prone areas are unlikely to exceed 90–100 cm (36–39 inches) in height. (Plate 1)

Alpinia caerulea

Synonym: *Alpinia coerulea*
Minimum temperature: -7ºC (20ºF)
Height: to 200 cm (79 inches)

This species is a native of the rainforest understorey of northern New South Wales north into southern Queensland, Australia, but has been found to be remarkably hardy. While not among the more dramatic species in flower, *Alpinia caerulea* is a highly ornamental foliage plant with tall, gently arching stems clothed by glossy, 40-cm (16-inch) long leaves that have deep purple-red undersides. The flower spikes are open and are often also heavily infused with purple. They bear small, tubular red and white buds that open to little flowers with a pinkish white labellum and a red-brown stamen.

The specific epithet "caerulea" was given by George Bentham in 1873 and refers to the unusual, 15-mm (⅔-inch) indigo-coloured berries that the plants produce in large clusters after flowering, and which give the plant its colloquial name of the blue berry ginger. These fruits are a particular favourite of bower birds, and are equally appealing to humans, tasting (unsurprisingly) gingery, with a strong lemon flavour.

In Australia *Alpinia caerulea* is widely grown as an ornamental and is particularly used as a plant for shade (including deep shade). To succeed in more temperate zones it requires a sheltered, sunny position with a rich, moist but well-drained soil. Once again, plants grown as deciduous specimens will not flower and will be considerably shorter than in their native habitats.

Alpinia formosana

Minimum temperature: -12°C (10°F)
Height: to 180 cm (71 inches)

This spectacular and gorgeous plant was originally described by Karl Schumann in 1899. A native of Taiwan and also the southern islands of Japan, *Alpinia formosana* was recognized in a paper by Jeng Yang and Jenn Wang, as a natural hybrid between *A. intermedia* and *A. zerumbet*.

Very unusually, this species is naturally variegated. All specimens produce tough, leathery leaves that are 60 cm (24 inches) long by 12 cm (4³/4 inches) wide with lateral veins coloured cream or white, a feature that gives the plant its (inevitable) common name of pinstripe ginger. Flowering can occur from May to August. Plants produce fully upright, 15- to 20-cm (6- to 8-inch) tall panicles that bear 30–40 shell-shaped flowers. These open from striking, snow-white rounded buds to reveal a dramatic, ovate labellum 3 cm long and wide (1¹/4 inches). The labellum is also white, but with a large, coloured flare that is maroon in the throat, and turns to orange, surrounding a pale yellow patch towards the lip. Above the labellum is held the white stamen, with a club-shaped anther. *Alpinia formosana* blooms only on the previous year's stems, but will retain these tough stems through at least a few degrees of frost. If planted in a suitably protected location, it might be expected to flower successfully when cultivated outdoors in a sheltered garden; however, *A. formosana* will happily grow in much colder locations than this where it makes a superb foliage plant, particularly in a partially sunny, warm location with moist soil where the leaves can reach their maximum size.

Alpinia galanga

Minimum temperature: -12°C (10°F)
Height: to 180 cm (71 inches)

While it is not tremendously ornamental, *Alpinia galanga* is an important plant for two reasons. First, it is the only *Alpinia* species with a significant economic role. The rhizome is the source of the spice galangal, or galangale, and is widely used in cooking throughout southern and southeastern Asia. It also has a long history of medicinal uses. Second, although the species is very widely cultivated throughout Southeast Asia, it is one of the few alpinias that flowers on the current season's growth.

When not in flower the plant resembles a small hedychium, with narrowly upright or slightly arching stems clothed in glossy, lanceolate leaves. The flower spikes can appear from July to October and consist of very densely flowered racemes 10–15 cm (4–6 inches) tall, bearing numerous small, pale green, elongated buds. These open to reveal nondescript flowers with a small white labellum, marked with dark red at the throat, and a prominent pale green or white stamen.

Alpinia hainanensis

Synonyms: *Alpinia henryi, A. katsumadae*
Minimum temperature: -7°C (20°F)
Height: to 180 cm (71 inches)

Named by Karl Schumann in 1904, this species has had a history of some nomenclatural confusion. Essentially, the species was collected from the Chinese island of Hainan on three separate occasions and allocated three separate names (two of them by Schumann), before examination of the collected material demonstrated that all three were, in fact, the same species. Many plants currently in cultivation are still labelled as either *Alpinia henryi* or *A. katsumadae*, but *A. hainanensis* is the earliest published name and thus takes precedence.

Aside from its home in the South China Sea the species is also found in mainland China, in the Guangdong and Guangxi provinces, as well as south into neighbouring Vietnam. It is a forest plant said to reach 300 cm (118 inches) tall in the wild. Cultivated specimens are considerably smaller, often flowering at no more than 90–120 cm (36–48 inches). Even at this lesser size, this tough and vigorous species is easily cultivated where temperatures allow. The variable leaves can be as much as 65 cm (26 inches) long by 12 cm (4³/₄ inches) wide. Although plants in cultivation rarely match these dimensions, they are always attractive and slightly but noticeably hairy. Flower spikes are produced on old stems from April to June and take the form of an upright raceme up to 30 cm (12 inches) tall. Opening from cream-coloured buds the flowers are lightly scented of honey and are relatively large, with an ovate labellum up to 4.5 cm (1³/₄ inches) long; they are white, beautifully marked with lines of deep red that radiate out from the centre.

I have found that, with some protection, the stems of *Alpinia hainanensis* will tolerate considerable frost. They will successfully persist outdoors to allow successful flowering the following season. (Plate 2)

Alpinia japonica

Minimum temperature: -12°C (10°F)
Height: 30–60 cm (12–24 inches)

This small species is probably the hardiest member of the genus, not just at the rhizome, but (crucially) at the stem. Plants will remain evergreen to at least -7°C (20°F), a feat that, among the *Zingiberaceae*, only a few *Roscoea* species can match. The most northerly *Alpinia* species, *A. japonica* is a forest native of virtually the entire southern half of China, with Sichuan and Jiangsu as the northerly boundaries. The species is also found on Taiwan and Japan, where it is possibly a naturalized Chinese introduction. It was Japanese material that Carl Thunberg used when he named the species as *Globba japonica* in 1784.

Plants produce short stems clothed with comparatively large, softly hairy, lanceolate leaves up to 40 cm (16 inches) long. From March to August these stems give rise to the narrow and very upright flower racemes that hold many tubular 1-cm (¹/₂-inch) long flower buds. The bicoloured buds are white towards the axis and dark pink for the remaining two-thirds of their length. They flare open to reveal a small, bilobed white labellum with pinkish red stripes. The flowers occur exclusively on the previous year's stems, but if given some protection, they will readily persist into the next season, and even if somewhat defoliated they will still allow for successful flower formation.

The species prefers a moist soil and position in light shade or partial sun, although it is resentful of strong, midday sun and cannot tolerate too much heat. *Alpinia japonica* is uncommon in cultivation, which is a shame given its attractive leaves and flowers and its unusual degree of hardiness. It seems probable that even more cold tolerant forms of this very widespread species might be introduced from the northerly limits of its natural range, where plants must presumably flower and fruit successfully at temperatures comparable to those in the United Kingdom.

Alpinia nutans

Synonyms: *Elettaria cardamomum* hort., *Amomum compactum* hort.
Minimum temperature: -10ºC (15ºF)
Height: to 80 cm (31 inches)

Alpinia nutans is the true name for a plant that has been almost continually misidentified throughout its history in cultivation. William Roscoe mistakenly made the name *A. nutans* conspecific with *A. zerumbet* in 1828, and most plants in current cultivation are now labelled either as *Elettaria cardamomum*, which is a much taller, entirely non-hardy, tropical plant and the source of the spice cardamom, or as *Amomum compactum*, which is a Javanese native and another non-hardy plant. The confusion arises because three species, *A. nutans*, *A. compactum*, and *E. cardamomum*, are all commonly referred to as cardamoms. The true spice is derived solely from *E. cardamomum*, but *A. compactum* is used as a substitute in some Asian countries, and all parts of *A. nutans* itself are very strongly scented of cardamom. This confusion has doubtless been exacerbated by the fact that the true *A. nutans* very rarely flowers in cultivation, regardless of the conditions in which it is maintained, a situation that makes confident identification of plants all the more difficult.

The species is grown entirely for its wonderfully aromatic foliage, which is produced in dense clumps. The upright, lanceolate leaves are 20–40 cm (8–16 inches) long, tough, and glossy.

Alpinia nutans is an understorey species of the forest floor and, in cultivation, will tolerate deep shade even where conditions are too dry to allow other gingers to grow. Plants are robust, rather vigorous, and reliably hardy, and will not be defoliated unless severely frosted for a prolonged period. Even when this does occur new shoots will readily emerge from the rhizomes the following season. This species is fairly widely available in the

United Kingdom and the United States, although almost never under its true name. The 2003 edition of the *RHS Plant Finder* does not list the species, but most, and very possibly all, of the nurseries offering *Elettaria cardamomum* are actually growing *A. nutans*. Gardeners should be careful to ensure that they acquire the correct, hardy, and strongly aromatic plant.

Alpinia pumila

Minimum temperature: -10°C (15°F)
Height: to 15 cm (6 inches)

Named by Joseph Hooker in 1885 this Chinese species is native to shady, humid mountain valleys in Guangdong, Guangxi, Hunan, and Yunnan provinces at altitudes of 500 to 1100 m (1600–3600 feet). This highly distinctive groundcover species has very short, undeveloped stems, each holding two or three leaves. The broad 7-cm (2¾-inch) wide leaves are about around 15 cm (6 inches) long and arch over to fully reveal their upper surfaces which are dark green striped with silver, the stripes leading forward from the midrib towards the leaf lip. The foliage can withstand temperatures to at least -5°C (22°F) and is extremely decorative, easily reason enough to cultivate the plant. Rarely seen, the flowering raceme is produced on a 30-cm (12-inch) tall peduncle that appears from April to June. It bears small, tubular, white flowers with a 1-cm (½-inch) wide labellum that has a notched apex. *Alpinia pumila* is slow growing and should be positioned in full shade, in a sheltered position with a seasonally moist soil.

Alpinia tonkinensis

Minimum temperature: -7°C (20°F)
Height: to 240 cm (96 inches)

Named by François Gagnepain in 1902, this fine species is a native of Vietnam and China, with territory in Guangxi and north into Hunan province. The tall stems are clothed in glossy, leathery, narrowly lanceolate leaves up to 60 cm (24 inches) long by only 7 cm (2¾ inches) wide. Flowers form on the previous year's stems and occur very early in the year— February in China, March to May with plants in cultivation. The inflorescence is large and takes the form of an upright panicle that on mature specimens can reach 40–50 cm (16–20 inches) tall. The numerous buds open to reveal a circular or ovate 1-cm ($\frac{1}{2}$-inch) diameter cream labellum, prominently marked with dark red veining. The hardiness of *Alpinia tonkinensis* is untested, and plants may prove to be tougher than the estimate suggests.

Alpinia zerumbet

Minimum temperature: -12ºC (10ºF)
Height: to 200 cm (79 inches)

This magnificent species has had an array of nomenclatural problems since it was first named as *Costus zerumbet* by Christiaan Hendrik Persoon in 1805. Some 23 years later William Roscoe published an illustrated description of the plant and mistakenly decided it was synonymous with the very different *Alpinia nutans* (a plant that had formerly been known as *Globba nutans*). The species was then transferred to the short-lived genus of *Languas* where it was described as both *L. speciosa* and *L. schumanniana*. The next stop saw J. C. Wendland identify the plant as *Zerumbet speciosum*, which subsequently became *Alpinia speciosa*, before finally being brought to its correct and rightful place as recently as 1972, when Brian Burtt and Rosemary Smith published the name *A. zerumbet* and thus (hopefully) ended the confusion. The species has long been widely cultivated as an ornamental across much of Southeast Asia and is now naturalized in Hawaii and Florida. It is difficult to assess the exact boundaries of its original distribution, although it has natural populations in southern China and Taiwan.

Alpinia zerumbet is a very impressive species, the largest of the root-hardy alpinias, with tall, arching stems clothed by shining green, lanceolate leaves that in the warmest climes can reach 60 cm (24 inches) long by 10 cm (4 inches) wide. In temperate gardens the species is remarkably hardy at the root, down to an astonishing -18ºC (0ºF) according to one grower, although stems will generally be cut back by any more than a few degrees of frost, and the cooler growing temperatures will only allow for shorter growth. Typically plants will be more erect and reach perhaps 120 cm (48 inches) in height, although they are well able to flower at this height, albeit on the previous year's stems.

The inflorescence is one of the finest in the genus and takes the form of a drooping panicle, up to 30 cm (12 inches) long, that cascades from the leafy tip of the stem. The red-pink softly furry rachis bears many waxy, pink-tipped, milky-white flower buds that open from the panicle base in succession, each revealing a large labellum 4–6 cm (1½–2½ inches) long. The labellum is coloured glowing golden yellow and intricately veined with deep red. Because of the form of their flowers, alpinias are often referred to as shell gingers, but *Alpinia zerumbet* is particularly qualified to wear that epithet. Looking like it is festooned in clusters of exotic conchs, a plant in full flower is an unforgettable sight.

Although its natural habitat is shaded forests, in temperate gardens *Alpinia zerumbet* is undoubtedly best grown in a warm, sheltered, and sunny spot and given copious water and food when in active growth to encourage as much development as possible. Indeed when cultivated permanently under glass as an evergreen, *A. zerumbet* can readily reach 400 cm (158 inches) tall, with the huge gently arching stems tending to hold the flowers away from readily visible inspection. A cultivation that allows for periods of active growth and dormancy is the key to producing vigorous stems with well-displayed flowers. (Plate 5)

Alpinia zerumbet dwarf variegated

This form of the species is available in the United States and has very short (non-flowering?) stems to only 25 to 30 cm (10–12 inches). The relatively large leaves are strongly marked with creamy yellow variegations. This plant should prove to be as hardy as the species and in temperate gardens is best planted in at least part sun to ensure the variegation is maintained.

Alpinia zerumbet 'Variegata'

Very widely available and commonly planted wherever the species occurs, 'Variegata' is essentially grown as a foliage plant. It is generally much more reluctant to flower than the species, even when grown under ideal conditions. Stems are not as tall as those of the species and can reach approximately 120–180 cm (48–71 inches) long. The very bold, broad leaves are heavily variegated with pale yellow. The variegation takes the form of asymmetrical blocks and stripes that radiate outwards from the central vein towards the leaf tip. (Plate 6)

Above left: 1 *Alpinia calcarata*
Courtesy Robert Lee Riffle.

Above: 2 *Alpinia hainanensis*

Left: 3 *Alpinia purpurata* 'Eileen MacDonald',
a tropical cultivar

Left: **4** *Alpinia vittata*, a tropical species

Above: **6** *Alpinia zerumbet* 'Variegata'
Courtesy Robert Lee Riffle.

Below: **5** *Alpinia zerumbet*

Left: **7** *Boesenbergia rotunda*

Above: **8** *Cautleya gracilis*
(CCW106)

Left: **9** *Cautleya spicata*
Robusta form

Right: 10 *Costus* species

Below: 11 *Costus barbatus*, a tropical species

Left: 12 *Costus cuspidatus*

Below: 13 *Costus glaucous,*
a tropical species

Right: **14** *Costus lateriflorus*, a tropical species

Below: **15** *Costus pictus*

Left: 16 *Costus scaber*

Below: 17 *Costus speciosa*
Courtesy Robert Lee Riffle.

Above: 18 *Costus speciosus* 'Variegatus'
Courtesy Linda B. Gay, Mercer Arboretum.

Right: 19 *Costus woodsonii*

20 *Curcuma* aff. *aurantiaca* 'Khymer Orange'
Courtesy Linda B. Gay, Mercer Arboretum.

Above: 21 *Curcuma australasica*

Below: 23 *Curcuma yunnanensis*

Above: 22 *Curcuma sumatrana*
Courtesy Linda B. Gay, Mercer Arboretum.

Above: 24 *Globba platystachya*
Courtesy Linda B. Gay, Mercer
Arboretum.

Right: 25 *Globba wintii*
Courtesy Robert Lee Riffle.

Left: 26 *Hedychium* fruiting

Below: 27 *Hedychium coronarium*

Above: 28 *Hedychium coronarium* var. *chrysoleucum*

Above: 29 *Hedychium densiflorum*, collected from East Nepal

Right: 30 *Hedychium densiflorum* 'Assam Orange'

31 *Hedychium densiflorum* 'Sorung'

32 *Hedychium densiflorum* 'Stephen'

33 *Hedychium gardnerianum*, bracts just opening

Left: 34 *Hedychium greenii*

Right above: 36 *Hedychium maximum*

Right below: 37 *Hedychium spicatum*

Below: 35 *Hedychium hasseltii*

Above: 38 *Hedychium thyrsriforme*   *Below:* 39 *Hedychium yunnanense*

Left: 40 *Hedychium* 'Dr. Moy', flowers
Courtesy Tony Avent.

Left: 41 *Hedychium* 'Dr. Moy', foliage
Courtesy Tony Avent.

Above: **44** *Hedychium* 'Lemon Sherbet'

Left: **45** *Hedychium* 'Luna Moth'

Above: 46 *Hedychium* 'Peach Delight'
Courtesy Tony Avent.

Right: 47 *Hedychium* 'Pink Hybrid'

Above: 48 *Hedychium* 'Pradhanii'

Above: 49 *Hedychium* 'Samsheri'

Right: 51 *Hedychium* 'Tara'

Above: 50 *Hedychium* 'Tai Empress'
Courtesy Tony Avent.

Right: **52** *Kaempferia galanga*
Courtesy Linda B. Gay, Mercer Arboretum.

Right: **53** *Kaempferia gilbertii* '3D'
Courtesy Linda B. Gay, Mercer Arboretum.

Right: **54** *Kaempferia pulchra* 'Alva'
Courtesy Linda B. Gay, Mercer Arboretum.

Above: 55 *Kaempferia pulchra* 'Silver Spot'
Courtesy Linda B. Gay, Mercer Arboretum.

Below: 56 *Kaempferia roscoeana*
Courtesy Linda B. Gay, Mercer Arboretum.

57 *Kaempferia rotunda*

Above: 58 *Roscoea alpina*

Left: 59 *Roscoea auriculata* 'Floriade'

Above: 60 *Roscoea capitata*   *Below:* 61 *Roscoea cautleyoides*

Above: 62 *Roscoea cautleyoides*, bicoloured form

Above right: 63 *Roscoea cautleyoides* Blackthorn strain

Right: 64 *Roscoea cautleyoides* 'Jeffrey Thomas'

65 *Roscoea cautleyoides* 'Kew Beauty'

66 *Roscoea humeana*

Right: **67** *Roscoea praecox*

Below: **68** *Roscoea purpurea*

Left: 69 *Roscoea purpurea*
Striped Form

Above: 71 *Roscoea purpurea* 'Peacock'

Left: 70 *Roscoea purpurea*
'Brown Peacock'

Above: 72 *Roscoea purpurea* 'Peacock Eye'

Right: 73 *Roscoea purpurea* 'Polaris'

Below: 74 *Roscoea purpurea* 'Red Gurkha'

Above: **76** *Roscoea scillifolia* pink-flowered

Left: **75** *Roscoea scillifolia* dark-flowered

Below: **77** *Roscoea tibetica*

Above: 78 *Roscoea tumjensis*   *Below:* 79 *Roscoea wardii*

80 *Roscoea* 'Beesiana', pale form

Above: 81 *Roscoea* 'Beesiana',
dark form

Above: 82 *Roscoea* 'Beesiana Monique'

Above: 83 *Roscoea* 'Grandiflora'

Above: 84 *Roscoea scillifolia* × *R. cautleyoides*

Above: 85 *Siphonochilus carsonii*
Courtesy Linda B. Gay, Mercer Arboretum.

Left: 86 *Siphonochilus decorus*
Courtesy Linda B. Gay, Mercer Arboretum.

Left: 87 *Siphonochilus kirkii*

Left: **88** *Zingiber cassumunar*
Courtesy Linda B. Gay, Mercer Arboretum.

Above: **89** *Zingiber mioga*, dark form

Right: **90** *Zingiber spectabile*

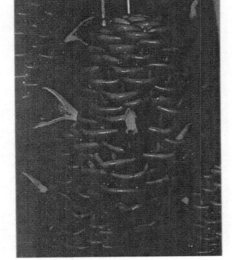

Alpinia Hybrids

Alpinia 'Strawberries and Cream'
Minimum temperature: -10ºC (15ºF)
Height: to 90 cm (36 inches)

Very few hardy *Alpinia* hybrids have been developed, but this cross of *Alpinia japonica* by Tom Wood is now available in the United States. Plants are said to be sun tolerant. The short flowering spike bears glossy, bright red tubular buds. The open flowers are white with a large, ovate labellum that is flushed with pink and veined with red. Another unrelated form of the tropical species *A. purpurata* is also named 'Strawberries and Cream'; it is in nursery cultivation in the United States.

Amomum

Amomum is the second largest genus of the *Zingiberaceae*, with approximately 150 species. Most of these are native to the tropical regions of Southeast Asia and Australasia and so are, unfortunately, beyond the resources of the temperate region gardener. Almost 30 species, however, are native to China and the Himalaya, and it is among these that the hardy representatives can be found.

The genus was formed by William Roxburgh in 1820. The generic name is a Latinization of the Greek words "a", meaning "without", and "momus", meaning "harm", referring to the curative and medicinal properties of the plants. All *Amomum* species are extremely aromatic, and several have been used for various ethnobotanical and culinary purposes, in particular the production of various forms of the spice cardamom from the dried seed pods.

Amomum species produce two different types of shoot. The pseudostems are frequently tall and robust and carry all the leaves, while the inflorescences are produced at the tip of the generally very short stems that arise separately from the rhizome. The *Amomum* inflorescence comprises a series of densely arranged, sometimes overlapping, scaly bracts from which emerge the flowers, often in very tight clusters that can obscure the bracts entirely. The flowers of most species consist almost entirely of an enlarged labellum, held by short, waxy corolla lobes with a central stamen. This arrangement is similar to that of *Alpinia*, although the *Alpinia* inflorescence is produced on the leafy stems. Genetic and chemical analysis has confirmed that the genera are closely related and are both members of the tribe *Alpiniaea*. The individual flowers are typically pale yellow, although white- and red-flowered species occur. In each case the labellum is typically marked with various lines and venation that act as guides for pollinators.

Amomum dealbatum

Minimum temperature: -10°C (15°F)
Height: to 200 cm (79 inches)

This species was named by William Roxburgh in 1820. It is a native of cool, shady moist forests at elevations of 600 to 800 m (2000–2600 feet) in Yunnan province, China. It also occurs naturally in Nepal, Sikkim, and northern Thailand. The species is widely cultivated in northeastern India, where the young flower spikes are eaten as a spicy vegetable, and the seed pods are dried and powdered to form an inferior form of cardamom.

In its native habitats the species can be very robust with the evergreen, thick, leafy stems reaching 350 cm (140 inches) in height. In temperate cultivation the plants are generally deciduous, although stems will persist through all but the hardest frosts, and are more likely to peak at 100 to 150 cm (39 to 60 inches) in height. The foliage is very fine, with the lanceolate leaves capable of reaching 70 cm (28 inches) long by 14 cm (5½ inches) wide, and having a close, reddish-brown pubescence on their undersides. In the wild the flowers appear in May and June, but in cooler cultivation the bronzy-red, scaly flower stems can emerge straight from the soil at any time between April and September. The very short inflorescence is packed with numerous flowers that open in succession for a period of three or four weeks. The flower buds are tubular and white, and each opens to reveal a 2.5-cm (1-inch) long white labellum with a crinkled margin and a prominent central golden patch that has delicate red veins running from the throat to the edges of the labellum.

Amomum dealbatum is not a difficult plant to grow, but it does require a considerable amount of food, water, and as much summer heat as possible. Given such it will produce the large amount of seasonal growth that makes it so appealing.

Amomum subulatum

Minimum temperature: -10°C (15°F)
Height: to 150 cm (60 inches)

Smaller than *Amomum dealbatum,* this allied species is native to deep, shady moist forests in Guangxi and Yunnan provinces of southwestern China as well as Xizang (Tibetan Autonomous Region), Bangladesh, Bhutan, northern India, Myanmar, Nepal, and Sikkim. The species was described by William Roxburgh in 1820. It is widely grown as a crop throughout the eastern Himalaya, the seed pods being the source of the black cardamom. While it is little encountered in the West, this spice is important in the cuisines of Nepal and northern India, where the seed pods are harvested in autumn while still unripe before being fire dried and sold, still in pod form.

The leafy stems of *Amomum subulatum* bear long, hairless, narrowly lanceolate leaves to 60 cm (24 inches). Throughout summer the plants can produce essentially stemless inflorescences straight from the top of the rhizome. The scaly brown bracts split open to allow the flowers to emerge, one at a time, in succession for a period of approximately a month. The flower buds open into three creamy white corolla lobes that surround a 3-cm (1¼-inch) long pale yellow labellum. The labellum reflexes downwards revealing a golden orange central stripe from which radiate many red veins.

Amomum subulatum is not as vigorous as *A. dealbatum,* but is also easily grown in a warm, sheltered, moist, and shady garden location. In such a site and with some winter protection, the plants should be more or less evergreen, allowing better re-growth in spring.

Boesenbergia

This genus consists of around 50 species of short plants that are denizens of shady forests from the Himalaya to Indonesia, with most endemic to the tropical rainforests of Southeast Asia. Nathaniel Wallich, in 1829, originally named a *Zingiberaceae* genus *Gastrochilus,* but this name was subsumed into *Boesenbergia* when Carl Kuntze published the latter in 1891.

Boesenbergias do not form leafy stems (the pseudostems of other *Zingiberaceae* genera). Instead, each leaf is held on its own petiole, and the basal sheaths of the collective petioles are bunched tightly together at ground level. In most species, including the three discussed here, the inflorescence emerges on a short stem that appears at the centre of the leaf sheaths. The flowers are thus almost at ground level, and are both small and fleeting, each lasting no more than a day at best. Typically, flowers of this genus have a cupped or curled labellum that is marked with stripes and blotches, and which sometimes forms into a tube with the corolla lobes.

Boesenbergia species are far from spectacular in flower, but they do posses a certain diminutive charm and all make for handsome foliage plants. Few species are hardy enough for use in the temperate garden, but those that are require a seasonally moist, well-drained, humus-rich soil (a leaf-mould-woodland mix is ideal) and a sheltered position in full shade. Boesenbergias are often late to emerge from dormancy, and in the United Kingdom this can be problematic since the plants require a prolonged period of consistently warm weather to trigger re-growth. In the United States they are easily grown and make appealing groundcover beneath trees and in other woodland settings.

Boesenbergia longiflora

Synonyms: *Gastrochilus longiflora, Curcumorpha longiflora*
Minimum temperature: -10°C (15°F)
Height: to 60 cm (24 inches)

This species is a native of central and southwestern Yunnan province, northern India, Laos, Myanmar, and northern Thailand. The plants are denizens of shady, sheltered forest floors and can frequently be found growing on the banks of streams in mountainous regions at altitudes of 1100 to 1900 m (3600–6200 feet).

Regardless of growing conditions *Boesenbergia longiflora* is always deciduous, re-emerging each spring—typically in May in cultivation—to produce two or three broad, ovate, dark green leaves up to 12 cm (4³/₄ inches) long by 9 cm (3¹/₂ inches) wide. The leaves are held together, each on their own petiole, rather than being attached to a stem. The inflorescences occur on separate stems that appear from the rhizome adjacent to the foliar stems. Between three and six flowers are produced in succession from each shoot. Each flower has an almost tubular, 3-cm (1¹/₄-inch) long labellum that can be either white or purple-red, marked with a prominent deep red blotch in the throat. The stamens are short and not decorative. Behind the labellum are the three 2.5-cm (1-inch) long white corolla lobes that form from the bud. The lobes make the flowers look remarkably similar to those of orchids from the genus *Bletilla*.

The deciduous habit of *Boesenbergia longiflora* points to its hardy nature. While the species has a fairly wide distribution, plants that originate from Yunnan are undoubtedly suitable for use in temperate gardens, where they can be successfully grown in partial or full shade in a sheltered, moist but well-drained soil.

Boesenbergia plicata

Synonym: *Boesenbergia plicata* var. *lurida*
Minimum temperature: -10°C (15°F)
Height: to 45 cm (18 inches)

This species is a common native of southern Thailand and the islands of Langkawi, Teratau, and Tioman off the coast of peninsular Malaysia. It has handsome, ovate leaves up to 40 cm (16 inches) long by 15 cm (6 inches) wide. The leaves are very glossy and conspicuously ribbed along the veins. In some forms, the leaves are also flushed with red on their undersides. The inflorescence emerges on a separate spike produced from the centre of the clustered leaf petioles rather that directly from the rhizome. Each spike bears two or three flowers that open in succession. The flowers are tiny, only 2 cm (³/₄ inch) long at most, and tubular, with a rolled labellum that is closely held by the corolla lobes. The flowers can be golden yellow, or orange to red. Plants with orange to red flowers were previously separated as *Boesenbergia plicata* var. *lurida*, but the colour forms are too inconsistent and variable to warrant varietal status.

Despite the southerly climes from which it originates, rather remarkably, *Boesenbergia plicata* has proven reasonably hardy. It can be successfully grown in temperate gardens when provided with full shade and considerable moisture when in growth. In Southeast Asia *B. plicata* times its seasonal emergence to coincide with the southwesterly April monsoon, when increasing temperatures combine with very heavy moisture levels. The additional problem for gardeners in the United Kingdom is that the species will often not break dormancy until summer and may then not have sufficient time and heat to put on the growth required to sustain strong healthy plants. Nevertheless *B. plicata* is a handsome foliage plant and well worth trying in the appropriate location.

Boesenbergia rotunda

Synonym: *Boesenbergia pandurata*
Minimum temperature: -10°C (15°F)
Height: to 60 cm (24 inches)

Originally described in 1753 as *Curcuma rotunda*, then transferred to *Kaempferia* (as *K. pandurata*), this extremely well-known ginger did not have its current name published until 1958, when Rudolf Mansfeld brought together the original (and thus the only valid) specific name with the correct generic name. The species has a long history of cultivation as a spice, and the fat roots that grow from the small rhizome are known as "khao chae" (Chinese keys), and are much valued in Thai and Malaysian cuisine. The species is, however, not native to Southeast Asia but originates, rather, from southern Yunnan and possibly northern India, where the plants grow in dense, moist forested shade at altitudes of around 1000 m (3300 feet).

Emerging in midspring, the leaves reach around 50 cm (20 inches) long, each held on a 7- to 15-cm (2¾- to 6-inch) long petiole. The leaves are broadly ovate and generally plain green on both surfaces with ribbing evident on the upper surface; however, an unnamed variant has leaves infused with red beneath. The fragrant flowers appear in July and August from short stems at the centre of the leaf petioles. The flowers are somewhat larger than those of many *Boesenbergia* species. The labellum is 2.5–4-cm (1–1½ inches long) with a flared and gently rippled margin; it is pink, often with a golden throat that has red speckling, and it is approximately twice the length of the pale pink corolla lobes from which it unfurls.

Boesenbergia rotunda is widely cultivated throughout southern and southeastern Asia, but is reasonably hardy in temperate locations. It can be successfully grown given the usual *Boesenbergia* conditions of warm, moist shade. (Plate 7)

Caulokaempferia

This uncommon genus of approximately 10 species is native to China, India, Myanmar, Sikkim, Laos, and northern Thailand. Kai Larsen, founder of the botanical institute at the University of Aarhus, Denmark, created the genus in 1964. The generic name literally means "stalked *Kaempferia*", referring to the upright, leafy (pseudo)stems that are absent from plants in the genus *Kaempferia* itself. Caulokaempferias are small plants of the forest understorey. They produce narrow stems clothed with generally short leaves. The small inflorescence is carried at the end of a leafy stem and consists of a small arrangement of lanceolate bracts, each of which holds one flower. The flowers always have a long corolla tube and three corolla lobes with a longer central lobe that is seated above the large, ovate labellum. The lateral staminodes are developed into conspicuous and petaloid structures. Unlike many members of the *Zingiberaceae*, caulokaempferias do not have an elongated stamen; instead, the anther is fixed to the throat of the labellum.

Caulokaempferia linearis

Minimum temperature: -7°C (20°F) ?
Height: to 30 cm (12 inches)

This species is a native of the cooler forests of the eastern Himalaya, where plants grow in the accumulated leaf litter on the forest floor and are particularly found on moist banks near mountain steams. The species is deciduous and does not break dormancy until May in the wild, often June in cultivation.

The stems are extremely slender and emerge from tiny rhizomes that never exceed a few centimetres (about 1 inch) in length. Each stem bears two or three narrow glossy leaves that are sometimes flushed bronzy-red beneath. In July and August the same stems produce the small inflorescence. The bracts open in succession, each revealing their individual flower which comprises a large and very beautiful, lightly ruffled, snow-white labellum that has the texture of tissue paper, coupled with a small, pinkish-purple central corolla lobe. The individual flowers last for only one or two days, but plants will remain in bloom for several weeks.

Although it is certainly hardy, *Caulokaempferia linearis* requires a fiercely drained medium that is kept very moist during the vigorous, active growth phase and barely moist through the winter dormancy. In the garden this might be accomplished using a barrier to maintain moderate water levels. The plant is undoubtedly easier to maintain in a pot, where moisture levels can be much more readily determined.

Cautleya

Arguably the second hardiest genus of the *Zingiberaceae*, *Cautleya* consists of three closely related species from the mountainous Himalayan regions of Bhutan, China, India, Kashmir, Nepal, and Sikkim, and continuing into Myanmar, northern Thailand, and Vietnam. The genus was founded by Joseph Hooker in 1888 and commemorates Sir Proby Thomas Cautley (1802–1871), a British military engineer who served in India.

Botanically *Cautleya* is closely allied with *Roscoea*, most species having, indeed, been originally described as roscoeas. The two genera were originally separated only by flower colour (all of the cautleyas have yellow flowers, but so, as it turns out, do a number of species of *Roscoea*) and, more fundamentally, by their respective seed capsules, which are oblong and slow to open in *Roscoea*, and rounded and quick to open in *Cautleya*. In her revision of *Roscoea* published in 1982, Jill Cowley also pinpointed a number of consistent (and more practically useful) differences in the leaves of the two genera. Chief among them is that *Roscoea* leaves do not have petioles (leaf stems) but instead emerge directly from their sheaths, whereas all *Cautleya* species have well-defined petioles.

Cautleyas are fully deciduous plants that produce elongated, narrow green leaves from extremely small, fleshy rhizomes. Emerging in summer, the inflorescence is a terminal spike borne in the midst of the leaves and is notable for having bracts that are often brightly coloured, each holding a single yellow or orange flower. The flowers are very similar to those of *Roscoea*, with a prominent labellum 2.5 cm (1 inch) long. The labellum reflexes downwards beneath a hooded dorsal petal.

All cautleyas are fine and reliable plants for the temperate garden where they are easily grown and highly attractive in flower. Cautleyas enjoy a position in either dappled shade or light sun, but must not be allowed to get too hot or parched.

Cautleya cathcartii

Minimum temperature: -15ºC (5ºF)
Height: to 50 cm (20 inches)

First described by John G. Baker in 1890, this species is least frequently encountered in cultivation. A native of Xizang (Tibetan Autonomous Region), Nepal, and Sikkim, plants are found in open forest at elevations of 1700 to 2500 m (5600–8200 feet). The species is similar to the more familiar *Cautleya gracilis*, but differs from that species by having flowering spikes that bear between 15 and 20 pale orange or bright yellow flowers each with a 2.5-cm (1-inch) long cleft labellum. The flowers are produced in June and make a conspicuous display among the 20-cm (8-inch) long, narrowly lanceolate leaves.

Probably the hardiest of the cautleyas, *Cautleya cathcartii* has recently been introduced into cultivation by Bleddyn and Sue Wynn-Jones of Crûg Farm Plants in northern Wales. Their seed collection (BSWJ2281) was made from northern India. The plants have leaves with red-purple infused undersides, together with bright yellow flowers supported by contrasting red bracts.

Cautleya gracilis

Synonym: *Cautleya lutea*
Minimum temperature: -15ºC (5ºF)
Height: to 80 cm (31 inches)

This species was originally named *Roscoea gracilis* (the slender *Roscoea*) by James Edward Smith in 1822. The name *Cautleya lutea* was also published by John Forbes Royle, who believed it to be a separate species; however the two were merged by James Dandy in 1932, and the name *C. gracilis* has priority since it was the earliest published. Nevertheless, many plants (perhaps most) are currently grown under the name *C. lutea* and much confusion exists over the identity of various cultivated plants since the species is naturally rather variable, particularly in flower. Many separate introductions have been made in recent years.

Cautleya gracilis is primarily a native of the Himalaya, from Kashmir in the west through Nepal, Xizang (Tibetan Autonomous Region), and Sikkim, with populations spreading on into Yunnan and Sichuan provinces in China, Thailand, and Vietnam. The species frequents cool, moist forested valleys at altitudes of up to 3100 m (10,100 feet). It also grows on moss-covered boulders and as an epiphyte on trees. The narrow, arching leaves are up to 30 cm (12 inches) long by 2–4 cm ($^{3}/_{4}$–1$^{3}/_{4}$ inches) wide. In July, the 10-cm (4-inch) tall inflorescences are prominently displayed well clear of the foliage, each holding from two to ten flowers. The flowers vary from primrose through to darker canary yellow, and open in succession from the base of the flower spike, each lasting up to five days. The colour of the rachis and calyces can also vary from pinkish green through to darker red, the latter forming a fine contrast with the yellow flowers. (Plate 8)

Cautleya spicata

Synonyms: *Cautleya robusta, C. spicata* 'Robusta'
Minimum temperature: -10°C (15°F)
Height: to 60 cm (24 inches)

This species was originally named as *Roscoea spicata* by James Edward Smith in 1822. A native of Guizhou, Sichuan, and Yunnan provinces and Xizang (Tibetan Autonomous Region), where plants occur at altitudes of 1100 to 2600 m (3600–8500 feet), *Cautleya spicata* is also present in Bhutan, northern India, Nepal, and Sikkim where, like all cautleyas, it inhabits the leaf litter of shady forest floors. It also occurs as an epiphyte. From a horticultural standpoint, the primary difference between this species and *C. gracilis* is that *C. spicata* produces a much more densely flowered, 12-cm (4 $^{3}/_{4}$-inch) tall inflorescence, with 40 or more flowers per spike being not uncommon.

In many, but not all, forms of the species, the leaf stems and the inflorescence are heavily infused with dark red; the rachis is entirely red; and the bracts that hold the flowers are pinkish. In such forms the flowers are invariably heavily pigmented also and open from golden orange buds. While these dark-flowered plants are extremely striking, they are not botanically distinct from the species as a whole, and many intermediate colour forms also exist. Opinions are divided as to whether *Cautleya robusta* is deserving of separate specific, varietal, or even cultivar status. It differs from *C. spicata* only in that is has a taller inflorescence and a consistently deep red rachis. (Plate 9)

Cornukaempferia

Like the similarly monikered *Caulokaempferia*, this genus was named by Kai Larsen in association with John Mood of the Waimea Arboretum, Hawaii. Published in 1997, the new genus was established after the discovery of *Cornukaempferia aurantifolia* in Thailand. The generic name means "horned *Kaempferia*" and refers to the prominent, curved anther crest (similar to those found in *Zingiber*) and the close resemblance of the leaves to those of *Kaempferia*. Genetic studies have revealed that, despite the considerable foliar resemblance to *Kaempferia*, *Cornukaempferia* is instead a close sister genus to *Zingiber*. The two species that have been discovered to date are highly ornamental, low-growing groundcover plants, native to deep forest shade in northern Thailand. They have been successfully crossed with one another, and the resulting hybrid may prove to be the best of the genus both ornamentally and in terms of ease of cultivation.

Cornukaempferia aurantiflora 'Jungle Gold'

Minimum temperature: -7ºC (20ºF)
Height: to 25 cm (10 inches)

'Jungle Gold', the primary form of the species currently in cultivation, was originally purchased from a Bangkok market in the early 1990s. From there the plant was taken to Australia, where it was believed to be a new species of *Kaempferia*. In 1996 a live specimen was despatched to John Mood in Hawaii, together with a photograph of the plant in flower, which appeared to bear more resemblance to a *Zingiber*. Mood was somewhat sceptical and considered that the photograph might have been a hoax, until his specimen flowered in 1997, and it immediately became clear that this was, indeed, a new genus.

The plants are fully deciduous and are late to break dormancy, with new leaves not appearing until temperatures reach 20ºC (68ºF)—typically May and June in the United Kingdom. The prominently ribbed, ovate leaves can reach 25 cm (10 inches) long by 15 cm (6 inch) wide and, after emerging upright, are subsequently held at right angles to their short petioles, and thus parallel to the ground. The leaf colour is dark green with blackish-red overtones above, deeper purple beneath. Overlaid upon this are strong patches of silver sited between the upper leaf veins, concentrated towards the margins. In some specimens around 75% of the leaf area is silver, with just the central vein area remaining in the dark colours. The beautiful leaves are only part of the attraction, however, as the flowers that emerge in succession through June and July from short stems at the centre of the leaf axils are equally appealing. These consist of a large, ovate labellum 5 cm (2 inches) long. The ruffled labellum curls to forms a loose, open tube in conjunction with the shorter corolla lobes. The flowers are a bright orangey-gold, lined with red, opening from deep red-orange buds, and have a prominent crested anther in the throat.

Cornukaempferia aurantiflora should be grown in full shade in a warm, moist location. It is very susceptible to rot if allowed to become wet while dormant. Ideally plants should be protected from the worst excesses of winter, although they may be left in the ground where the correct conditions can be provided.

A second collection of the species was made in 1998, from Chiang Rai Province in northern Thailand, by J. Maxwell; this was the first time that the species was observed in its natural habitat. 'Jungle Gold' has been successfully micropropagated in the United States and Europe and is now widely available worldwide.

Cornukaempferia longipeteolata

Minimum temperature: -10ºC (15ºF)
Height: to 60 cm (24 inches)

Florida-based ginger collector John Banta found this second *Cornukaempferia* species in 1996, growing in dense shade in a mountainous evergreen forest at 765 m (2500 feet) in the Petchabun province of northern Thailand. It was initially believed to be a new species of *Kaempferia*, as had been the case with *C. aurantiflora*, but after comparison with the earlier collected plant, it became clear that this too was a *Cornukaempferia*. Phylogenetic analysis, coupled with the morphological differences, lead to it being published in 1999 as a separate species.

Cornukaempferia longipeteolata has somewhat larger leaves than *C. aurantiflora*, each reaching approximately 30 cm (12 inches) long by 20 cm (8 inches) wide. These, as the name suggests, are held on elongated petioles, in pairs, and are a very dark, velvety black-green, with sparse, randomly arranged small silver patches and paler, raised vein "ribs". Aside from the rich colouration, the leaves somewhat resemble those of a *Hosta*. The flowers, though, are substantially more interesting. Shortly after the leaves have unfurled, the short inflorescence appears in the axis between the pairs of leaf petioles. Each inflorescence produces between five and ten flowers in succession, and each has a crinkled labellum 4 cm (1½ inches) long by 3 cm (1¼ inches) wide, coloured deep golden with a large red throat patch. Beneath the labellum is a pair of 3-cm (1¼-inch) long orange lateral staminodes, and above are three dark orange corolla lobes, the lateral pair both 4 cm (1½ inches) long, and the prominent dorsal lobe 5 cm (2 inches) long.

Seemingly both hardier and more vigorous than *Cornukaempferia aurantiflora*, this superb species is perhaps the more adaptable to temperate cultivation, given full shade and a rich, open woodland type soil. Again, the plants must not be allowed to get truly wet while dormant.

Costus

First described by Carl Linnaeus in 1753, *Costus* is, with at least 70 species, the largest and most significant genus of the family *Costaceae*. While they are now generally regarded as separate from the *Zingiberaceae*, the *Costaceae* are, nevertheless, still very much thought of as gingers and this, together with their considerable ornamental appeal, fully justifies the inclusion here of these fascinating plants.

Native to Central and South America, Africa, and Southeast Asia, *Costus* species are either tropical or subtropical in origin. Thus most are quite unsuitable for the temperate garden; however, a few species have been found to be remarkably hardy and, with a moderate amount of care, these can make extremely beautiful and rewarding garden plants.

Costus species characteristically produce leafy stems that are often gently kinked or curling—unlike members of the *Zingiberaceae*, which produce straight or arching stems. Often very handsome, generally lightly pubescent leaves clothe these stems and are arranged in a spiral pattern, normally concentrated in the upper half of the stems.

The *Costus* inflorescence is typically produced from the tip of the leafy stems, although some species can also bloom on additional, separate, almost leafless stems that arise directly from the rhizome. The inflorescence itself is relatively uniform throughout the genus and consists of a series of bracts that are often colourful, and which, depending on the species, may be tightly clasped together in a pinecone shape or held more loosely. Flowers emerge in small numbers over a long period and have either a large, showy, tissue-paper-textured, trumpet-shaped labellum emerging from a tubular corolla, or a colourful corolla, also tubular, which entirely contains and obscures the labellum. Based on these two flower morphologies Paulus Maas proposed two botanical sections within *Costus* in his 1977 monograph on the *Costaceae*. Section *Costus* contains those species with showy, exerted labella, and section *Ornithophilus* (the term for flowers pollinated by hummingbirds, as indeed these *Costus* are) comprises the species with tubular flowers and hidden labella.

Aside from some forms of *Costus speciosus* and the African *C. spectabilis*, all *Costus* species are naturally evergreen in the wild. In temperate cultivation they will generally be cut back by frosts, overwintering as a dormant rhizome before re-sprouting the following spring. Typically, *Costus* species re-grow earlier than most of the subtropical gingers, with shoots appearing in April and May. Since the flowers occur on the new shoots, an enforced winter dormancy does not impede the plant's ability to flower so long as it is provided with sufficient food and water to build strong new leafy stems.

Almost all species are forest dwellers and have traditionally been grown in shade. In temperate gardens, so long as the soil is kept well watered while the plants are in growth, the additional warmth of a sunny position will allow for better flowering and promote healthy rhizome growth. (Plate 10)

Costus cuspidatus

Synonym: *Costus igneus*
Minimum temperature: -10°C (15°F)
Height: to 60 cm (24 inches)

The smallest *Costus* species currently in cultivation, this native of southeastern Brazil grows in full shade among the leaf litter of humid, subtropical forests. The short purplish stems are clothed with glossy, pointed (cuspidate), ovate, waxy leaves up to 20 cm (8 inches) long by 8 cm (3 inches) wide. The leaves are green on the upper surface and typically infused with purple beneath. The short inflorescence is produced at any time between July and October, and the flowers appear in succession, with between one and four open together on each stem. The small, tubular buds open to reveal very showy, large flowers in which the 8-cm (3-inch) wide labellum is held completely flat against the foliage, fully revealing the tiny yellow stamen attached to its throat. The labellum is almost circular, with heavily notched margins, and is an unmarked and a uniform bright tangerine orange.

Costus cuspidatus has been successfully tested to remarkably low temperatures. It is not a difficult plant to cultivate in a sheltered position, with a moist soil in dappled shade or part sun—the higher light levels encouraging flowering. Under such conditions the species will gradually form leafy clumps; however, they must not be allowed to get too wet while dormant since the rhizome is particularly susceptible to rot, and depending on location, the growing site may be covered in winter. This extremely ornamental ginger is widely available in the United States and is now beginning to appear in Europe. (Plate 12)

Costus lacerus

Synonyms: *Costus chinensis, C. speciosus* hort.
Minimum temperature: -12°C (10°F) ?
Height: to 300 cm (118 inches)

Costus lacerus may well prove to be the most northerly growing *Costus* species and this, coupled with the relatively high altitudes at which it naturally occurs, makes the plant an enticing prospect for the hardy gardener. Named by François Gagnepain in 1903, this species is a native of forests streamsides at 1100 to 2200 m (3600–7200 feet) in Yunnan and Guangxi provinces of China, Xizang (Tibetan Autonomous Region), Bhutan, northern India, Sikkim, and northern Thailand.

This extremely ornamental species is very closely allied to the more familiar *Costus speciosus*. It produces large, glossy leaves up to 45 cm (18 inches) long by 15 cm (6 inches) wide, and pubescent beneath. The inflorescences appear from July to September and consist of a loose cone, to 15 cm (6 inches) long, of deep red bracts from which emerge the large, trumpet-shaped labella. As it was originally described *C. lacerus* has a labellum of pale pink; however, plants in cultivation generally have white flowers with a pale, acid yellow tint in the throat.

Although the species is widely grown, most specimens in the trade are mislabelled as *Costus speciosus*. Given that *C. speciosus* is very widely cultivated through much of the natural range of *C. lacerus*, it seems reasonable to suppose that hybrids between the two may well abound, and some of the plants in cultivation may fall into this category. The two species can be separated by the flower bracts, which in *C. speciosus* remain firm and pointed, whereas in *C. lacerus* they soon break into loose fibres (that is, they lacerate). Whether, once genetic analysis has been undertaken, this morphological difference is sufficient to maintain the two plants at specific level is debateable, but from a hardy horticultural point of view *C. lacerus* is well worth obtaining in preference to all other *Costus* species. It is hoped that specifically sourced high-altitude Chinese stock might soon be introduced to Western cultivation.

Costus pictus

Synonym: *Costus hieroglyphica*
Minimum temperature: -12ºC (10ºF)
Height: to 240 cm (96 inches)

Although it is native to high-altitude forests of Mexico and Belize, *Costus pictus* is among the hardiest and easiest species to grow in a temperate location. It makes a bold, handsome plant that produces tall, cane-like stems. These are clothed with attractive, glossy, stiff, lanceolate leaves up to nearly 40 cm (16 inches) long by 8 cm (3 inches) wide. The leaves have distinctive, sometimes very pronounced, ripples at the margins. The specific name "pictus", and indeed the invalid specific name "hieroglyphica", both refer to the distinctive brown stippling that occurs on the base of the leaf sheaths. The inflorescence in usually produced at the tip of the leafy stems, although a separate flowering stem can also emerge from the rhizome. *Costus pictus* can bloom from July to October. The inflorescence consists of a tight, pinecone-shaped amalgamation of green bracts. The trumpet-shaped flowers emerge from the side of the "cone". The 4-cm (1½-inch) long, butter yellow corolla holds a flared, rounded labellum which has a base colour of pale yellow and is very heavily overlaid with lines of dark purple-red. Each inflorescence lasts for up to one month, with one or two flowers appearing at any one time.

Costus pictus is a vigorous species. Plants succeed best in a moist, rich, and well-drained soil in a wind-sheltered position in light shade or part sun. Rhizomes of this species are much less susceptible to problems in winter than are the rhizomes of other *Costus* species and the plants do not require any special treatment in this regard. The thick stems are highly tolerant of frosts; although they will be defoliated and cut back with prolonged cold, they are able to re-grow strongly in late spring. (Plate 15)

Costus pulverulentus

Minimum temperature: -7°C (20°F)
Height: to 150 cm (60 inches)

Close to *Costus spicatus*, this marginally hardy species is a native of floors of moist forests at up to 1400 m (4600 feet) in Central America. *Costus pulverulentus* has narrowly ovate leaves, 30 cm (12 inches) long by 10 cm (4 inches) wide. Short hairs cover both surfaces. The inflorescences can appear from June to September and consist of a narrow, sharply pointed cone approximately 8 cm (3 inches) long with overlapping scarlet bracts. The bracts are held very tightly together and each has a margin of short brown cilia. Emerging one by one, the flowers have a scarlet to bright pink tubular corolla that a shorter, reflexed, golden yellow labellum, and, unusually, a red protruding stamen.

Costus scaber

Synonym: *Costus spicatus* hort.
Minimum temperature: -10°C (15°F)
Height: to 180 cm (71 inches)

The plant in wide nursery circulation in the United States under the name *Costus spicatus* is not, in fact, that species (which has a green cone inflorescence), but is probably referable to *C. scaber*. A native of Costa Rica, *C. scaber* is relatively widespread at forest margins at altitudes up to 600 m (2000 feet).

Plants are vigorous and produce many strong stems, with archetypal *Costus* curves, particularly towards the tips. The upper portion of the stem is clothed in handsome, obovate, waxy leaves, up to 30 cm long (12 inches) by 10 cm (4 inches) wide, each with a pronounced drip-tip. The inflorescences emerge for a long season from June to October and comprise 10-cm (4-inch) long cone-shaped assemblages of tightly held, orange-red bracts. The flowers appear one at a time, their ornamental portion consisting of a pinkish orange corolla tube 4 cm (1½ inches) long by 15 mm (²⁄₃ inch) wide. The corolla tube almost entirely contains a 3- to 4-cm (1¼- to 1½-inch) long golden labellum.

Suitable for a moist soil in either sun or light shade, *Costus scaber* is a popular and easily grown plant with fine foliage and decorative flowers. It can be readily cultivated in many temperate gardens with minimum attention. While naturally evergreen, the species easily adapts to a deciduous habit and readily re-shoots in spring. (Plate 16)

Costus speciosus

Minimum temperature: -15ºC (5ºF)
Height: to 210 cm (83 inches)

Probably the hardiest of the cultivated *Costus* species, this variable, widely ranging Asian plant is native to clearings and edges of moist forests in Malaysia and Indonesia. It is naturalized in Hawaii and has long been present in China (where it can be found at elevations of up to 1700 m [5600 feet]), Taiwan, India, and the rest of Southeast Asia, but these populations too are probably naturalized cultivated plants rather than true natives. Nevertheless, *C. speciosus* was named (as *Banksea speciosus*) by James Edward Smith in 1791 from one such plant that was collected by Johann Koenig in southern India.

Costus speciosus produces robust, tall, cane-like stems that are stained red-purple and clothed with very, handsome oblong-lanceolate leaves that are 20 cm (8 inches) long by 10 cm (4 inches) wide and covered with a softly downy pubescence. Appearing from August to October, the inflorescence comprises a large, 10-cm (4-inch) tall dark maroon-red, cone-like structure that is made of the many flowering bracts. The exceptionally beautiful, tuba-shaped flowers open, one to four at a time, to reveal a long, tubular white corolla that holds an 8-cm (3-inch) wide, pure white, almost circular labellum with crimped margins. The flower's delicate texture gives the plant its common name of crepe (paper) ginger. The contrast between the shining flowers, the deep red bracts, and the broad dark foliage is exceptionally fine.

Plants that originate from India and China naturally become winter dormant and are the most suitable forms for temperate cultivation. Plants that are native to Southeast Asia remain evergreen in the wild. While they can be successfully grown in frosty gardens, they are clearly not so well adapted to such conditions. Like most *Costus* species, *C. speciosus* is susceptible to rhizome rot while dormant, and the plants should be protected from excess water in winter. In other respects they are extremely hardy. Tony Avent of Plant Delights Nursery has overwintered the species without protection at a remarkable -18ºC (0ºF) in North Carolina. Plants are best grown in a warm, partly sunny position with a seasonally moist soil. A number of plants in cultivation under this name are, in fact, referable to the very similar *C. lacerus*, which see. (Plate 17)

Costus speciosus 'Foster Variegated'

Minimum temperature: -5°C (22°F) ?
Height: to 150 cm (60 inches)

An apparently non-flowering form available in the United States. The variegated foliage has broad, creamy white stripes and contrasts well with the dark red stems. This cultivar is best grown in partial shade to protect the foliage from scorching.

Costus speciosus 'Java Pink'

Minimum temperature: -5°C (22°F) ?
Height: to 210 cm (83 inches)

'Java Pink' is the most commonly seen pink-flowered form. It originates in Indonesia and has a naturally evergreen habit. This cultivar is considerably less hardy than the more northerly, deciduous forms, and is, as a consequence, shy to flower and difficult to overwinter in the garden. When they are produced, the flowers are as for the species, but with a pale pink corolla and a delicate, blush pink labellum.

Costus speciosus 'Tetraploid'

Height: to 120 cm (48 inches)

This excellent form is available in the United States and is considerably more compact and more floriferous than the species. Plants are able to flower from stems 75–90 cm (30–36 inches) tall.

Costus speciosus variegated form

Minimum temperature: -7°C (20°F)
Height: to 150 cm (60 inches)

This unnamed variegated form of the species differs from the more familiar 'Variegatus' in that it has upright stems and much more strongly variegated leaves. Creamy yellow longitudinal stripes and slashes cover much of the leaf surface. This form is reportedly non-flowering.

Costus speciosus 'Variegatus'
Minimum temperature: -7°C (20°F)
Height: to 120 cm (48 inches)

This widely distributed cultivar has broad leaves edged with an irregular band of creamy white, with occasional additional faint lines across the leaf surface. The plant is also notable for the habit of its dark red stems: they tend to develop a strongly spiralling pattern that frequently makes large specimens wider than they are tall. This arrangement of stems and foliage is exceptionally fine. Like other variegated forms, this one does not flower and is less hardy than the type, but is well worth cultivating wherever conditions allow. (Plate 18)

Costus spectabilis

Minimum temperature: -7°C (20°F) ?
Height: to 10 cm (4 inches)

Eduard Fenzl originally named this African species (as *Cadalvena spectabilis*) in 1865 for its large, showy flowers. In 1883 George Bentham transferred it to *Kaempferia* (as *K. spectabilis*). Finally, in 1893, Karl Schumann transferred it to *Costus* as *C. spectabilis*. Based upon this reclassification Schumann subsequently sunk the genus *Cadalvena* into *Costus* in 1904.

Known locally as the trumpet crocus, *Costus spectabilis* is present in many intertropical African countries, where it grows in savannah areas that are subject to marked dry and moist seasons. The species has a naturally deciduous habit and is almost certainly hardy, but is problematic both to cultivate and propagate, and is only suitable for container cultivation in a shade or alpine house.

At first glance this plant looks nothing like a ginger. The stem is vestigial, and the three or four 15-cm (6-inch) long, fleshy, ovate leaves are held fully prostrate. Appearing in summer, the flowers are among the largest of all *Costus* flowers. They comprise a short corolla and an 8-cm (3-inch) long bright yellow cupped-shaped labellum. The rhizome is exceedingly long and narrow; when allowed, it will grow straight downwards without making any contingent offshoots. This feature renders the species very difficult to propagate by normal vegetative means, and the growing plant is also highly liable to fracture away from the rhizome when handled.

All of the adaptations made by *Costus spectabilis*—the long, deep-rooting rhizome; the large, fleshy leaves; the prostrate habit—are indicative of drought tolerance. The species should be accommodated in an open, gritty medium that is watered regularly while the plant is in growth, but kept completely dry when the plant is dormant.

Costus spiralis

Minimum temperature: -4°C (25°F) ?
Height: to 150 cm (60 inches)

Named by William Roscoe in 1807, this South American species is purported to be reasonably hardy, but this remains untested and seems questionable. Plants have a growth habit resembling that of *Costus scaber*, with waxy, glabrous, broadly lanceolate leaves on gently curving stems. The inflorescences are tight, squat pink cones of bracts, borne from summer to late autumn. The pink flowers appear in succession and consist of a tubular pale pink corolla, within which is contained a dark pink labellum. The species is in nursery circulation in the United States and would certainly require a near-dry dormancy if it were to be successfully grown in temperate zones.

Costus woodsonii

Minimum temperature: -5°C (22°F) ?
Height: to 90 cm (36 inches)

First described by Paulus Maas in 1972 and now known in the trade as French kiss, this small species is a naturally evergreen, forest-dwelling native of Panama and Costa Rica. It has been proven to be marginally hardy, with a deciduous habit, in frost-prone gardens. *Costus woodsonii* has short, gently curving stems that bear glossy, obovate leaves and, from July to October, produce 7-cm (2³/4-inch) long, tight, narrow cones of bright red flower bracts. The small flowers appear one by one and have a tubular orange corolla surrounding a largely hidden yellow labellum. *Costus woodsonii* requires a near-dry dormancy to avoid rotting of the rhizome and a warm, moist, sunny position if it is to succeed in any temperate zone. (Plate 19)

Curcuma

Curcuma comprises approximately 50 small to medium-sized species, pre-dominantly native to Southeast Asia, with outposts in the Indian Himalaya and southern China, plus one species that is endemic to Australasia and the South Pacific. They are commonly called the hidden gingers or hidden lilies, referring to the inflorescences, which in many (but not all) species are near to the ground where they are often obscured beneath their large leaves. Another frequently encountered name is Siam tulip, referring to the petal-like appearance of the showy, shiny upper flower bracts that often emerge in a cup-shaped, tulip-like formation.

Carl Linnaeus first described this important genus in 1753 and in doing so chose to adopt and Latinize "kurkum", the long-standing Arabic name for the saffron colour of the spice turmeric, which is derived from the rhizomes of *Costa longa*. Bearing this derivation in mind, *Curcuma* should be pronounced with two hard "k" sounds: "KUR-kum-uh". Aside from *C. longa* itself, many, and probably most species have been, and continue to be, utilized as spices, vegetables, colouring agents, perfumes, oils, and a huge array of medicines. They also are widely cultivated as ornamentals.

Visually, *Curcuma* species are relatively similar to one another. Although little work has been done in the past to establish the relationships between the species, recent genetic research conducted at the Royal Botanic Garden, Edinburgh, has revealed that there is indeed little genetic variance between the species. The results suggest that the species are only recently diverged from a common ancestor.

Curcumas are exclusively deciduous plants. In temperate gardens they emerge from dormancy between April and July, depending on the species and the prevailing local temperatures. Many have extremely ornamental foliage, with large, paddle-shaped or elongate-ovate leaves that are invariably heavily ribbed by veins. While all have green foliage, a number of curcumas display a prominent red stripe either side of the midvein, and others have deep red-stained stems that contrast beautifully with the vivid green leaves.

Flowering can occur either early in the season, before (or at the same time as) the foliage emerges, with the inflorescences produced on separate, short stems that arise directly from the rhizome, or in late summer and autumn, with the flower spikes held at the terminus of the leafy stems. Some species can produce both forms of inflorescence and can also have two distinct flowering seasons. In all cases the inflorescence comprises a stiffly upright spike of broad, spirally arranged bracts that are fused to one another to create pouches in which the flowers themselves are borne. Most curcumas have two kinds of floral bracts: bracts occupying the lower portion of the inflorescence are fertile, generally green, and hold flowers, while those at the top of the spike are sterile (without flowers) and are almost always larger and more highly coloured or pure white. These showy upper bracts are held in a flaring rosette shape known as a coma.

Like many of the gingers, and indeed most of the vegetation in northern Thailand and its surrounds, the Southeast Asian *Curcuma* species have evolved their dormancy to cope with the extremely dry season that occurs between the monsoons, when their native habitat receives almost no rainfall and is occasionally swept by fire. This period lasts for three to five months in Asia. Although it is also the hottest time of the year, the plants are able to adapt to temperate winter dormancy, with the trigger being a drop in temperature rather than a lack of moisture.

Like many subtropical deciduous gingers, curcumas are, understandably, susceptible to winter wet. All species should be given an open, free-draining medium, with the sensitive varieties requiring additional protection. Species that originate from China and the Himalaya tend to be far more tolerant in winter than do the Southeast Asian species, although none will survive waterlogging while dormant. When in growth most *Curcuma* species require a position in full sun (with midday shade in the hottest locations) and high levels of nutrition and moisture. Given these conditions, they have been proven to be among the hardiest of the neotropical gingers and will thrive in a remarkably wide range of locations.

The down side of curcumas is that, because of the reduced length of their growing season—sometimes just three or four months, with plants typically emerging from dormancy in June and July—many are notoriously hard to flower outdoors in the United Kingdom, and those species that produce their inflorescences on the leafy stems are unlikely to flower here at all. Curcumas that bloom before the leaves emerge are far more successful in southern England and should be grown in the warmest, sunniest position available to encourage good growth. That said, many curcumas are well worth growing for their superb foliage alone, and their relative hardiness and general vigour allows for a variety of cultivation possibilities. In cooler climates, with a shorter active growing season, the plants will also, not surprisingly, be smaller than where they are able to emerge in spring and continue growth into late October.

In the southern United States all the species described in this book can be expected to succeed and flower wherever temperatures remain above those stated for each variety. Indeed, *Curcuma* species are more widely grown there than any other gingers, aside from *Hedychium* species.

Curcuma alismatifolia

Minimum temperature: -10°C (15°F)
Height: to 80 cm (31 inches)

Named by François Gagnepain in 1903, this species is originally native to open grasslands of Cambodia and northern Thailand. It is now widely grown throughout southern and southeastern Asia.

Curcuma alismatifolia produces narrow, gently arching, lanceolate foliage with leaves 45 cm (18 inches) long by 5 cm (2 inches) wide. In some forms the leaves have a dark red central vein. Flowering occurs between June and August, depending on when growth commenced. The inflorescence, which is unusual for being borne on a narrow, elongated peduncle that emerges directly from the rhizome, extends to 15 cm (6 inches) or so above the height of the leaves. The lower bracts are green with dusky red margins, but the deep lavender-pink sterile upper bracts are much larger than those of many species, and are held in a loose, 10-cm (4-inch) tall torch shape. The petal-like appearance of the bracts gives the plant its common name Siam tulip. The white flowers have a large ovate deep purple labellum and appear in succession for approximately four weeks.

In cultivation *Curcuma alismatifolia* requires a position in full sun to promote flowering and to prevent the flowering stem from becoming leggy and weak. It has found much favour as an ornamental plant and is widely available in Southeast Asia, the United States, and Europe. A very conservative estimate is that at least 30 cultivars have been named. Many of these are being mass grown in Thailand for export around the world.

Curcuma alismatifolia 'Chiangmai Pink'
Height: to 60 cm (24 inches)

This cultivar is smaller than the type and has darker pigmentation throughout. The leaves are coloured deep green with a burgundy red midvein. The inflorescence has a coma of pale, lavender-purple bracts.

Curcuma alismatifolia 'Kimono Pink'
Height: to 45 cm (18 inches)

A semi-dwarf cultivar, 'Kimono Pink' is smaller than the species in all its parts, with a much more compact inflorescence held no more than 30 cm (12 inches) above ground level. The upper bracts are pale rose pink, and the labellum is a deep violet.

Curcuma alismatifolia 'Rose'

This cultivar was selected for its exceptionally large, deep pink upper bracts that are held in a 15-cm (6-inch) in diameter bowl arrangement to resemble a semi-double *Magnolia*.

Curcuma alismatifolia 'Snow White'

Recently introduced from Thailand by Tim Chapman of Gingerwood Nursery, St. Gabriel, Louisiana, this very beautiful cultivar has upper bracts that are indeed white, but each has a deep purple tip and an infusion of blush pink in its upper half.

Curcuma alismatifolia 'Thai Beauty'

'Thai Beauty' is one of the cultivars that is mass produced for export from Southeast Asia. The upper bracts are a much deeper, magenta pink than is typical for the species.

Curcuma alismatifolia 'Thai Supreme'

'Thai Supreme' is similar to 'Thai Beauty' but with fuchsia-pink upper bracts, each with a deep purple tip.

Curcuma alismatifolia 'Tropic Snow'
Height: to 60 cm (24 inches)

This cultivar is slightly smaller than the species and bears pure white upper bracts, each with a green tip and a faint green central vein.

Curcuma alismatifolia 'White'
Height: to 50 cm (20 inches)

'White' is very similar to 'Tropic Snow', but with broader upper bracts that are white with a prominent green tip.

Curcuma amada

Minimum temperature: -7°C (20°F)
Height: to 90 cm (36 inches)

Named by William Roxburgh in 1810, *Curcuma amada* is probably originally native to Bengal, although the species is cultivated throughout India for medicinal and culinary purposes and is also found on the Andaman Islands, off the coast of Myanmar. In India the plant is known as the mango ginger, in reference to the mango-like aroma of the edible fresh rhizomes.

Curcuma amada has very fine, banana-like, broad, paddle-shaped leaves that have prominent ribbing and frequently a purple flush towards the axis. The 15-cm (6-inch) tall inflorescence precedes the foliage and is held on a 20-cm (8-inch) long peduncle. The lower bracts are green and bear small, dark yellow flowers, while the upper rosette of purplish-pink sterile bracts is large, showy, and broadly star-shaped. In India the species produces flowers in spring, but in temperate zones the plants emerge from dormancy in June or July.

Curcuma angustifolia

Minimum temperature: -10°C (15°F)
Height: to 180 cm (71 inches)

One of the largest plants of the genus, *Curcuma angustifolia* is native to open grassland and light woodland in the eastern Himalaya. It was described by William Roxburgh in 1810. The superb leaves are 60–80 cm (24–31 inches) long, broad, and heavily ribbed, appearing in midsummer in temperate gardens. The inflorescences precede the leaves in early summer and are held on short, 10-cm (4-inch) long peduncles. Each inflorescence has numerous pale, almost lemony green bracts that bear tubular, small yellow flowers. Topping the inflorescence, above the fertile bracts, are approximately 20 flaring sterile bracts. These are typically pale lavender in colour, although darker pink forms and pink and white bicoloured forms also occur.

Curcuma aromatica

Minimum temperature: -12°C (10°F)
Height: to 90 cm (36 inches)

Richard Salisbury first described this species in 1807. It was probably originally native to the Indian Himalaya, but is now widely cultivated for medicinal and culinary purposes (as a substitute for turmeric) throughout southern Asian and southern China. *Curcuma aromatica* bears handsome, oblong, ribbed leaves that reach 60 cm (24 inches) long by 20 cm (8 inches) wide and have elongated drip-tips. Each leaf is held on a tall petiole 40 cm (16 inches) long. The flowering spikes appear from bare ground around June or July in temperate gardens and precede the leaves. The inflorescence is about 15 cm (6 inches) tall and has a few large green fertile bracts that contain bright yellow, 2.5-cm (1-inch) long flowers. The upper, sterile bracts are white at their base, strongly flushed with dark purplish pink.

Curcuma aff. *attenuata* 'Maroon Beauty'

Minimum temperature: -10°C (15°F)
Height: to 60 cm (24 inches)

This short *Curcuma* originated in Thailand and possibly represents a new species. The inflorescences are 15–20 cm (6–8 inches) tall and produced well before the foliage, sometimes as early as April. The inflorescences have a few flaring, purple-tipped green fertile bracts bearing prominent yellow flowers with pink corolla lobes. The much larger, sterile upper bracts are pointed and deep pink. 'Maroon Beauty' is a robust plant and one of the best curcumas for cultivation in the United Kingdom.

Curcuma aurantiaca

Minimum temperature: -5°C (22°F)
Height: to 90 cm (36 inches)

Commonly known as the rainbow curcuma, in reference to its colourful flower bracts, this superb species is, unfortunately, questionably hardy and is probably restricted to outdoor use in the mildest areas of the United States. Named in 1915 by Dutch botanist Coenraad van Zijp from material collected on Java, the species is also found in Malaysia, Thailand, and Sri

Lanka. *Curcuma aurantiaca* produces magnificent foliage. The very heavily ribbed, glossy leaves are around 45 cm (18 inches) long by 30 cm (12 inches) wide and emerge in June and July. They are soon followed by the inflorescences, which are generally hidden below the foliage, but are almost equally appealing. The inflorescences are 20-cm (8-inch) tall towers of deep cherry red bracts bearing little golden flowers. Unusually for curcumas, the sterile bracts are less colourful (a pale pink) and smaller than the fertile ones.

Curcuma aff. *aurantiaca* 'Khymer Orange'

Minimum temperature: -10ºC (15ºF)
Height: to 60 cm (24 inches)

This spectacular form was collected in Cambodia and almost certainly represents a new species close to *Curcuma aurantiaca*. From July plants bear superb, 30-cm (12-inch) long paddle-shaped, arching leaves with corrugated ridges. The globe-shaped, 15-cm (6-inch) tall inflorescences emerge from September at the centre of the foliage and have entirely fertile bracts coloured deep amber with prominent, protruding tubular deep yellow flowers. This plant is hardier than *C. aurantiaca* but requires a well-drained medium and is probably too late into growth to succeed in the United Kingdom. (Plate 20)

Curcuma australasica

Minimum temperature: -12ºC (10ºF)
Height: to 180 cm (71 inches)

The so-called Aussie plume, or Cape York turmeric, this native of tropical northern Australia—Cape York, Arnhem Land, and Thursday Island—grows among dry scrub and at the margins of rainforests. The species was named by Joseph Hooker in 1867, although it was discovered in Cape York and introduced to cultivation in England by the famous Exeter nurseryman John Veitch. *Curcuma australasica* has evolved its deciduous habit in tandem with the local rainfall conditions, where up to 150 cm (60 inches) fall each summer, but the winters are essentially dry. As with many gingers from Southeast Asia, *C. australasica* has a habit that allows the species to be adapted to temperate cultivation with relative ease. Indeed, *C. australasica* has proven to be one of the hardiest species of the genus.

The handsome, erect, and ribbed slightly grey glaucous leaves emerge from May to July and reach around 60 cm (24 inches) long. The 20- to 30-cm (8- to 12-inch) inflorescences appear either in tandem with, or shortly before, the foliage and have shiny, pale green fertile bracts that bear bright yellow tubular flowers. The sterile upper bracts are glossy and white at the base, becoming deep pink towards the tip; they are produced in large numbers in a generally very symmetrically poised rosette. (Plate 21)

Curcuma elata

Minimum temperature: -15°C (5°F)
Height: to 240 cm (96 inches)

Named by William Roxburgh in 1814, this supremely impressive species from Myanmar is both the tallest and one of the hardiest curcumas in cultivation. It is notably early to break dormancy, with the inflorescences appearing first, typically in May, although they can emerge as early as April in the southern United States. Held on very thick stems, the flowering display is very bold, with 35-cm (14-inch) tall spikes. The funnel-shaped fertile lower bracts are green, and the tubular white flowers have a deep yellow mark at the tip on the labellum. The sterile upper bracts are large, numerous, and coloured a luminous lavender pink, deepening to purple at their tips. The ovate leaves are 45 cm (18 inches) long and equally impressive, with very heavy veinal ribbing and a faint purple band on either side of the midvein.

Curcuma flaviflora

Minimum temperature: -12°C (10°F)
Height: to 90 cm (36 inches)

This Chinese species was named by Shao Quan Tong in 1986 and has quickly been dubbed the fiery curcuma in the United States. The plant is endemic to forests at up to 1400 m (4600 feet) in Menghai county, southwestern Yunnan province. It is one of the most satisfactory of the genus for cultivation in temperate zones.

Handsome, narrowly ovate, heavily veined leaves emerge in May and reach 25 cm (10 inches) long by 10 cm (4 inches) wide, each held on a short petiole only 5 cm (2 inches) long. The inflorescences occur near the base of the leafy stems between June and September, and they emerge by bursting though the junction of the leaf sheaths to rest at an angle to the stem. The spike is short, at just 6 cm (2½ inches) or so, but is comprised entirely of fertile, overlapping, bright scarlet, upright bracts. The flowers are far more prominent than those in most *Curcuma* species and fully emerge from the bracts to reveal a white-striped, bright yellow labellum with a pair of yellow lateral staminodes, the whole about 4 cm (1½ inches) long.

Curcuma flaviflora requires a shadier position than that suitable for most curcumas. Although certainly hardy, the plants must be given a very well drained medium to prevent rotting of the rhizome while dormant. The species is now available in the United States, and it is hoped the plant will soon be tested more extensively in the United Kingdom where it may prove to be the best of the genus in terms of growth pattern and flowering reliability.

Curcuma gracillima

Minimum temperature: -7°C (20°F)
Height: to 60 cm (24 inches)

Native to Laos and northern Thailand, this somewhat variable small species was named by François Gagnepain for its narrow flowering stems and slender leaves. Typically emerging in June, the leaves are very linear and 30 cm (12 inches) long. A 30-cm (12-inch) tall peduncle develops at the centre of the leaf axis and eventually bears the inflorescence in September. The inflorescences are modest in size, generally 6–7 cm (2½–2¾ inches) tall, but well displayed above the foliage with a few green fertile, broad bracts bearing white flowers. The purple labellum is heavily veined with white. The true species is rarely seen and not terribly ornamental beside most other *Curcuma* species. Virtually all plants in current cultivation under this name are referable to *C. rhabdota.*

Curcuma inodora

Minimum temperature: -10°C (15°F)
Height: to 120 cm (48 inches)

Ethelbert Blatter, founder of the St. Xavier's College herbarium, which is now the largest collection of plant specimens in western India, named this

Indian species in 1931. True plants of the species are rarely offered by nurseries, but *Curcuma inodora* is one of the hardier members of the genus and is worth seeking out. It has broad, ribbed leaves with a prominent burgundy stripe along the midrib. The leafy stems are often also infused with burgundy. The foliage appears in May and June and is followed a few weeks later by 10-cm (4-inch) tall inflorescences that occur at the base of the stem, pushing through the leaf sheath. Each comprises a loose arrangement of jade green fertile bracts with a smaller number of pink to burgundy-red flushed, upward-facing, sterile bracts.

Curcuma longa

Synonym: *Curcuma domestica*
Minimum temperature: -15ºC (5ºF)
Height: to 120 cm (48 inches)

Carl Linnaeus named *Curcuma longa* in 1753, appropriately making it the type species of the genus, for this is the plant that yields the spice turmeric as well as the saffron yellow pigment for which the genus is named. In 1918 Theodoric Valeton described a new species, *C. domestica*, which he believed was the true source of turmeric; however, further examination in 1950 by Richard Holttum demonstrated that the two species were synonymous and that *C. longa* was its rightful (first published) name. Despite this, the invalid name *C. domestica* is still very widely used to this day, perhaps because the "domestica" epithet better fits with people's expectations of the plant. The species has been cultivated for the best part of 4000 years. More recently it has been distributed widely throughout the tropics and subtropics, thus obscuring its precise natural origins, although it is certainly a native of India.

In May and June *Curcuma longa* produces elliptic, bright green, ribbed leaves up to 90 cm (36 inches) long by about 15 cm (6 inches) wide. The inflorescences appear from August to October, both on separate flowering stems that emerge directly from the rhizome and at the terminus of the leafy stems on 15-cm (6-inch) long peduncles. The flower spike is about 15 cm (6 inches) tall with pale green fertile lower bracts that hold small, pale yellow flowers and a coma of much larger, widely opening, showy sterile bracts. The sterile bracts are white, sometimes flushed with pink or pale purple.

Curcuma longa is an easily grown species for full sun or part shade. It is unlikely to produce flowers outdoors in the United Kingdom. Nonetheless, the plants are well worth growing for their foliage, as well as their interesting history.

Curcuma ornata

This invalid name appears to have been applied to specimens of a number of species, including *Curcuma zedoaria* and *C. elata*. Friedrich Voigt first published the name in 1845 (following an earlier reference by Nathaniel Wallich), but the plant was never described. It seems likely that the original *C. ornata* was always synonymous with another species

Curcuma petiolata

Synonym: *Curcuma cordata* Wallich
Minimum temperature: -15°C (5°F)
Height: to 120 cm (48 inches)

This species is native to the Indian Himalaya at altitudes up to 1500 m (4900 feet) and could easily hold a record for messy nomenclature. William Roxburgh first mentioned the plant in 1814, as *Curcuma cordifolia* but failed to provide a valid description. He subsequently named another species, *C. petiolata*, his (fully valid) description of which was published posthumously in 1820. Some 10 years later Nathaniel Wallich named yet another plant from India as *C. cordata*. After researching the genus in 1890, John Baker determined that all three plants were the same species, and thus the first published name, *C. petiolata*, is the correct one. Rather oddly, the confusion continues even now, more than 100 years later, and most of the plants in cultivation are still wrongly labelled as *C. cordata* and/or "Jewel of Thailand".

For all that, this is an extremely fine garden plant, with heavily ribbed, narrowly ovate, arching leaves that emerge in May and June. The substantial leaves are 60 cm (24 inches) long. At up to 35 cm (14 inches) tall, the inflorescence is among the largest in the genus and appears at the terminus of the leafy stems in July and August. The fertile lower bracts are pale green with pink margins and they hold large, prominently displayed pale lemon yellow flowers with a golden marked labellum. The sterile bracts are circular, shiny, and bright pink.

Curcuma petiolata is a vigorous, hardy species. It can be easily grown in any good, open soil in full sun or light shade.

Curcuma petiolata 'Emperor'
Synonyms: *Curcuma petiolata* 'Variegata', *C. petiolata* 'Figi'
Height: to 90 cm (36 inches)

Tim Chapman named this cultivar, although the plant, the only known variegated *Curcuma*, is also widely grown in Thailand under various names. 'Emperor' is marginally shorter growing that the species, but possibly even more vigorous. It produces many lanceolate leaves, each with a narrow cream margin. This cultivar is highly tolerant of shade and can be thoroughly recommended for use as a foliage plant in warmer gardens in the United Kingdom.

Curcuma rhabdota

Synonyms: *Curcuma gracillima* 'Candy Cane', *C. gracillima* 'Chocolate Zebra'
Minimum temperature: -7°C (20°F)
Height: to 60 cm (24 inches)

This plant was originally circulated (under both of the listed synonyms) as a form of *Curcuma gracillima*, but after publication of this new species in 2000 by Puangpen Sirirugsa and Mark Newman, it became clear that 'Candy Cane' and 'Chocolate Zebra' were referable to *C. rhabdota*. The true plant has been introduced to cultivation on several occasions since the late 1990s. Material was acquired from plant traders based in Laos and northern Thailand, where the species grows among open scrub and dry forests that Sirirugsa and Newman (2000) described as looking "like African savannas with abundant grasses below well-spaced trees".

Curcuma rhabdota produces gently ribbed ovate leaves 15–25 cm (6–10 inches) long, each held on a 6- to 10-cm (2½- to 4-inch) long petiole. The inflorescence is produced at the centre of the leaves and is held well clear of the foliage on a peduncle 18–30 cm (7–12 inches) long. Between 10 and 20 bracts are held in an open arrangement, the lower two-thirds being fertile and deep chestnut brown with prominent jade green lines. These bear tubular flowers of white, with pale lilac margins and bright gold and scarlet stripes on the labellum. The coma of sterile bracts is white, irregularly marked with deep cherry red externally.

Curcuma rhabdota has proven to be unsatisfactory outdoors in the United Kingdom, with the plants failing to flower and generally declining swiftly. The species is, however, both successful and popular (albeit under the wrong name) in the southern United States, where the heat of late spring and early summer ensures good growth and flowering patterns. Plants require a particularly sharply drained soil and protection from winter wet.

Curcuma rhabdota 'Violet'

Synonyms: *Curcuma rhabdota* 'Burnt Burgundy', *C. rhabdota* 'Lavender Stripe', *C. gracillima* 'Violet', *C. gracillima* 'Lavender Stripe', *C. gracillima* 'Burnt Burgundy'
Height: to 30 cm (12 inches)

This cultivar is available under an absurd array of names, but is almost certainly referable to the species. Habit is as for the type, although the plants are smaller in all respects, with narrower leaves. The bracts are deep pink, tipped in bronze, that same colour also appearing in stripes on the outside of the lowest bracts. The flowers are large and pale violet in colour.

Curcuma roscoeana

Minimum temperature: -10°C (15°F)
Height: to 60 cm (24 inches)

A native of northern Thailand and Myanmar and commonly known as the pride of Burma, this species is one of the most striking of all gingers. It is most apt that Nathaniel Wallich named the plant in honour of William Roscoe, the godfather of the *Zingiberaceae*.

The leaves are 30–45 cm (12–18 inches) long, oblong, arching, ribbed, and plain green, emerging in early summer. The inflorescences, which appear from August to October at the centre of the leaves on extremely short stems, comprise 15- to 20-cm (6- to 8-inch) tall spikes of broad, circular flaring bracts that are a deep copper to amber orange, with paler whitish bases. All the bracts are fertile and bear small, tubular cream-coloured flowers with golden labella.

Unfortunately, *Curcuma roscoeana* is one of the hardest species to satisfy in cultivation, particularly in the open garden. It is highly intolerant of winter wet, but will not survive a totally dry dormancy. It should be cultivated in containers and its moisture levels carefully managed while dormant.

Curcuma rubescens

Minimum temperature: -15°C (5°F)
Height: to 180 cm (71 inches)

Aptly named in 1810 by William Roxburgh, the ruby ginger is a superb, tall, and very hardy Indian species. Plants have gently arching, broadly lanceolate, heavily ribbed, shiny, 60-cm (24-inch) long leaves held on very striking, 90-cm (36-inch) tall, deep red petioles. The midvein of the stem is also deep red, and the same pigment extends into the 20-cm (8-inch) tall inflorescences, which are produced in late summer and early autumn at the terminus of the leafy shoots. All the flower bracts are white, the lower ones suffused with red and gold at their base, the upper ones stained red-purple at their tips. The white flowers have a ruffled labellum with a yellow margin and are held in a deep red corolla.

Curcuma rubescens is rather shy flowering and probably would not flower at all in the United Kingdom. The beautiful foliage is reason enough to cultivate the plant wherever conditions will allow.

Curcuma sumatrana

Minimum temperature: -10°C (15°F)
Height: to 60 cm (24 inches)

Named by Friedrich Anton Wilhelm Miquel in his 1860 *Promodrus florae Sumatranae*, this small Indonesian species produces large numbers of relatively short 20- to 30-cm (8- to 12-inch) tall pale green, ovate, ribbed leaves that are held erect, or slightly arching, on very short petioles. The flower spikes appear from July to autumn at the terminus of the leafy stems and are 10–15 cm (4–6 inches) tall. The flat, broad, pale green fertile bracts bear trumpet-shaped yellow flowers. The sterile coma bracts are a shiny ovate pink in colour. Although not as showy as many species, *Curcuma sumatrana* is highly floriferous and reasonably hardy in typical *Curcuma* conditions. It requires moderate shade in high summer. (Plate 22)

Curcuma yunnanensis

Minimum temperature: -10°C (15°F)
Height: to 180 cm (71 inches)

First described in 1987 by Nian Liu and Senjen Chen, this species is endemic to grasslands of the Wanding Zhen region of western Yunnan province in China. It has extremely bold, 60-cm (24-inch) long banana-like, oblong foliage, heavily corrugated with veinal ribbing. The leaves are held on short red-stained petioles 15 cm (6 inches) tall and, in most specimens, have a stripe of purple along the midvein. New foliage typically emerges in June, with the inflorescences following from July to autumn. The inflorescences are produced at the terminus of the leafy stems and are around 15 cm (6 inches) tall. The small, purple-flushed, pale green fertile bracts bear 4-cm (1½-inch) long, tubular yellow flowers held in pink corolla tubes. The sterile coma bracts are deep purple with a white base. *Curcuma yunnanensis* has been successfully introduced to cultivation, where it has proven to be vigorous and also far larger (under good feeding and watering regimes) than the wild-recorded specimens. (Plate 23)

Curcuma zedoaria

Minimum temperature: -15ºC (5ºF)
Height: to 150 cm (60 inches)

Known as the zedoary, or white turmeric, *Curcuma zedoaria* is an important medicinal plant whose rhizome is dried and powdered for use in China and Japan. It is also eaten as a spicy vegetable in Thailand. First described by William Roscoe in 1807, the species has long been widely distributed throughout southern Asia, but probably originates in the Himalayan regions of northern India. In addition to its ethnobotanical uses, *C. zedoaria* makes a splendid ornamental plant.

Emerging in April and May, the ribbed, ovate leaves can reach 90 cm (36 inches) long and are notably bright green, always with a prominent stripe of burgundy-red either side of the midvein on the upper surface, and with that same vein coloured deep red on the leaf underside. The 20-cm (8-inch) tall inflorescences are produced on separate short flowering stems 5–8 cm (2–3 inches) tall. These stems arise directly from the rhizome and appear early in the season, before or simultaneous with the foliage unfurling. The flower spikes are made up of a small number of large bracts. The fertile lower bracts are pale, whitish green, faintly flushed with brown, and bear small, pale yellow tubular flowers. The larger shiny sterile upper coma bracts are pink to reddish purple.

Curcuma zedoaria is certainly attractive in flower, but the real glory of the plant is in its fine foliage. The species is vigorous and trouble-free. It is one of the hardiest species in the genus. Furthermore, it blooms and emerges early from dormancy, making it ideal for cultivation in the United Kingdom and in the United States.

Curcuma Hybrids

Many of the named cultivars of *Curcuma* that are in cultivation in the United States and Southeast Asia have not been properly identified. While some of these undoubtedly are hybrids, many originated as wild-collected plants that were sold at Asian markets without note of their precise origins. While far from exhaustive—many dozens of named varieties are in mass cultivation in Thailand in particular—the selection that follows represents some of the most notable and widely cultivated curcumas.

Curcuma 'Black Thai'
Minimum temperature: -10°C (15°F) ?
Height: to 90 cm (36 inches)

'Black Thai' is a putative hybrid or possibly a new species that originated in Thailand and has been cultured in Hawaii, from where plants were introduced to cultivation in the mainland United States. The narrow, upright lanceolate leaves follow the inflorescences, which are up to 20 cm (8 inches) tall and produced directly from the rhizome, on separate very short, 5-cm (2-inch) tall, flowering stems. The fertile bracts are green at the base of the spike and yellowish towards the top with golden yellow flowers that have red corolla lobes. The small rosette of infertile bracts first emerges a very striking deep burgundy and opens to ruby red. Although it is said to be hardy, this plant has yet to be fully assessed.

Curcuma 'Feather Boa'
Minimum temperature: -10°C (15°F)
Height: to 120 cm (48 inches)

This magnificent hybrid from Tom Wood has large, upright lanceolate leaves that emerge in August, following the substantial 30-cm (12-inch) tall inflorescences. The fertile bracts are pale, jade green marked with chestnut brown. These hold the tubular flowers, pale yellow with a deep yellow stripe in the centre of the labellum and pink corolla lobes. The sterile upper bracts are incredibly prolific, far more numerous than in other curcumas, and are a pale, blush pink, white at their base, and deeper pink towards the tips.

Curcuma 'Green Goddess'
Minimum temperature: -5°C (22°F)
Height: to 20 cm (8 inches)

This dwarf hybrid has a rosette of very narrow, linear, deep green foliage. The tiny 2.5-cm (1-inch) tall inflorescence is produced at the centre of the leaves in August, and consists of a small number of flaring, deep green bracts. 'Green Goddess' is a rare and tender curiosity rather than an ornamental plant.

Curcuma 'Hot Lips'
Minimum temperature: -10°C (15°F)
Height: to 120 cm (48 inches)

This sun-loving hybrid comes from Tom Wood. It has narrowly lanceolate, upright leaves. The plant is floriferous, with 20-cm (10-inch) tall inflorescences produced early in the season, from May in the United States. The bracts are very rounded, the lower fertile ones cream, tipped with pink, and the glossy, upper, sterile bracts deep pink.

Curcuma 'Panama Purple'
Minimum temperature: -10°C (15°F)
Height: to 60 cm (24 inches)

This semi-dwarf plant has attractive, ovate leaves with prominent burgundy midveins. The inflorescence is narrow with short bracts. The lower fertile bracts are green with small pink and pale yellow flowers. The upper sterile bracts emerge pink, with deep, blackish purple rims, this colour weakening as the spikes open.

Curcuma 'Pink Pearls'
Minimum temperature: -7°C (20°F)
Height: to 30 cm (12 inches)

Collected in Cambodia and possibly a cultivar of *Curcuma sparganifolia* (a species described by François Gagnepain in 1903), this diminutive plant has very narrowly linear, strongly arching leaves 30 cm (12 inches) long. In late summer to early autumn the flowering stem emerges from the centre of the foliage and extends to about 15 cm (6 inches). A miniature pink inflorescence tops the flowering stem. The inflorescence is essentially globe shaped and consists of a few overlapping, circular bracts that hold tiny white flowers, each with a yellow striped labellum.

Curcuma 'Purple Gusher'
Minimum temperature: -10°C (15°F)
Height: to 180 cm (71 inches)

Possibly the finest *Curcuma* hybrid to date, this tall plant was bred by Tom Wood and, in the United States, has two distinct flowering seasons. Early inflorescences appear from bare soil around May, and a later crop appears at the centre of the leafy stems in August. In both instances the plants are extremely floriferous with many spikes appearing from each rhizome. The inflorescence itself has almost tubular, jade green fertile lower bracts with prominent extended canary yellow flowers. The shiny sterile upper bracts are large and flare out widely in a fountain-like arrangement. They are deep burgundy when first emerging and open to reveal pure white bases with deep purple tips—an extremely striking combination.

Curcuma 'Scarlet Fever'
Minimum temperature: -10°C (15°F)
Height: to 180 cm (71 inches)

Originating in Malaysia and introduced to the United States by Florida grower Mike McCaffery, this currently unidentified curcuma has proven to be reasonably hardy. It is highly impressive with greatly elongated, narrowly lanceolate, burgundy-striped foliage that arches out from tall, intensely red petioles. The plant is much more compact—to 120 cm (48 inches)—when grown in full sun, but can become huge—240 cm (96 inches) has been recorded—in shade. The narrow 25-cm (10-inch) tall inflorescences precede the foliage, occurring on separate stems that emerge directly from the rhizome. The fertile lower bracts are pale, whitish green, and the coma of sterile bracts is deep, burgundy red. 'Scarlet Fever' is reportedly a shy flowerer, but is a vigorous grower and worth cultivating for the foliage alone.

Curcuma 'Siam Ruby'
Minimum temperature: -7°C (20°F)
Height: to 30 cm (12 inches)

Like *Curcuma* 'Pink Pearls', *C.* 'Siam Ruby' may well be a cultivar of the Cambodian species *C. sparganifolia*. Plants have very narrow, grass-like arching foliage and in September produce a central flowering stem. The inflorescence is 3 cm (1¼ inches) long with a few deep pink bracts, each with a dark, chocolate brown tip. The small flowers are predominantly white, with a golden marked labellum.

Curcuma 'Sri Pok'
Synonym: *Curcuma* 'Sri Pak'
Minimum temperature: -7°C(20°F)
Height: to 60 cm (24 inches)

Originally collected in Vietnam, 'Sri Pok' is most certainly not a hybrid but represents an unidentified wild species. Plants have large, heavily ribbed leaves held on arching, red-stained petioles. The inflorescences appear in August, after the foliage, from very short separate stems that emerge directly from the rhizome. The unusual, rather tubular bracts are held in a very loose, flaring arrangement, almost at ground level. The deep burgundy red bracts are all fertile and bear very prominent large, intensely golden yellow flowers.

Globba

This genus comprises 40 to 100 species of small gingers generally no more than 60 cm (24 inches) tall. *Globba* species are geographically centred in Southeast Asia. The majority of them are native to Thailand, but the most northerly and westerly populations occur in southern China and one species is native to Australia. Carl Linnaeus first described the genus in 1771. The name is ostensibly a derivation of "galoba", a transliteration of an Indonesian name for the plants. For this reason, and following the rules of Latin pronunciation in general, the generic name is pronounced "GLOW-buh", not "GLOB-uh".

Most cultivated *Globba* species produce weakly upright or arching stems that bear floppy foliage. They can look either attractive or merely nondescript, depending on the situation and vigour of the plant. A few varieties have appealingly patterned pewter markings on the foliage, although only one of these—*G. platystachya*—is of interest to the hardy gardener. In general, globbas are grown exclusively for their extremely highly evolved flowers that are quite unlike those of any other ginger, or, for that matter, any other genus of flowering plants.

All the species flower from the terminus of the leafy stems, with inflorescences typically appearing from late summer to midautumn. All produce a raceme, which varies in length from compact with few flowers in some species to the greatly elongated raceme of *Globba winitii*. The inflorescence may be fully upright, horizontal, or, in the case of the most showy species, pendent. Some globbas have very large and highly coloured bracts, generally in a colour that contrasts strongly with the flowers, while others have only vestigial green bracts. From the bracts emerge the flowers, which, in the species discussed here, are relatively uniform. The typical arrangement comprises an elongated (sometimes greatly elongated) corolla tube upon which are seated a reduced labellum, the corolla lobes from which the flower originally unfurled, and a pair of lateral staminodes that generally are the most petal-like element of the flower (see Figure 1). Fused to the tip of the labellum is the plant's most extraordinary feature, a massively exerted, arched stamen that leads well away from the rest of the flower and terminates in a pair of anthers, which can themselves have bizarre, wing-like lateral appendages. The presence and shape of these anther appendages is often crucial in identifying different species.

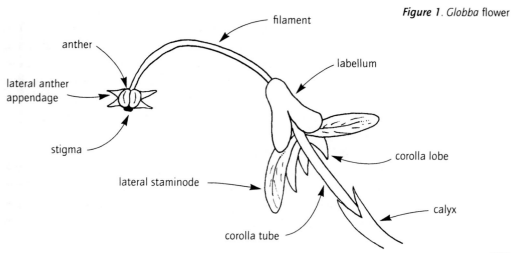

Figure 1. *Globba* flower

filament

anther

labellum

lateral anther appendage

stigma

lateral staminode

corolla lobe

calyx

corolla tube

Though certainly fascinating, all of these features are exceedingly small, with a typical *Globba* flower being no more than a few centimetres (about 1 inch) long; however, in combination, and particularly in the species with enlarged bracts, the floral display is highly distinctive and very ornamental. Unlike many flowers in the *Zingiberaceae*, the individual flowers of *Globba* are remarkably long-lived and persist for up to a week. Each inflorescence lasts at least a month, a trait that has encouraged the cultivation of globbas for cut flowers.

Globbas hybridize with abandon in their wild habitats and many species are clearly either closely related or merely synonyms of one another. As is true in many genera of the *Zingiberaceae*, correct identification of the species can be difficult, and much work remains to be done to solidify both the numbers of valid species and the relationships between them.

Globbas do not increase rapidly at the rhizome, although they can certainly be divided when the plants have developed sufficiently; however, many species produce bulbils from which they may be more readily propagated. These bulbils form on the lower part of the inflorescence, in the bracts, in place of some of the lower flowers. In the wild the bulbils simply fall off as the inflorescence decays and thus colonize the surrounding ground. In warm climates (although not in temperate regions) the plants also produce large amounts of seed. A recent study demonstrated that several species have evolved arils (fleshy seed coverings) that are unusually high in various nutrients. The seeds of these species are attractive to, and collected by, no less than 21 different ant species. The ants convey the seeds back to their nests, and thus unwittingly work on the plants behalf to disperse their progeny as much as 8 m (26 feet) from the parent plant.

It is easy to see how, using these sophisticated reproductive techniques, globbas are capable of forming large stands of plants. This makes it all the more alarming to realize that many species are now endangered in the wild due primarily to mass collecting. No justifiable reason exists for cultivating wild-collected *Globba* species when they are so readily reproduced in cultivation. Gardeners should be careful to ensure that they source only cultivated stock.

All *Globba* species are true denizens of the shady forest floor and thus must be cultivated in shade. Bright, dappled shade will produce the best plants in temperate zones, although in warmer regions many globbas may scorch unless provided with full shade. In both climates, a rich, open but moist substrate will produce the best results. A number of evergreen species occur, but all the species listed here are naturally deciduous and will become dormant regardless of the temperatures at which they are maintained. Their natural patterns of dormancy have developed in tandem with the Southeast Asian monsoons, rather than any variation in temperature, but in cultivation these plants require a sustained period of warmth, with daytime temperatures around 18°C (65°F) before emerging for the new season. In temperate zones this makes globbas often very late to appear, sometimes as late as July. As long as temperatures remain high for several months after plants emerge, this should not be a problem, but in cooler regions of the United Kingdom, and despite their overall hardiness at the rhizome, globbas will probably not survive unless induced into growth earlier.

In their native habitats the plants become very dry before the onset of the monsoon, as the landscape in general becomes parched. In cultivation globbas are, resultantly, very intolerant of winter wet, which is not to say that they cannot be grown in the garden, but rather that suitable protection must be provided in the form of a deep, dry mulch, or a physical barrier to rain that will allow the plants to overwinter successfully. Alternatively they may be planted out in pots that can be lifted for storage with the rhizomes intact once plant growth has been frosted back. In either instance the species listed here have been proven to be tolerant of surprisingly low temperatures, certainly to a degree that many would never come close to encountering in the wild.

Globba colpicola

Synonym: *Globba winitii* 'Golden Dragon'
Minimum temperature: -7°C (20°F)
Height: to 60 cm (24 inches)

Originally introduced to cultivation as an unknown species, the plant was dubbed 'Golden Dragon' and is generally sold as a cultivar of *Globba winitii*, despite having now been correctly identified as *G. colpicola*, a species originally described by Karl Schumann. Plants produce slender, arching stems clothed with papery, thin, lanceolate leaves, approximately 20 cm (8 inches) long, dark green above and paler beneath, with prominent veining. When well grown the plants bloom continually from August to October and produce a large pendent, branched inflorescence, very heavily congested with golden yellow to pale orange flower buds. The flowers are archetypal for the genus, with a small, arrowhead-shaped labellum that is gold with a central patch of crimson. The elongated stamen unfurls like a long fern frond and holds a club-shaped anther pair with flaring lateral appendages like tiny petals. Each inflorescence is exceptionally long-lived and will continue flowering for a good six weeks. *Globba colpicola* is now widely available (under the name 'Golden Dragon') in both Europe and the United States.

Globba globulifera

Synonym: *Globba* 'Purple Globe'
Minimum temperature: -7°C (20°F)
Height: to 60 cm (24 inches)

First described by François Gagnepain, this *Globba* is native to the forests of Vietnam, where it is now listed as a threatened species due partly to habitat loss, but also to overcollecting for the Southeast Asian horticultural and flower markets. *Globba globulifera* is among the easiest species to cultivate, and it reproduces rapidly.

Plants produce many narrow, arching stems with lanceolate leaves 15–20 cm (6–8 inches) long. One source states that the plants have "pumpkin orange" autumn colour, but more typically the leaves will turn to a (not terribly ornamental) yellow with the onset of frosts. The highly distinctive inflorescences, which start to appear in June and continue to September; consist of a congested, ball-shaped mass of showy, pinkish purple bracts that are either pendent or held horizontally against the foliage. Within each bracteole lies a small white bud that opens to reveal a creamy white corolla tube with a narrow, lemon yellow, arrowhead-shaped labellum. The extended stamen is white and has star-shaped appendages to the anthers. As with many *Globba* species, the inflorescence of *G. globulifera* is certainly fascinating and very long-lived, with flowers appearing for four to six weeks. The inflorescence is also small and can easily be overlooked on the short, nodding stems.

In common with some other species, *Globba globulifera* produces bulbils from the aging inflorescence, particularly when the plants are being grown in humid conditions. These bulbils will readily form new plantlets and can be separated and potted up to increase stock of the species. In warmer areas the new plantlets are capable of flowering in the same season that they form. This method is the best one for reproducing the species. Since the bulbils form so readily, there can be no justification for the further plundering of wild stocks.

Globba globulifera (?) white form

Presumed to be a white form of the species, although it has yet to be formally identified, this plant originated from importations of Asian stock to U.S. nurseries, where they occasionally appear alongside the regularly coloured form of *Globba globulifera*. The white form is similar to the species in all respects aside from the inflorescence, which has translucent white or pale chartreuse green bracts. The flowers are coloured as per the normal form of the species.

Globba macroclada

Synonym: *Globba andersonii* hort.
Minimum temperature: -7°C (20°F) ?
Height: to 60 cm (24 inches)

Another species named by François Gagnepain, *Globba macroclada* is a native of the Himalayan foothills of Assam where plants typically grow on steep banks or at forest margins, often in association with long grasses that keep the rhizome shaded and moist. This natural habitat results in plants with a cascading habit, the wiry, narrow stems strongly leaning over. Unlike many of the cultivated globbas, *G. macroclada* produces an erect inflorescence that, like the *Hedychium* inflorescence, will arch into an upright position regardless of where the stem tips are located. The 10-cm (4-inch) long inflorescences appear from June to September and are branched but comparatively sparsely clad with flowers. The flowers appear in a long succession, with each spike lasting around four weeks, and are of a uniform, deep golden yellow. The labellum is 1 cm (½ inch) long. The species is available in Europe (generally under the name *G. andersonii*) but has been little tested for hardiness.

Globba platystachya

Synonym: *Globba* 'Silver Stripe'
Minimum temperature: -10°C (15°F)
Height: to 75 cm (30 inches)

Originally named and described by John G. Baker, this Indian species is the hardiest of the globbas with patterned foliage. Held on arching, narrow stems, the relatively large, 30-cm (12-inch) long, lanceolate leaves are strongly pleated at the midvein, with an elongated tip. Two narrow silver bands border the green midvein, contrasting with the deep to mid-green of the remainder of the leaf surface. The inflorescences occur in late summer and comprise sparse, upright racemes of very small golden yellow flowers that are rather dwarfed by the foliage. *Globba platystachya* forms new plantlets in the leaf axils at the base of the leaf sheaths and is best reproduced by removal and potting up of these plantlets. This *Globba* is not yet widely available in Europe, but with its appealing foliage and comparative hardiness promises to be possibly the most satisfactory species to grow here. (Plate 24)

Globba racemosa

Synonyms: *Globba bulbosa, G. cathcartii*
Minimum temperature: -10ºC (15ºF)
Height: to 100 cm (39 inches)

This wide-ranging species is a native of lightly wooded areas in northern Thailand and Myanmar as well as India, Bhutan, and much of southern China where plants are found at elevations of 400 to 1300 m (1300–4300 feet). *Globba racemosa* is a robust plant with arching stems that bear lanceolate leaves to 20 cm (8 inches) long by 5 cm (2 inches) wide. Flowering occurs from June to September, and plants produce a large compound inflorescence 30–45 cm (12–18 inches) long. The inflorescence bears widely distant, dark reddish-bronze bracts with bronze calyces. These split open to reveal dark, golden yellow flowers. The staminodes have a red tint and the heavily reflexed labellum has a red spot at the centre. Like the inflorescences of other *Globba* species, those of *G. racemosa* are very long-lived and last for up to six weeks, with the waxy flowers surviving for up to a week each. After the flowers have fallen away, fat white bulbils can develop on the lower portions of the flowering stem. These bulbils represent an easy way to increase stock.

Material in circulation in Europe that originated in India under the name *Globba cathcartii* is almost certainly referable to this species. Like many globbas, *G. racemosa* has not been widely tested for hardiness, but plants originating from higher altitudes should be relatively hardy and are well worth trying.

Globba schomburgkii

Synonym: *Globba bulbifera* hort.
Minimum temperature: -10°C (15°F)
Height: to 50 cm (20 inches)

Named by Joseph Hooker in 1877 in honour of the botanical explorer and former British consul in Bangkok, Robert H. Schomburgk, *Globba schomburgkii* is the most cold hardy and the most frequently seen *Globba* species in cultivation. A native of northern Thailand, Vietnam, Myanmar, and southern Yunnan province in China, the species dwells in the leaf litter on the floors of moist forests at elevations of up to 1300 m (4300 feet).

Globba schomburgkii has short but fairly stout stems that are more erect than those in many species, and these are clothed by up to six lanceolate leaves that reach 20 cm (8 inches) long by 3–4 cm (1¼–1½ inches) wide. Despite its small stature, this species arguably has the showiest floral display. Flowering in August and September the plants produce gently pendulous, 10-cm (4-inch) long racemes that are densely packed with entirely orangey gold flowers. The labellum is narrow and bicleft, and the anthers have star-like, winged appendages. This species reproduces by bulbils, which are borne at the base of the inflorescence, developing in the lowest bracteoles at the same time as the flowers open further up the inflorescence. Some forms produce notably more bulbils than others. The flowers last for up to five days before withering, and each inflorescence remains in flower for a month or so.

Because it produces bulbils, a habit shared by a number of species, *Globba schomburgkii* has been confused in cultivation with *G. bulbifera*. More specifically, specimens of this *G. schomburgkii* have been labelled as *G. bulbifera*. The two taxa are valid and distinct species, however, and may be quite easily distinguished by their inflorescence, which is always pendent in *G. schomburgkii* but upright in *G. bulbifera*. In a suitable site, this species will readily spread via bulbils to naturally form carpeting colonies of plants.

While the species has been reported as overwintering successfully at -14°C (7°F) in the United States, it has not been extensively tested for hardiness in Europe, and is certainly consistently late to break dormancy, which impedes flowering potential. Nevertheless, it is a species well worth attempting. It tolerates far more sun than most globbas, allowing plants to be sited in warmer positions where successful flowering is more likely to be induced.

111

Globba siamensis

Synonym: *Globba* 'Bamboo Leaf'
Minimum temperature: -7°C (20°F)
Height: to 45 cm (18 inches)

A native of Cambodia and northern Thailand, this species was first described by James Hatton Hemsley in 1985. Only recently was it introduced into the U.S. nursery trade, where it is invariably sold under the invalid descriptive name 'Bamboo Leaf' rather than its species name. The leaves are very narrowly lanceolate, and the inflorescence comprises many glossy purple-brown bracteoles from which emerge the golden yellow flowers. Reportedly shy flowering, this species has limited horticultural appeal.

Globba winitii

Minimum temperature: -12°C (10°F)
Height: to 60 cm (24 inches)

First described in 1926 by Charles Henry Wright, *Globba winitii* is a native of the Lampang province of northern Thailand. The species (or at least globbas bearing this name) is widely cultivated throughout Southeast Asia, both as a garden ornamental and commercially for the cut flower trade.

Globba winitii produces robust, upright stems clothed in strongly pendent, 20-cm (8-inch) long lanceolate leaves that are "folded" along their midvein and have a noticeably cordate base. Produced from July to October, the 20-cm (8-inch) long inflorescences are also fully pendent, and indeed the whole plant has a delightful, softly nodding appearance. Each inflorescence consists of a long flowering raceme that bears large, ovate, and very showy pinkish-purple bracts. These bracts strongly reflex backwards on their axis until they face fully upwards. Each bract bears a bright yellow flower held on a deep purple stem. The flowers have a typical *Globba* construction, and their most ornamental part is the wing-like lateral staminodes. The whole inflorescence is much larger than that of most cultivated species of *Globba* and is also very long lived, both on the plant, where flowers are produced over a four-week period, and also as a cut flower, with each stem lasting approximately fourteen days.

Globba winitii has reportedly been successfully overwintered at -14°C (7°F) in the United States, but can be frustratingly slow to break dormancy.

For that reason it is unlikely to succeed as a year-round garden plant in the United Kingdom. Where early summer and late spring temperatures promote a more certain ending of dormancy in the United States, the species is much more easily grown and widely available, even in non-specialist plant outlets. Like most globbas, *G. winitii* requires at least partial shade and a moist, woodland medium in which to grow; it should be kept just moist when dormant.

Vast numbers of globbas of all species have been removed from their native habitats to feed the nursery and cut-flower trade in Asia and the United States. The wild populations of most species are now very severely depleted. The name *Globba winitii* has been applied almost indiscriminately to an array of globbas that have been introduced into cultivation from such wild-collected stock since the mid-1980s, the large majority of which are not, in fact, this species. Wild populations of *Globba* also naturally hybridize with one another to a considerable degree, and such hybrids may have been introduced under the same, banner species name.

To further confuse the situation, the common name dancing girls, referring to the individual flowers, is often applied to *Globba winitii*, but there are also two series of globbas that have been micropropagated in the United States under the collective names "Dancing Girls" and "Dancing Jewels" (the latter group with the cultivar names 'Ruby Queen', 'Pristina Pink', 'Purest Angel', and 'Blushing Maiden'). These varieties and colour forms have not been formally identified, but they are almost certainly not *G. winitii*, and may even represent (potentially several) new, unnamed species. The true species is extremely scarce in the wild. It may only have been introduced into cultivation twice, with the vast majority of the true plants in cultivation having originated vegetatively from a collection made in northern Thailand that was originally sent to the Royal Botanic Gardens, Kew, in the 1930s.

A cultivar known as *Globba winitii* 'Red Leaf' is also probably not referable to this species. 'Red Leaf' has pinkish bracts, paler than the type, with dark leaves that are burgundy red beneath. The stems are of the same red colour. True plants of *G. winitii* all have the distinctive cordate base to the leaves, a feature not found in any of the named varieties. (Plate 25)

Hedychium

Johann Koenig, who named this genus in 1783, selected the name based upon the only species then known in Europe, the sweetly fragrant, white-flowered *Hedychium coronarium*. The word "hedychium" is derived from the Greek "hedys", meaning "sweet", and "chion", meaning "snow". Following the rules of Latin pronunciation, the "ch" of the generic name is pronounced as a hard "k", and the emphasis is given to the second to last vowel (or group of vowels), which in this case is a "y", giving the pronunciation "heh-DIK-ee-um". The genus now comprises approximately 50 species, all but one of which are native to central and southeastern Asia, with concentrations in southern China and the Himalayan regions. The outlying member is *H. peregrinum*, which is endemic to Madagascar, and thus one of the surviving African *Zingiberaceae* relics from the time before that continent split from Asia.

Many species were named in the first half of the nineteenth century and were introduced into British cultivation shortly after they were identified. By the mid-nineteenth century there were no less than 22 species in British nursery cultivation, and hedychiums were highly popular plants, riding their first wave of horticultural fashion. The Victorians were, however, growing them exclusively as hot-house or conservatory plants. Perhaps their generally tropical appearance mitigated against them, because, despite the relatively high altitudes and northerly latitudes from which the plants had originally been collected, hedychiums were simply not tried or used in outdoor garden conditions. As a result, by the start of the twentieth century all but a few of these species were already lost to cultivation, when the hugely increasing costs of maintaining heated glasshouses took their toll, and smaller, more floriferous plants were deemed a better use of heating, labour, and space resources in the few glasshouses that remained.

To a large extent this outlook towards *Hedychium* persisted throughout most of the twentieth century. When Tony Schilling wrote "A Survey of Cultivated Himalayan and Sino-Himalayan *Hedychium* Species" (1982), he referred to the genus as being "overlooked and underappreciated", also noting that, astonishingly, "there are no commercial sources for this fascinating group of plants anywhere in the country".

It's fair to say that in just 20 years this situation has changed radically. The 2003 *RHS Plant Finder* lists no less than 81 taxa of *Hedychium* that are available to British gardeners. Many additional forms are found in the United

States and Japan. I have endeavoured to list here all of the species that have any chance of success in temperate gardens. Some of these, all native to China, have yet to be introduced to cultivation anywhere, but I include them because there are now a large number of regular Western botanical expeditions to southwestern China, and it seems reasonable to suppose that some of the Chinese species may soon be available in the West. (Estimations of hardiness for these plants are on the conservative side and are based on the known tolerances of existing garden plants that originate from similar altitudes and ecology in China.) I also list all of the (more than 80) named hybrids that are presently available, which, if anything, represent just the tip of the iceberg. An abundance of new Japanese and American hybrids will certainly soon further swell the ranks of hedychiums from which hardy gardeners can choose.

Hedychiums grow from stout, fleshy rhizomes that increase laterally each season, producing generally very thick, upright or arching pseudostems clothed with large, often conspicuously ribbed, broadly lanceolate leaves. The largest members of the genus are, along with *Alpinia zerumbet*, the biggest of the hardy gingers, with stems up to 300 cm (118 inches) or so. Forms with very impressive, banana-like foliage can earn themselves a place in the garden on the merits of their foliage alone. *Hedychium greenii* has conspicuously red-coloured foliage, and a few hybrids also have reddish bronze pigmentation on the undersides of the leaves.

Like many gingers, *Hedychium* species are late to break winter dormancy and require a prolonged period of mild weather to trigger growth. Typically this happens in May in hardy gardens. Although some varieties may not emerge until summer, their subsequent growth will not be impeded provided they are well fed and watered.

In temperate gardens all hedychiums are always deciduous, because growth is halted with the first frosts. Although stems may remain intact in warm winters and in sheltered gardens (as is often the case in London gardens, for instance), plants will make no further growth and will be replaced by the next season's crop. If grown under frost-free conditions, some (though not all) species will remain evergreen and are potentially capable of active growth at any time of the year. The length of the growing season affects flowering potential, but will also have an impact on the ultimate size of any given specimen. Plants grown in colder gardens tend to produce shorter pseudostems, as do specimens that have a poor source of nutrition.

Hedychiums flower from the terminus of their leafy stems. The flowering spike consists of many broad, overlapping waxy bracts, which are arranged in a spiral to form a cone-like or spindle-shaped inflorescence. Some varieties have a short, tightly bunched spike, while others have a far looser and more open arrangement of bracts. The flowers, which emerge from the bracts in groups of one to five, comprise a pair of petal-like lateral staminodes and a large lip, or labellum (see Figure 2). Together these take the appearance of "petals", the true petals being reduced to very narrow filaments that dangle and twist beneath the rest of the flower. Like all ginger flowers, *Hedychium* flowers possess a single stamen. In many species these stamens are highly decorative, with the prominent anthers and tiny terminal stigma being fused together at the tip of a hugely extended and often vividly coloured filament. Among the hardy gingers, this feature is unique to *Hedychium* (although *Globba* species have greatly extended but morphologically very different stamens). In fact, in some species it is their most ornamental feature.

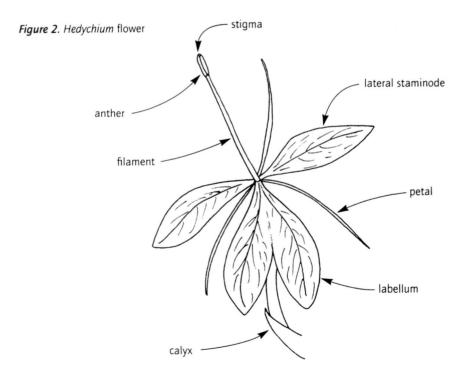

Figure 2. Hedychium flower

stigma

lateral staminode

anther

filament

petal

labellum

calyx

The individual flowers typically last only a few days each, but emerge in succession to provide five to fourteen days of flowering per spike. The flowers are often intensely and beautifully fragrant, with the scent from different plants being variously likened to gardenia, honeysuckle, and jasmine. Actually they have their own particular perfume that is perhaps best called hedychium-like.

Flowering typically starts in June with the earliest species, which are also the hardiest. Such plants originate at high altitudes where the short growing season requires plants to bloom and set seed as quickly as possible before growth is curtailed by cold. Many hedychiums do not start to flower until later in the year, with September being the peak month. In choosing plants for gardens it is therefore important to consider when frosts are likely to occur, since any variety that does not bloom until, say, October, is highly unlikely to flower at all in a garden that starts to experience sharp drops in temperature and daylight length by that month.

A final season of attraction occurs when the plants set seed. These are produced in fat pods that split open to reveal a fleshy, tangerine orange interior in which are held deep red arils (fleshy appendages) that contain the actual shiny black seeds (Plate 26). The pods and their bright contents remain on the plants for some weeks and provide an eye-catching contrast with the dark green foliage. *Hedychium acuminatum* is the only species that will reliably set seed outdoors in most parts of Britain, although *H. densiflorum* will also often oblige in southern counties, and many species will fruit in the southern United States and southern Europe.

In the wild most *Hedychium* species come into growth to synchronize with the advent of the summer monsoon. In cultivation, the tougher species will persist with little attention, but to give their best when in full growth they require a good level of moisture and adequate supplies of nutrition to feed the very substantial annual growth that they make.

Many hedychiums can also be found naturally growing as epiphytes. Most of these are native to the more southerly, warmer regions. Some hardier species also share this habit, although few, if any, are exclusively epiphytic in nature. The reason for this is more of an adaptation to conditions of high moisture which allow the usually subterranean rhizomes to grow upon rocks and tree branches.

In warmer climates most hedychiums succeed best in partial shade, where their large leaves are less likely to desiccate. In cooler gardens, however, most will grow best in full sun, which will promote good development of the flowering spikes and a prolonged growth season. The exceptions to this are the true cool climate natives: *Hedychium acuminatum, H. densiflorum, H. forestii, H. spicatum,* and *H. yunnanense.* None of these will tolerate any great heat, and all of them will benefit from partial shade even in cooler gardens. In the warmest gardens, such as those located in the southern United States, these cool climate natives require full, bright shade. No hardy hedychiums prosper in deep shade and none are likely to flower in such conditions.

Hedychiums have been brought back into fashion largely as a result of the interest in tropical, or at least tropical-looking, plants for hardy gardens. In the past they have occasionally been used for bedding purposes, although cannas have always been a more popular option in this regard. Now, however, *Hedychium* species are seen as an increasingly essential component of any bold display of exotics, rubbing leafy shoulders with the likes of *Dicksonia, Phyllostachys, Musa,* and so forth. This trend in no way represents the limits of possibility for *Hedychium*; after all not every garden is converted to a tropical look, and it would be tragic if these plants were to once again fade from the spotlight as gardening fashions move on.

In nature, *Hedychium* species are frequently found in bright, moist woodland margins. They will often look most at home among the woodlanders. Grown with the shelter of shrubs such as *Rhododendron* (partly to mitigate against potential wind damage), hedychiums can look both natural and impressive. As long as there is sufficient filtered sunlight to allow for good flowering, hedychiums may also be used successfully beneath a tree canopy.

In the wild many *Hedychium* species can be found on steep banks and alongside waterways where they naturally lean over, forming beautiful cascading arches of foliage with the terminal flower spikes held upright. Where space and conditions allow, these hedychiums will rarely look better than when grown in such a manner, particularly in association with water. But even this does not begin to tap the possibilities for temperate gardeners, since hedychiums will grow equally well in a mixed border, where their height, late flowering season, colourful flowers, and perfume can be partnered with a huge array of perennials. In addition, they can be employed in groups or as large, isolated specimens to fill small, spot beds with their dense lush foliage. Finally, almost all species make dramatic plants for large containers on a patio or similar area. This method of cultivation allows the more tender species to be brought into use, as well as extending the northerly limits of the hardy ones.

As with many members of the *Zingiberaceae*, the genus *Hedychium* also has nomenclatural problems, particularly when it comes to determining the limits of the species, some of which range across considerably diverse habitats and geographies. Writing of *Hedychium* in 1853 Nathaniel Wallich commented:

> Few species only admit (to) being somewhat rigorously defined; the rest slide suddenly or by gradations, into each other, so as to elude all endeavours to fix them with any sort of botanical precision. The fact is that, like other very natural groups, ours point blank refuses to disclose the exact limitations of its members, and leaves the systematizing botanist to grope his way through the maze as best he may.

Until recently, of course, all attempts to define species were determined entirely by physical morphology, so the natural Victorian inclination to "fix" such limits was inevitably frustrated. Hedychiums are a naturally variable group of plants that may still be in the process of natural evolution and hybridization. More recent introductions have often proved equally difficult to place, but with the advent of genetic analysis the true order of relationships between the species and their forms is finally emerging. From the gardener's point of view this process can lead to confusion in the identity of plants offered for sale by nurseries, but will ultimately result in a far more concrete and scientific portrait of the genus that can only serve to assist all horticulturists.

An even larger cause of confusion for the eager gardener is the propensity for some American suppliers of *Hedychium* to sell them under an almost arbitrary array of descriptive "fancy" names. These plants are almost always not true cultivars and are doubtless intended to attract potential customers that might be scared off by Latin; however, even when a plant's true name is offered alongside the sales pitch, it is, unfortunately the "fancy" name that tends to persist, leaving the plant's true identity unnecessarily obscured in the future. There are already a number of false cultivars and hybrids with multiple names, and it is hoped that as further new plants are introduced to cultivation this confusion can be avoided.

Hedychium bijiangense

Minimum temperature: -15°C (5°F) ?
Height: 120–170 cm (48–67 inches)

This close relative of the much more familiar and naturally widespread *Hedychium coccineum* is native to forested areas of northwestern Yunnan at high altitudes of 2600 to 3200 m (8,500–10,500 feet). Te Lin(g) Wu and Senjen Chen named *H. bijiangense* in 1978. The species is apparently cultivated in China for its very large and showy flowers, produced on 30-cm (12-inch) tall spikes in late September. Each yellow flower has an undivided labellum approximately 3 cm (1¼ inches) long by 2 cm (¾ inch) wide.

Although *Hedychium bijiangense* is seemingly not currently in Western cultivation, at least one specimen was grown at the Royal Botanic Garden, Edinburgh. Furthermore, the potential hardiness and very large flowers would seem to make it an ideal candidate for (re)introduction and use in a wide range of gardens; however, because it flowers late in the season, this species might prove a disappointment as a garden plant in areas where warm temperatures are not sustained into early autumn.

Hedychium bipartitum

Minimum temperature: -7°C (20°F) ?
Height: 100–200 cm (39–79 inches)

Guang Zhao Li named this little-known species in 1985 from cultivated specimens found growing at 1200 m (3900 feet) in northeastern China in the Guangxi province. The species's natural habitat is unknown. The fragrant yellow flowers occur in August on a 15- to 20-cm (6- to 8-inch) tall spike. This ginger is unlikely to prove very hardy.

Hedychium bordelonium

Minimum temperature: 0°C (30°F) ?
Height: 50–100 cm (20–39 inches)

This epiphytic species from Myanmar was recently collected and named in honour of Mike Bordelon, the manager of the greenhouse at the Smithsonian Botanical Research Centre. It is a spectacular and very unusual species in flower, more reminiscent of a *Curcuma*, with stiff, waxy burgundy-

purple flower bracts. Hardiness is unknown, and the species is not currently in wider cultivation.

Hedychium brevicaule

Minimum temperature: -4°C (25°F) ?
Height: 20–40 cm (8–16 inches)

Named by Ding Fang in 1980, this small, epiphytic species is native to
forests at low altitudes of 500 to 700 m (1600–2300 feet) in western
Guangxi province, China, near the border with Yunnan province. The very
open flower spike, which is about 10 cm (4 inches) tall, occurs in August on
cultivated plants. The slightly fragrant pure white flowers are attractive
though not flamboyant. Plants have recently been introduced into the
United States and are proving adaptable to cultivation.

Hedychium coccineum

Minimum temperature: -18°C (0°F)
Height: 150–220 cm (60–87 inches)

This well-established and naturally widespread species is native to the
Indian and Nepalese Himalaya and Bangladesh, but long cultivated across
southern and south central Asia. It is a magnificent plant, with tall and very
robust pseudostems that produce glaucous green leaves and large flaming
flower spikes of orange to brick red early in the *Hedychium* season.
Flowering occurs from June to August, depending on the temperature.
Although the flowers are either faintly or not at all scented, they compensate in overall flower power, with dozens of individual flowers being produced together on each spike.

The species is variable in all aspects, including flower size and colour and
certainly hardiness, as is to be expected from a plant with a wide natural
distribution. Several selections have been named, but you would be hard
pressed to come across a bad one. James Edward Smith named the species
in 1811. Another published species, *Hedychium carneum*, is also referable to
H. coccineum.

Plants are easily cultivated in the garden, and the species will tolerate a
wide range of positions from full sun to light shade without impeding the
flowering spectacle. This exceptionally fine and exceptionally hardy plant is

now widely available in cultivation and is certainly a must for anyone interested in growing hardy gingers.

Hedychium coccineum var. *angustifolium*

Originally described as a separate species (*Hedychium angustifolium*) by William Roxburgh in 1824, this variety has distinct and very narrow foliage that make it relatively easy to identify even when not in flower. The pseudostems are exceptionally tall, reaching 250 cm (98 inches) or more. The upward-facing leaves create an appealing ladder-like impression up the height of the plant. The flower spike is similar in size to the species, but the (typically) richly tangerine-coloured individual flowers are smaller in their parts. The hugely protruding stamens are the most distinctive floral feature. Plants are easily cultivated and increase well, but are much less reliable flowerers and probably also marginally less hardy than the typical species, *H. coccineum* var. *coccineum*.

Hedychium coccineum var. *angustifolium* 'Peach'

While maintaining the height and foliage features that are typical for var. *angustifolium*, this selection is very different in flower. The flower spikes are shorter than those of the typical variety, but the individual flowers are considerably larger, each with an exceptionally showy and large bilobed labellum. The flower colour is unusual too, opening pale gold and aging to a warm, soft peach-white. Plants are prolific and heavy bloomers, with flowers appearing in September and October. The plants are also notably vigorous in growth, which leads to speculation that this cultivar may be of hybrid origin. It is the parent of a large array of hybrids.

Hedychium coccineum var. *aurantiacum*

Named by William Roscoe, this Indian variety is similar to var. *angustifolium*, with narrow, upright leaves on tall stems, again to 250 cm (98 inches), but with flower spikes that are more open and lax. The individual flowers typically are an intense, flame orange-red.

Hedychium coccineum var. *aurantiacum* 'Flaming Torch'
Synonym: *Hedychium* 'PDA form'

Introduced into cultivation by Plant Delights Nursery, this cultivar has a larger flower spike than is typical for the variety and is also more vigorous in growth.

Hedychium coccineum 'Disney'
Synonym: *Hedychium coccineum* 'Honduras'

Here we encounter one of many hedychiums whose naming is hopelessly confused and/or lost. Certainly different nurseries in Europe and the United States appear to be offering different plants under this name—some describing it as a dwarf form, and others as a giant form, for instance. It seems doubtful that the name "Disney" was ever intended to be used as a clonal name and was simply a purely descriptive label given by *Hedychium* grower-breeder Dave Case to a plant propagated from those growing at Disney World in Orlando, Florida. The true clone has leaves with a reddish tinge to the undersides and flowers of mid to pale orange, and is a prolific and heavy flowerer. In other respects it is typical for the species.

Hedychium coccineum 'Orange Brush'

Confused in cultivation and possibly synonymous with 'Disney', this form, named by Tom Wood, has more lax flowers of mid-orange, and is said to have shorter pseudostems to around 120 to 150 cm (48–60 inches) tall. Height is not necessarily a reliable feature, as it can vary greatly depending on growing conditions.

Hedychium coccineum 'Woodlanders'

Said to be a hybrid between *Hedychium coccineum* var. *coccineum* and *H. coccineum* var. *angustifolium*, this form originated in Coimbra, Portugal, and was subsequently distributed by the Woodlanders Nursery of Aiken, South Carolina, in the late 1980s. Plants have very long, narrow upright foliage and from July to September produce large flowering spikes, heavily clothed with large peach-coloured flowers. The labellum is semi-cupped and bilobed with a deep orange-red throat. The flowers have long, flame red stamen filaments and soft gold petals.

Hedychium convexum

Minimum temperature: -5ºC (22ºF)
Height: 50–80 cm (20–31 inches)

Shao Quan Tong named this currently obscure Chinese species in 1986. *Hedychium convexum* is native to forests of Jinghong county in southwestern Yunnan province, where plants have been found at elevations of 1000 m (3300 feet). It is a short species, suggesting that it is probably largely epiphytic in nature, and might prove to be demanding in cultivation. The flowers occur in August, are small and predominantly yellow, and are notable for having an undivided labellum. This species is not currently in cultivation.

Hedychium coronarium Koenig

Minimum temperature: -15ºC (5ºF)
Height: 100–300 cm (39–118 inches)

Hedychium coronarium is the type species for the genus and the most widely cultivated and best-known ornamental ginger. Johann Koenig described it in 1783. It is hard to pinpoint the natural geographic boundaries of this species since it has been so widely cultivated for so long and has naturalized in many tropical and subtropical counties. The species is essentially Himalayan in origin, with natural populations in northern India, Nepal, Bhutan, and southwestern China, but is also established in Taiwan, Indonesia, Thailand, Malaysia, Sri Lanka, Vietnam, and Australia.

Hedychium coronarium has been put to both culinary and medicinal uses, but its great success and popularity results from its floral qualities. The familiar names butterfly ginger, white butterfly, and butterfly lily have been given in appreciation of the flowers, and not without reason, for these are quite magnificent both to see and to smell. In Sanskrit the plant is known as "gandasuli", meaning "queen's perfume". The magnificent, gardenia-like fragrance to which this name refers is probably the strongest fragrance of all *Hedychium* species, particularly in the evening.

The elongated, pinecone-shaped green spikes produce flowers from July to September. These flowers are bright white, generally (though not always) with a pale lime green throat, and are extremely showy and very large for the genus—each having a labellum that can measure 7 cm (2³/₄ inches) long and wide. The leaves have a soft white down on the undersides. Although not especially notable for its foliage, *Hedychium coronarium* is a tall, bold species that certainly has an architectural quality, even when not in flower.

In addition to the obvious appeal of this species, it is also one of the hardiest hedychiums. Some growers have found it reluctant to flower, which may be due to the source of the plant material or the fact that the plants in question are not the true species. For other growers, this ginger is among the earliest and the most reliable flowerers in the genus. Plants thrive in full sun (although some leaf scorch may occur unless humidity levels are high) to bright shade, but flowering is most prolific when the plants are positioned to obtain at least some direct sun.

Given the wide distribution and enormous habitat range of the species, it is not surprising that *Hedychium coronarium* is very variable. A number of named varieties have been described; however, there is little consent as to the botanical limitations of the species, and much confusion and misidentification exists over cultivated plants. In Europe, var. *chrysoleucum* has long been (mis)identified as *H. cororarium* and is also, perhaps, the more commonly grown variety of the species. In the United States, however, hybrids distributed as 'Butterfly Ginger' have also acquired the species' name. In an attempt to delineate exactly what is meant by the label *H. coronarium* the true species is now referred to as *H. coronarium* Koenig, to indicate that the plant in question agrees with the original type description for the species. (Plate 27)

Hedychium coronarium var. *coronarium* 'Andromeda'

Distributed by nurseries in the United Kingdom, this form originated from a garden in Barbados. It is somewhat shorter than the type, with pseudostems reaching around 100 cm (39 inches) tall. It apparently has yet to flower in European cultivation.

Hedychium coronarium var. *coronarium* 'Pink'
Height: to 200 cm (79 inches)

Plants distributed under this name by Plantation Gardens of Clermont, Florida, are presumed to be hybrids since pink is not known as a flower colour for the species. This clone has large, heavily fragrant flowers of apricot pink fading to pinky white. These are large, with a broad, bilobed labellum and are broadly similar in shape, if smaller than those of the species.

Hedychium coronarium var. *chrysoleucum*
Height: to 120 cm (48 inches)

Named as *Hedychium chrysoleucum* by Joseph Hooker, this smaller variety is native solely to northeastern India. As defined by stock in wide circulation in Europe, it is a distinct form that produces smaller flowers in greater profusion and holds them as an upward-facing cluster, produced from a much broader, less conical spike of bracts. Flower stems may be weighed down with the number of flowers and be presented almost horizontally. The flowers are powerfully fragrant and have golden yellow throats with contrasting orange stamens. One of the earliest hedychiums to bloom, always before *H. coronarium* itself, it is a consistently reliable flowerer in British gardens. It is extremely hardy and tolerant of a wide range of positions and garden conditions. (Plate 28)

Hedychium coronarium var. *maximum*

Endemic only to eastern India, this variety is defined as being larger than the type and having unmarked, pure white flowers. It is widely cultivated but probably not deserving of varietal status, since it can easily be accommodated within the described limits of the species itself. Further, the epithet "maximum" is also used at the species level (*H. maximum*), as well as seemingly being applied in the United States as a fancy name (*H.* 'Maximum') to large specimens of *H. coronarium*.

Hedychium coronarium var. *urophyllum*

Named in 1785 and native to low elevations in Assam, this variety differs from the species in its golden yellow flowers. At best the plant is only marginally hardy and perhaps not even to freezing point.

Hedychium densiflorum

Synonym: *Hedychium sinoaureum*
Minimum temperature: -18°C (0°F)
Height: 80–150 cm (31–60 inches)

Native to forest growth at 2000 to 2750 m (6600–9050 feet) in Xizang (Tibetan Autonomous Region), Bhutan, India, and Nepal, *Hedychium densiflorum* is (in some forms) probably the hardiest species of the genus.

Although not as flamboyant as some species, even in its most commonly seen form it ranks as a valuable garden plant. Nathaniel Wallich named the species in 1853 when he described plants that had been collected some 21 years earlier in Nepal. The first living specimens were not seen in Europe until 'Assam Orange' was introduced more than 80 years later. Various further collections have continued throughout the subsequent years, providing a diversity of forms of the species for cultivation.

In its basic and most commonly encountered incarnation *Hedychium densiflorum* is a relatively short species with slender stems and short flower spikes. These are typically around 15 cm (6 inches) tall and make up for their size by being very densely packed with small flowers. Flower colour is generally bright terracotta orange but can also be dark golden yellow and all shades between the two. The overall floral effect is similar to a large-flowered *Dactylorhiza* (marsh orchid), although in a strikingly different colour range. The species also varies considerably in its fragrance, with the toughest and highest altitude forms generally being unscented, or only having a very faint perfume that makes no appreciable impact in the garden, while other forms are strongly fragrant.

Like all of the hardiest and highest altitude hedychiums, *Hedychium densiflorum* unsurprisingly resents too much heat and grows much more successfully in Europe than in the southern United States. It also enjoys a shady, moist location. When given a good site, plants can increase quite quickly to form large, handsome clumps of arching stems. *Hedychium densiflorum* regularly sets seed and self-seeds with little provocation. It is sometimes maligned as a flowering plant due to its individually small flowers and frequent lack of fragrance, but I rate it very highly for ease of growth and adaptability in the garden and also for a charm and delicacy in flower that is quite different to the other species. (Plate 29)

Hedychium densiflorum 'Assam Orange'

In 1938 Frank Kingdon-Ward collected material of the species from 2000 m (6600 feet) in Assam (Arunachal Pradesh), northeastern India. These plants were subsequently transferred to the Royal Botanic Garden, Edinburgh. Despite the elevation at which they were found, and the obvious extremes of temperature that they must have endured in their native habitat, these plants were housed in a heated greenhouse and treated as tender, tropical subjects. Then, in the early 1970s, a clone of a plant from this collection was finally trialled outdoors, at Wakehurst Place in Sussex, where it was planted in a sheltered border with a southerly aspect. The trial proved a great success, and the plants thrived. Named 'Assam Orange', the clone was awarded a Royal Horticultural Society Award of Merit in 1974. This important plant essentially started the cultivation of gingers as garden plants in the United Kingdom.

Despite many additional plant introductions, 'Assam Orange' is still a fine plant. It is short, typically to 90 cm (36 inches) tall, with somewhat larger flower spikes at approximately 18 cm (7 inches) tall. These spikes are very heavily packed with moderately fragrant flowers that are of a particularly deep orange colour.

'Assam Orange' is easily grown and is now widely distributed throughout Europe where it is currently the *Hedychium* most likely to be found available from non-specialist nurseries and plant centres. Like all forms of *H. densiflorum*, 'Assam Orange' self-seeds readily. It is likely that some material in circulation under this name originated from seedlings rather than from vegetative divisions of the original. (Plate 30)

Hedychium densiflorum 'Sorung'

This extraordinary plant was found by Edward Needham at 2400 m (7900 feet) in the Hongu Khola valley on the east side of Saalpa Pass, near Sorung in eastern Nepal. It is larger than the typical species in growth, with stems that are more robust and that reach 150 cm (60 inches) tall. It also has substantially larger flower spikes, approximately 20 cm (8 inches) tall. Larger individual flowers are held well away from the spike (rather than being held tightly to the spike as is usual). The flower colour is unusual too, being a strong pinkish apricot, and the plant is beautifully fragrant particularly in the evening. As might be imagined from its natural elevation, 'Sorung' has proven to be perfectly hardy and represents an exciting new introduction to horticulture, as well as a further indication of the diversity of forms of *Hedychium densiflorum*. (Plate 31)

Hedychium densiflorum 'Stephen'
Height: 120–150 cm (48–60 inches)

'Stephen' is another magnificent form, with substantially larger and more open flowers than the typical species, this time of a peachy primrose with contrasting anthers and filaments of burnt orange, and the same intense fragrance as 'Sorung'. Tony Schilling collected this plant in 1966 at 2700 m

(8900 feet) from the Dudh Kosi Valley, in Khumbu, eastern Nepal. He found a small population growing on a "damp grassy west-facing slope of 20°, in mixed forest of *Quercus semecarpifolia*, *Rhododendron arboreum*, and *Magnolia campbellii*". Oddly, perhaps, the more common smaller-flowered form of *Hedychium densiflorum* was the only other *Hedychium* present there.

Schilling named his find after his son, and assumed, not surprisingly, that the plant was either a new species or a hybrid of *Hedychium densiflorum*. His view was partially supported by an examination undertaken at the Royal Botanic Gardens, Kew, which determined that 'Stephen' has 50 percent pollen sterility, a feature frequently found in hybrids. Taken together and viewed beside a typical specimen of *H. densiflorum*, 'Sorung' and 'Stephen' do not appear to belong to that species. Instead, they seem to be natural hybrids; however, this large-flowered 'type' of the species is apparently not uncommon in the wild, with populations occurring over a relatively large area. Genetic analysis in the United States has determined that the two forms are indeed part of *H. densiflorum*, with little significant genetic variation between them and the normal type of the species. 'Stephen' is a very fine and hardy plant that is now well established in cultivation and is available from specialist nurseries in Europe. (Plate 32)

Hedychium efilamentosum

Minimum temperature: -10°C (15°F) ?
Height: 100 cm (39 inches)

First named by Heinrich R. E. Handel-Mazzetti in 1936, this Chinese species has yet to be established in cultivation and is presumed to be rare and localized in the wild. It is native to woodland at 1800 m (5900 feet) in Xizang (Tibetan Autonomous Region) and produces yellow flowers from a 15- to 20-cm (6- to 8-inch) tall spike in July and August.

Hedychium ellipticum

Minimum temperature: -7°C (20°F) ?
Height: 120–150 cm (48–60 inches)

Uncommon both in the wild and in cultivation, this species is spectacular when in flower but still largely untested for ultimate hardiness in Europe.

Hedychium ellipticum is a native of the eastern Himalaya, from Nepal and northeastern India through northern Thailand, at altitudes of 600 to 1800 m (2000–5900 feet). The lower-altitude forms could not be expected to be terribly hardy, but those from the highest altitudes are now in cultivation in England and the United States where they are proving to be reasonably cold tolerant, if rather demanding in their requirements. A fully shaded, highly moisture retentive, humid, and mild (but never hot) position is necessary for good growth.

When content, the plants produce very thick, red-stained stems with handsome and extremely broad ribbed leaves like a small *Musa*. In its native climes *Hedychium ellipticum* often frequents steep mud slopes, growing more or less horizontally from the banks. Even when plants are grown on a level surface, the pseudostems will invariably arch over under the weight of the leaves, which allows the flower spikes (when produced) to be held clear of the foliage. The inflorescence is among the finest in the genus, with a multitude of creamy white flowers held upright in a cluster, each flower having a massively exerted orange-red stamen. The whole looks like a brightly coloured pin-cushion. This floral effect is complemented by a faint but pleasing spicy fragrance.

In Nepal and India. flowering of *Hedychium ellipticum* occurs in August, which should translate into a satisfactory flowering season in the West; however, this does not always appear to be the case. Specimens in cultivation seem reluctant to bloom in the garden, although they do flower successfully under glass. Perhaps it is a matter of introducing different high-altitude forms of the species into cultivation, or alternatively plants may be induced into growth earlier to give a prolonged growing season.

Hedychium flavescens

Synonyms: *Hedychium flavum* Roscoe, *H. emeiense*, *H. panzhuum*
Minimum temperature: -10ºC (15ºF)
Height: 120–240 cm (48–96 inches)

This species has a highly schizophrenic history of naming. William Roscoe originally described it as a variety of the very widespread and variable *Hedychium coronarium*. Later it was named *H. flavum*, which is now recognized as a separate species (which see). Chinese botanist Zheng Yin Zhu also published the short-lived names *H. emiense* and *H. panzhuum*, both of which are now regarded as synonymous with *H. flavescens*. William Carey first described the species proper in 1824. A Baptist missionary to India and founder of the Serampore Botanic Garden, Carey sent collections of native Indian ginger species to William Roscoe at the Liverpool Botanic Garden and in so doing was responsible for introducing the first gingers into Western cultivation.

Hedychium flavescens is native to damp, shady woodland and stream margins in the eastern Himalaya of Nepal and India. Its domain also reaches into Sichuan province in southwestern China, where it grows at fairly low altitudes of 500 to 800 m (1600–2600 feet). It has, nevertheless, proven to be relatively hardy and readily produces very robust and tall pseudostems clothed with softly pubescent foliage. The flowers are similar to those of *H. coronarium*, being individually large with a broad, bilobed labellum. They open a pale primrose yellow to cream colour with a darker lemon yellow to orange patch at the base of the labellum. Plants in shade retain their flower colour, while those in bright light tend to bleach out rapidly to off-white. The flowers are also powerfully fragrant, with a sharper, more lemony perfume than that of *H. coronarium.*

The only problem with this species in cultivation is that, while it flowers in late summer in the wild, in cultivation it blooms later in the season, often not until November. This invariably means that *Hedychium flavescens* will not flower at all, or will abort its developing inflorescences when grown in colder gardens that are prone to frost in November. In contrast the species is listed as a "noxious weed" in Hawaii, where the tropical climate provides conditions that allow escapees to multiply exponentially and smother native species.

Hedychium flavum

Minimum temperature: -10ºC (15ºF)
Height: 150–240 cm (60–96 inches)

Named by William Roxburgh in 1820, this species is botanically close to *Hedychium flavescens* and much confused with it in cultivation. In fact, the names are used almost interchangeably. *Hedychium flavum* can be distinguished by its leaves that lack the pubescence of its close relative, together with flowers that are a solid yellow, deeper coloured than *H. flavescens*, and without the darker patch of that species.

Hedychium flavum is a native of India, Myanmar, Thailand, and southern China at altitudes of 900 to 1200 m (3000–3900 feet). It is cultivated across the region for its flowers. The true species is little cultivated (indeed possibly not in cultivation) in Europe, and much of the stock in the United States appears to be referable to *H. flavescens*. *Hedychium flavum* itself would appear to be a valuable species, worth tracking down for its imposing stature and beautiful fragrant flowers, plus the hope that an earlier flowering season will allow successful flowering over a wider number of gardens.

Hedychium forrestii

Minimum temperature: -18°C (0°F)
Height: 180–290 cm (71–114 inches)

Named by Friedrich Diels in 1912, *Hedychium forrestii* was apparently already being grown in Scotland by the 1930s. Many cultivated plants of this imposing species derive from an introduction made in 1957 by Joseph Rock. He sent material (bearing the label *H. gardnerianum*) to the Royal Botanic Garden, Edinburgh, although the wild origin of the plants was not recorded. These specimens thrived, and material was distributed to the gardens of Kew, Wakehurst Place, Talbot Manor, and Castle Howard where, in this wide range of climates and conditions, none of them particularly benign, the species proved to be extremely hardy and vigorous in growth.

Hedychium forrestii is one of the largest hedychiums with bold, glossy foliage and thick pseudostems. A well-grown specimen brings a supremely impressive and architectural quality to any garden. The species is native to shady woodland in Southeast Asia, its territory covering Laos, Myanmar, Thailand, and North Vietnam, as well as southern China, where plants grow at altitudes of 200 to 900 m (650–3000 feet). Given this distribution, it is perhaps surprising that *H. forrestii* is as hardy as it is. Nevertheless, if given a location secure from lacerating winds, the species can successfully cultivated across most of the United Kingdom.

In flower *Hedychium forrestii* is not as dramatic as some *Hedychium* species but is still an attractive proposition with fairly tall flower spikes of 30 cm (12 inches). These cylindrical spikes, which are produced for a long season from late July to October, are open and rather loose, and bear good-sized, very open pure white flowers, each with a 5-cm (2-inch) long protruding cream anther and a fine perfume. In the open garden the flowers are rarely produced en masse, but small numbers open in succession throughout the flowering season. *Hedychium forrestii* is highly recommended for colder climates and for gardeners new to ginger cultivation.

Hedychium forrestii var. latebracteatum

Identified by Kai Larsen in 1965, this variety is endemic to Sichuan and Yunnan provinces in China, and in the neighbouring territory of North Vietnam. It differs from the type in two respects. First, the flower bracts are larger at approximately 3 cm (1 1/4 inches) wide versus about 1 cm (1/2 inch) for var. *forrestii*. Second, the flower colour is yellow, not white as in the type. While this plant is undoubtedly a valid variety, the specimens currently in cultivation under this name appear to be referable to *Hedychium maximum* and *H. yunnanense*.

Hedychium gardnerianum

Minimum temperature: -10°C (15°F)
Height: 100–180 cm (39–71 inches)

Alongside *Hedychium coronarium*, this species is the best known and most frequently encountered in the genus. It is widely cultivated throughout the subtropics. William Roscoe named it in honour of Edward Gardner, a noted collector of botanical specimens for the Calcutta Botanic Garden as well as the East India Company's British resident at the Nepalese royal court from 1816 to 1829.

The most frequently used common name is kahili, after the traditional Hawaiian royal standards that consist of red and yellow feathers. However, the plant is native not to Hawaii, but rather to the Himalaya, at altitudes of up to 2000 m (6600 feet), in Nepal, Sikkim, and eastwards to Assam. In Nepal *Hedychium gardnerianum* is also used ceremonially, giving rise to another of its common names, that of garland flower. During the eight-day Nepalese festival of Indrajatra, a festival that honours Indra, the Hindu god of rain, the flowers of this ginger species alone are used to make garlands that adorn a chosen girl who is believed to be the incarnation of the goddess Kumari.

Given constant heat and humidity, *Hedychium gardnerianum* can be fantastically vigorous, but it is far more benign in temperate climates where it has become a highly prized garden subject. It is only since 1990 or so that the possibilities of *H. gardnerianum* as a hardy garden plant have been explored. Previously regarded as an entirely tropical plant suitable for greenhouse cultivation or summer bedding schemes at best, it is actually far tougher than was initially realized. In fact, it will flower fully and reliably in

September wherever conditions will allow, despite the fact that plants are often very late to break dormancy and new stems do not appear until June or even July in temperate gardens. The possible reason for the previous caution in cultivation might have partially arisen from the look of the plant in flower—it simply seems unfeasible that such a flowering plant can be hardy. The very wide flower spike, which can reach 40 cm (16 inches) tall, although 25–30 cm (10–12 inches) is the norm, is heavily laden with a dense mass of narrow bright canary yellow flowers, each with a contrasting bright red stamen. Although the species generally has only a light fragrance, it is a truly spectacular sight in flower. When given a bright, sunny, and sheltered garden spot, it will handsomely reward any gardener. In temperate gardens, where frosts severely curtail the growing season, the species is fully deciduous; however, in tropical climes it behaves very differently, remaining evergreen and in full growth year-round.

After being widely distributed as an ornamental in the 1890s, *Hedychium gardnerianum* has escaped from cultivation and is naturalized in several countries. It is now regarded as a pest species in New Zealand, Madeira, Australia, and particularly Hawaii where its vigorous growth threatens the delicate natural flora. By the 1960s *H. gardnerianum* had also overwhelmed much of the native vegetation of the Azores islands in the Atlantic by invading the natural forest and waterways as well as *Pinus* plantations, smothering competing plants with a dense marching army of evergreen foliage and an impenetrable network of tough, tangled rhizomes. This floral embodiment of the phrase 'One man's meat is another man's poison' should serve as a cautionary tale about the introduction of non-native species into unsuitable (or rather too suitable) environments. Nonetheless, while gazing upon a crop of freshly opened *H. gardnerianum* flowers on a dull autumn day in England, it is, I confess, hard to muster anything but enthusiasm for the plant. (Plate 33)

Hedychium gardnerianum 'Compactum'

The Florida-based Gainesville Tree Farm nursery introduced this form and subsequently circulated it through the United States. The description of the plant is as for the species, but with pseudostems to no more than 120 cm (48 inches) tall. Since this is normal height for *Hedychium gardnerianum* outdoors in the United Kingdom, perhaps plants of the form are shorter still in that climate. 'Compactum' is hardy to -15°C (5°F), although this may well be estimated rather than learned through experience.

Hedychium gardnerianum 'Extendum'

Another Gainesville introduction, 'Extendum' was selected and named for its larger size. Pseudostems reach 240 cm (96 inches) tall, which is significantly taller than the usual range of the species.

Hedychium gardnerianum var. *pallidum*

Plants with paler flowers—in the primrose, rather than the lemon range of yellows—are referable to this variety. Occurring, as it does, over such an enormously wide and diverse range of geographies, it is far from surprising that some natural variation in form and colour can be found in different populations of *Hedychium gardnerianum*. Whether such variation is sufficient to warrant varietal status is another matter, since a gradation of yellow pigment is readily observed in both wild and cultivated stocks of the species. Plants grown in the United Kingdom under this name may, possibly, derive from a single source. They have a limited distribution in cultivation at present, but the creamy yellow flowers are certainly fairly distinct from the typical bright yellow of the species.

Hedychium glabrum

Minimum temperature: -15ºC (5ºF) ?
Height: 100–120 cm (39–48 inches)

Named in 1989 by Shao Quan Tong, this Chinese species is a seemingly rare native of forest margins at 2100 m (6900 feet) in southern Yunnan province. It is an extremely attractive species, with relatively short but stout pseudostems that hold handsome and very broad banana-like leaves.

Almost all *Hedychium* species have attractive foliage, but that of *H. glabrum* is particularly fine. The leaves are strongly ribbed with veins emerging from sheaths that have deep red margins. These sheaths remain tight to the stems after the leaves unfurl, producing broad red stripes up the length of the otherwise green pseudostems. The flowers occur in June, which is very early for the genus. The inflorescence is large at 20 to 30 cm (8–12 inches) tall by 8 to 12 cm (3–5 inches) wide and densely packed with flowers. These are pale yellow, each held by a rusty red-stained calyx, and each with an elongated pale red filament. The contrast between the soft red and the pale yellow elements within the flowers is extremely attractive.

Considering its ornamental foliage, early flowering season, short, stocky pseudostems, and presumed hardiness, *Hedychium glabrum* is one of the best *Hedychium* introductions, and one of the most exciting for the hardy gardener. Despite a very short history, the species is already cultivated by specialist growers in the United States. It is hoped that it will receive a wider distribution as stocks increase.

Hedychium gracile

Synonyms: *Hedychium gracilis, H. griffithianum*
Minimum temperature: -10ºC (15ºF)
Height: 80–120 cm (31–48 inches)

First described by William Roxburgh in 1814, this high-altitude Himalayan species is native to India, Bhutan, and Nepal, where plants grow in cool forests and at stream margins. They often are almost semi-epiphytic, with the rhizomes above ground, and the roots working into the leaf litter.

Hedychium gracile is a small species, with slender pseudostems that generally arch over under the weight of the leaves. Like many slender stemmed hedychiums, plants of this species will, in the wild, grow horizontally, or frequently downwards from steep banks, the inflorescence then arching into an upright position at the tip of the stem. In cultivation the temptation is to "correct" the growth of the plants and force them to stand as upright as possible, but this is not their natural inclination. Where the plants can be well sited, the arching stems make an appealing and unusual garden feature, particularly near water. To my mind at least, *H. gracile* is much better displayed in this manner rather than being artificially trussed up with the support of canes and ties.

The species is a good, reliable summer flowerer in cultivation, with blooms appearing from July through August. The individual flowers are white with a narrow labellum and very narrow, long white staminodes that curl downwards, producing a spidery effect. Contrasting with this the flowers have greatly protruding, pale red filaments that hold the anthers aloft for pollinators to inspect. The flowers are produced in some profusion and the overall effect is very attractive. Some forms of the species are fragrant, particularly at night, but others are largely scent-free. Plants recently, and maybe still currently, offered by Indian nurseries as "*H. griffithianum*" appear to be referable to this species.

Hedychium greenii

Minimum temperature: -10°C (15°F)
Height: 90–140 cm (36–55 inches)

This highly ornamental species is unique in the genus for several traits, including having very strongly coloured foliage that is a deep maroon on the undersides, the same colour also infusing the pseudostems of the plant. William Wright Smith originally described *Hedychium greenii* in 1913, naming it after H. F. Green whose collectors had, approximately two years earlier, found the species growing wild in the low hills of southwestern Bhutan. Plants originating from this location were cultivated at Green's home in Darjeeling and later also at the Calcutta Botanic Garden before being sent to England. Although the species has become, and still is widely known as "H. greenei", the original publication shows the intended and correct spelling, and the eagle-eyed will also spot that there is, in any event, no "e" on the end of Green's surname. Until recently all plants in Western cultivation derived from this one introduction. Although new cultivated stocks are now becoming available from Indian nurseries, most plants in gardens are clones of this original collection.

Hedychium greenii is a fairly uncommon native of the Himalayan foothills in Bhutan and northeastern India, where it typically grows as an evergreen in damp, often marshy ground at forest margins at altitudes of 900 to 1500 m (3000–4900 feet). It is not a large species, although wild plants can reach 180 cm (71 inches) tall in the much-prolonged growth period that they enjoy as evergreens. Cultivated specimens are often late to emerge from dormancy, and 90–100 cm (36–39 inches) is a more typical height in temperate gardens.

The flowers occur from July to October, depending upon temperatures and the length of the growing season. Although unscented and few in number—typically groups of two to five flowers will emerge sporadically throughout the season—the flowers are strikingly coloured a bright reddish orange and are individually relatively large. Each flower has a very broad, undivided lip that is held erect, giving the flower a different appearance from all other *Hedychium* flowers. With its small terminal spikes of vivid flowers, *H. greenii* could, at an uninitiated glance, be mistaken for one of its relatives the cannas, a mistake that would not be readily noted for any other *Hedychium* species.

It is not uncommon in the United Kingdom, and perhaps elsewhere, for plants to fail to flower, or to abort their developing flower buds where temperatures fail to sustain into autumn. The same effect has been reported when plants are grown in warmer temperatures without being heavily watered. Indeed, when in growth the species can readily be accommodated as a marginal water plant, mirroring its wild habitats. Even where plants do fail to flower satisfactorily every year, the species is still well worth growing for its foliage, which is certainly the most ornamental of all the hedychiums.

A further unusual trait of this species is that, following flowering, the old inflorescence will develop new viviparous plantlets that have (somewhat bizarrely for a fairly recent Himalayan introduction—blame the marketing folks) come to be given the Hawaiian name "keikis", meaning "babies". These youngsters can easily be separated from the main plant and, when potted up and kept moist, will readily root to form new plants.

The combination of coloured foliage, plantlets, unusual flower colour and morphology gives rise to the notion that *Hedychium greenii* is genetically separate from other hedychiums. Chromosome studies support this notion, showing that the species is indeed divergent from most others in the genus. *Hedychium greenii* is not known to have set seed in cultivation either in Europe or the United States, due, perhaps, to the weakening of the genetic material since most cultivated plants are viviparous clones of the same, limited source material, and potential cross-pollination with other variants has only recently become an option.

This low-altitude species has been thought of as an entirely tropical or glasshouse subject, but it will actually take a considerable degree of frost (perhaps more than is indicated above). It is easy to grow in general garden cultivation, although, like other hedychiums grown in temperate gardens, it becomes entirely deciduous under these conditions. *Hedychium greenii* does not increase rapidly at the rhizome, a trait that hardly matters to most growers given the species's other reproductive propensity. As a hardy plant this attractive species has much to recommend it, and greatest success can be achieved in a sheltered position with at least partial shade, where the application of copious food and water during the growing season should ensure strong, flowering plants. (Plate 34)

Hedychium hasseltii

Synonym: *Hedychium* 'Giant Moth'
Minimum temperature: -7°C (20°F)
Height: 40–60 cm (16–24 inches)

This species might be regarded as interesting rather than spectacular, although its sturdy but dwarf nature has been used with some success in the parenting of some superb *Hedychium* hybrids, most notably *H.* 'Luna Moth'. Originally described by Carl (Karl) Ludwig von Blume, the species produces a small spike of white flowers that open in ones and twos from golden yellow buds. The individual flowers are large, particularly in relation to the overall size of the plant, and comprise a broad lip, divided to its centre, and two long and broad lateral staminodes, seated below an extended dark golden filament and orange anther. Under outdoor cultivation plants produce a brief flowering display in July or August and also have an attractive, if not terribly strong fragrance.

Hedychium hasseltii is endemic to Indonesia, specifically the island of Java. While this region is not traditionally associated with temperate hardy plants, the volcanic Javan plateau highlands reach to 3700 m (12,350 feet) above sea level and are subject to relatively severe cold. In addition, Java has an extremely high rainfall, with monsoon conditions much of the year punctuated by a dry season from June to September. This pattern helps to explain why, with some coaxing, plants of these regions can tolerate a temperate climate.

Hedychium hasseltii is primarily an epiphyte, growing in the wild in full or semi-shade on the trunks of trees. For successful cultivation, it is essential to factor in the conditions under which is grows in the wild, namely, very high rainfall, shade, and fierce drainage. This does not mean that the plant can only survive when grown as an epiphyte, but rather that these conditions must, to some extent, be replicated if the plant is to thrive. Epiphytic plants in general derive most or all of their nutrition from a combination of rainwater and occasional decomposing leaves, so the emphasis in cultivation should be on a growing medium that (unlike that required for many *Hedychium*) allows for maximum drainage rather than heavy nourishment. In the garden *H. hasseltii* may be successfully grown in a variety of soils, with either stone, gravel, rock, or sand providing the drainage, or, perhaps more naturally, with its rhizomes planted into chopped bark or coarse leaf-mould, or a soil featuring a large proportion of one or more of these elements. Watering regimes become more important when such growing mediums are employed, since they are more prone to drying out. High humidity will also encourage more successful growth and better foliage.

For many hardy gardeners *Hedychium hasseltii* might be more easily grown in a container, where drainage and water supply may be more closely monitored. Given either approach, this species is surprisingly easy to accommodate and grow. *Hedychium hasseltii* is now available from nurseries in the United Kingdom and the United States, although its specialist nature will probably render it forever a rarity in cultivation. (Plate 35)

Hedychium longicornutum

Minimum temperature: -4°C (25°F) ?
Height: 50–60 cm (20–24 inches)

Named by William Griffith in 1892, this spectacular ginger is purported to be frost hardy, although I am not aware of the hardiness being properly tested as yet. I include the species here because it is both hugely ornamental and also easily available. *Hedychium longicornutum* is a native of the forest highlands of peninsular Malaysia, northwards into southern Thailand. Its marvellously self-describing local name, perched gingerwort, derives from the plant's natural growth habit as a pure epiphyte, always growing with its exposed roots tightly wrapped around an arboreal host, and with foliage cascading downwards in a green fountain.

In its native Asian climes *Hedychium longicornutum* is an evergreen, with flowering occurring at any time of the year, but in cultivation it flowers in March and April. Thus, from a practical point of view, plants must be accommodated in such a way that they remain evergreen throughout winter. Otherwise, like many *Alpinia* species, and for the same reason, they will not flower, and this would be a shame, since the floral display of this ginger is a site to behold. The horizontal or cascading pseudostems produce from their tips an explosion of soft red buds that are held upright, to resemble a loose red brush. These buds open to reveal twisted and spidery orange-yellow flowers, each with a greatly protruding white filament capped by a yellow anther, and all of this sited against the deep green foliage. The display gives rise to another of the plant's Malaysian names—the *enggang* (hornbill ginger).

Hedychium longicornutum is used in local medicine for a variety of purposes. The ground roots are used to treat earache and applied as a liniment for muscular or skin conditions, while the entire plant is used to treat intestinal worms.

In cultivation outside of the mildest regions, this species almost certainly should be grown in a container, with a restricted root run, copious water, and (possibly) a limited food supply. The growing medium, like that for any epiphytic plant, should contain a high proportion of coarse material to aid drainage. The plants should be sited in sheltered, bright shade where they will not desiccate.

Hedychium maximum

Minimum temperature: -10ºC (15ºF) ?
Height: 200–280 cm (79–112 inches)

This species is a strong contender for the title of "Hedychium with the most confused and abstruse history of naming and cultivation". Writing in 1825 William Roscoe described a species as "Hedychium maximum" following observations of plants collected in eastern India and brought back to cultivation in England. The white-flowered plant that was thus described and illustrated is properly known as *Hedychium coronarium* var. *maximum*, a large-flowered and robust variety of the species, notable for having very broad, white lateral staminodes. The plant under discussion here, however, is a different (and now the only) *H. maximum*, with entirely yellow flowers, and much more narrow lateral staminodes. To add to the confusion, it was recently introduced to British cultivation as *H. forrestii* var. *latebracteum* (which is also a valid, but separate plant).

Drawing a discreet veil over the nomenclatural horrors above, *Hedychium maximum* is a magnificent ginger. The plants have very fine, broad foliage and produce great, thick stems that tower above most of their kith and kin. In early autumn the stems start to bear very large and powerfully spicy fragrant flowers of pale creamy yellow, each with a wide, bilobed lip and a deep golden centre. Beneath the lip are two primrose yellow staminodes and a golden orange filament and anther. Where temperatures allow, *H. maximum* will continue flowering sporadically throughout autumn and on into midwinter.

The primary problem with cultivating the species in colder gardens is that, despite the plants' undoubted hardiness, they may not be able to reach flowering size unless protected in autumn, or started into growth artificially early in spring. Nevertheless, in sheltered spots, or with some assistance and protection, *Hedychium maximum* will provide a spectacular display if and when it is able to flower. This species is always going to be well worth any extra effort it requires to allow successful flowering.

In other respects *Hedychium maximum* is easily grown in conditions enjoyed by most of the hardy members of the genus, although it is slow to increase at the rhizome. The species is available from nurseries in the United Kingdom and the United States, and plants in cultivation are fairly uniform in appearance. When seeking to buy this species, it is particularly important to establish that plant being offered for sale bears yellow flowers (and thus is the true species) rather than white. (Plate 36)

Hedychium neocarneum

Minimum temperature: -10°C (15°F) ?
Height: 100–200 cm (39–79 inches)

This name was first published in 2000 in the new *Flora of China* (Wu and Larsen 2000). The plant was originally described in 1994 by Yi Yong Qian, who named it as "Hedychium carneum"; however, this earlier name is not valid, as it had already been used (in 1823, by Conrad Loddiges) for an unrelated Indian species of *Hedychium*.

Hedychium neocarneum is a native of the forests of southern Yunnan province at 1600 to 1900 m (5200–6200 feet). The original collection was made in Simao prefecture. The species is described as being close to *H. yungjiangense*, also recently named. *Hedychium neocarneum* differs from *H. yungjiangense* in having leaves that are considerably more hairy beneath, and having a white labellum that has a large flesh-red basal blotch (wholly white in *H. yungjiangense*). In addition, the pale red anther-bearing filament is substantially longer at 5 cm (2 inches) versus approximately 1 cm (1/2 inch). In Yunnan *H. neocarneum* flowers in September, producing pinecone-shaped flower spikes up to 35 cm (14 inches) tall by 20 cm (8 inches) wide.

Although it has not yet been introduced to cultivation, *Hedychium neobracteum* should certainly be hardy in temperate gardens, coming, as it does, from altitudes that harbour the like of *Roscoea debilis*. The *Hedychium* seems to be a highly ornamental prospect. In addition to its flowers, this species has purple leaf sheaths, a feature that is always appealing on other hedychiums. The only likely cultivation problem might arise from the autumn flowering season, which might limit the regions in which the plant can be successfully flowered. In any case, it is hoped that material will soon become available for trial.

Hedychium parvibracteatum

Minimum temperature: -12°C (10°F) ?
Height: to 50 cm (20 inches)

First described in 1978, by Te Lin(g) Wu and Senjen Chen, this extremely small species is native to southeastern Xizang (Tibetan Autonomous Region), in the *Rhododendron*-rich forests of Bomi county, near the Himalayan border with Assam. It has not yet been introduced to cultivation, although the area is, for the first time in many decades, subject to seed-collection expeditions, and the arrival of *Hedychium parvibracteatum* in the West seems a feasible possibility.

The plant produces short, narrow leaves 15 cm (6 inches) long by 4 cm (1½ inches) wide and, in July, 10-cm (4-inch) tall spikes of golden yellow flowers. Individual flowers are tiny—the undivided labellum just 5 mm (⅕ inch) long by 3 mm (⅛ inch) wide, with only marginally longer lateral staminodes—but they are densely packed into the spike. The species is clearly related to the much larger *Hedychium densiflorum*, which it closely resembles when in flower.

Hedychium puerense

Minimum temperature: -10°C (15°F) ?
Height: 120–200 cm (48–79 inches)

This Chinese species is native to forests at 1300 to 1600 m (4300–5200 feet) in southern Yunnan, the same habitat as *Hedychium neocarneum*. Like that species, *H. puerense* was named by Yi Yong Qian, this time in 1996.

The plant produces flowering spikes that reach 50 cm (20 inches) tall by 23 cm (9 inches) wide, which is exceptionally large for such a relatively small *Hedychium*, and these are supported by densely hairy pseudostems. The individual flowers are produced in profusion and are predominantly white, each with a bilobed labellum approximately 2 cm (¾ inch) long and wide. The labellum has a yellow blotch at the base and is accompanied by pure white lateral staminodes and an elongated white filament to nearly 7 cm (2³⁄₄ inches) that in turn holds a white anther.

Like *Hedychium neocarneum* (unsurprisingly given that they come from the same geographic area), *H. puerense* flowers in September in Yunnan, so may prove problematic in gardens that suffer from early autumn frosts. The species has not yet been introduced to cultivation, but represents an outstanding ornamental prospect for the future.

Hedychium qingchengense

Minimum temperature: -10°C (15°F) ?
Height: 80–120 cm (31–48 inches)

Zheng Yin Zhu first published the name of this small species in 1992, in the bulletin of Sichuan school of traditional Chinese medicine. *Hedychium qingchengense* is a native of low elevation forests at 500 m (1600 feet) in central Guan county of Sichuan province. This region is rich in flora that have proven suitable for cultivation in temperate gardens, and is home to the Wolong Panda Reserve that has itself yielded some superb introductions for the hardy garden.

Hedychium qingchengense has narrow leaves approximately 40 cm (16 inches) long. From July to September it produces small flower spikes 6–15 cm (2¹⁄₂ to 6 inches) tall. The individual flowers are modestly sized and white, with narrow lateral staminodes and a labellum around 2 cm (³⁄₄ inch) long by 3 cm (1¹⁄₄ inches) wide. The labellum has a prominent orange basal blotch. The filaments protrude, but not to any great ornamental degree. While the species is utilized in Chinese herbalism, it is not greatly showy, and its horticultural appeal is perhaps more limited. That said, it is certainly notable for being one of the most northern species of *Hedychium* and should prove hardy if and when it is introduced to cultivation.

Hedychium simaoense

Minimum temperature: -7°C (15°F) ?
Height: to 180 cm (71 inches)

Another of the species named by Yi Yong Qian in 1996, *Hedychium simaoense* is native to forests of Simao prefecture in southern Yunnan at altitudes of around 1400 m (4600 feet). This highly unusual species is notable for having narrowly linear leaves up to 50 cm (20 inches) long but typically only a few centimetres (about 1 inch) wide. Produced in August, the flowering stems are densely hairy and give rise to large flower spikes of 20 to 35 cm (8–14 inches) tall by 15–23 cm (6–9 inches) wide. The individual flowers are produced in profusion and can be either white or yellow, with a cleft labellum and lateral staminodes 2–3 cm (3/4–1 1/4 inches) long.

The species is perhaps most notable for having flowers that are infused with purple, a colour not found in any other *Hedychium* species. The corolla tube that holds each individual flower is purple, as is the prominent 5-cm (2-inch) long filament and the anther (although more rarely this can be orange). In addition, the labellum and the lateral staminodes are pale purple at their bases.

Sadly, *Hedychium simaoense* is not in cultivation at present. It should prove at least moderately hardy. With its summer flowering season and its unusual flowers and foliage it represents an excellent prospect for introduction as well as for hybridizing programmes.

Hedychium spicatum

Minimum temperature: -15°C (5°F)
Height: 90–150 cm (36–60 inches)

Along with *Hedychium densiflorum*, *H. spicatum* is regarded as the hardiest *Hedychium* species in cultivation. It is a native of the eastern Indian Himalaya, as well as Nepal, Myanmar, northern Thailand, Xizang (Tibetan Autonomous Region), and Guizhou, Sichuan, and Yunnan provinces of southern China. It has been found at altitudes of 1200 to 2900 m (3900–9500 feet) and is the most commonly occurring species in the wild, at least in the Himalayas. Due, perhaps, to the frequency with which it occurs in the wild, *H. spicatum* is used for a variety of medicinal and culinary purposes (see chapter 5), and the dried rhizome is a common feature of Himalayan and northern Indian marketplaces. James Edward Smith described this species in 1811 from a collection made of Nepalese plants, and the species was brought into cultivation at the Calcutta Botanic Garden with the introduction of further material, also from Nepal, collected by Edward Gardner some six years later.

Hedychium spicatum is a small species, rarely much exceeding 100 cm (39 inches) in cultivation, with narrow, glossy, smooth foliage and, in June and July, 20-cm (8-inch) tall flower spikes. The spikes are generally sparsely clothed with flowers, although the individual flowers are fragrant and rather pretty. The flowers are often described as resembling white moths, due to the small, upright white lateral staminodes and white labellum that typify a group of species including *H. forrestii*, *H. picatum*, *H. villosum*, and *H. yunnanense*. The labellum, which is strongly bifurcated to its centre, ages to cream or pale yellow in many forms and is often marked by an intensely golden orange throat. This throat, along with a flesh red corolla tube and similarly coloured filament, makes a pleasing contrast with the paler flower parts.

Hedychium spicatum has proven to be a reliable and consistent early flowerer in cultivation. It sets seed more readily than any other *Hedychium* species in temperate cultivation. As the pods split open to reveal their vivid scarlet seed arils (the fleshy pulp that surrounds the seeds), set against the waxy bright orange of the inside of the pod, the plants provide a further ornamental display that sometimes rivals the flowering itself.

While *Hedychium spicatum* is far from the most spectacular species of *Hedychium*, it is an invaluable plant for those colder gardens where more tender species would not survive. Thus, it is an important vanguard plant to increase the range and number of locations in which gingers can be successfully cultivated. The species is always deciduous, regardless of how warm or bright the conditions of cultivation, indicating that it has adapted to a natural habitat that is cooler than the one in which many hedychiums grow. The species will not tolerate prolonged, unprotected heat.

Since the species was originally named, material of *Hedychium spicatum* has regularly been introduced into cultivation. A number of forms and variants are available to the gardener, although as yet none have been given cultivar names. One of the most interesting and ornamental of these is *H. spicatum* BandSWJ23203, a form collected from the Singlila Ridge (that forms the border between Nepal and Sikkim) by Bleddyn and Sue Wynn-Jones of the renowned Crûg Farm Nursery. This form is more densely and prolifically flowered than is typical, and has leaves that, unusually, unfurl to reveal a purple-red underside.

Hedychium (spicatum?) PB 57188 was collected (as *H. yunnanense*) more recently, by Pete Bordman. It has strongly coloured flowers, each with a labellum that fades to butter yellow, and linear, apricot orange petals. It is also notable for having exceptionally large foliage—18 cm (7 inches) wide by 56 cm (22 inches) long. (Plate 37)

Hedychium spicatum var. *acuminatum*

William Roscoe, in 1824, initially named this variety as a separate species, *Hedychium acuminatum*. Twenty-nine years later Nathaniel Wallich proposed including it as a variety of *H. spicatum*, and so it has remained. The variety is present throughout much of the species's natural range at elevations of 2000 to 3200 m (6,600–10,500 feet) and is the primary (possibly only) representative of *H. spicatum* native to India.

Var. *acuminatum* differs from var. *spicatum* in its flower spikes, which are more lax, with fewer individual flowers although these are more colourful, with the apex of the corolla tube, base of corolla lobes, lateral staminodes, and labellum all purplish red. The labellum also has a more sharply pointed (acuminate) tip. It is much the more commonly encountered variety in cultivation, reflecting the primarily Indian origins of introduced plants. Native Chinese plants are said to flower from August to October, significantly later than var. *spicatum*, although plants in cultivation do not appear to share this difference.

The status of var. *acuminatum* is perhaps open to question, since, as a species, *Hedychium spicatum* is both widespread and widely variable, and var. *acuminatum* is not a regionally discrete form. Tony Schilling collected a form (S. 1147) of this species in 1966 from the warm temperate forests to the south of Kathmandu, and introduced it to cultivation at Wakehurst Place. Schilling refers to this form as being an "exceptionally handsome form of very distichous habit".

Hedychium stenopetalum

Minimum temperature: -10°C (15°F)
Height: to 360 cm (142 inches)

Referring to *Hedychium stenopetalum* in an on-line garden forum, renowned ginger grower and nurseryman Tim Chapman of Gingerwood Nursery, St. Gabriel, Louisiana, wrote, "Saw this in the wild for the first time and was shocked by just how amazingly huge the plant is . . . massive!"

The largest of the *Hedychium* species, *H. stenopetalum* is native to monsoonal forests of the Indian Himalaya, where its towering pseudostems are clothed with equally impressive huge, deep green leaves. The flowering spikes emerge in August and September, and are broadly in scale with the rest of the plant at around 45 cm (18 inches) tall by 25 cm (10 inches) wide, although they are rather sparsely clothed with flowers. The individual flowers are a bright, clear white, with a slightly cupped labellum that has a bilobed apex and a faint lime green central patch. The lateral staminodes are pure white, narrow, and arching. The true petals are linear and curl around the other flower parts upon opening. The modestly sized flowers have a long, exerted white filament and cream stamen. The overall flowering spike is impressively chunky.

Hedychium stenopetalum is established, though not yet widely available, in cultivation and has proven to be easily grown given large quantities of food and water. The plant must be sensitively sited in sheltered semi-shade where its substantial frame will not be damaged by wind. Plants have been sold in the United States under the name *H.* 'White Stars', however, this is not a cultivar name, but merely intended to convey a description of the flowers; such plants are referable to *H. stenopetalum*.

Hedychium tengchongense

Minimum temperature: -7°C (15°F) ?
Height: to 70 to 80 cm (28–31 inches)

Named by Yi Bo Luo in 1994, this small species is a native of forests in Tengchong county, western Yunnan province, close to the Chinese border with northern Myanmar, at elevations of 1600 to 1700 m (5200–5600 feet). It has broad leaves that reach 40 cm (16 inches) long by 10 cm (4 inches) wide, and in July produces 25-cm (10-inch) tall, densely packed flower spikes. The flowers are pure yellow and comparatively large for the overall size of the plant, each with a 4-cm (1½-inch) labellum that is divided to half its depth, and a pair of 4-cm (1½-inch) long, very narrow lateral staminodes. Emerging from these comes the 4.5-cm (1¾-inch) protruding orange filament, tipped with an orange anther.

Hedychium tengchongense is not yet in cultivation, and indeed little more is known about this species (it could well grow primarily as an epiphyte, for instance). The combination of large, strongly coloured flowers; short, stocky stature; early flowering season; and probable hardiness makes it another intriguing prospect for milder hardy gardens.

Hedychium thyrsiforme

Minimum temperature: -10°C (15°F)
Height: to 100 to 210 cm (39–83 inches)

Writing in 1828 William Roscoe stated: "Specimens of this rare species were received by the author from Dr. Wallich, at Calcutta, in 1819. By its compact spike, convoluted and reflexed bracts and elliptic leaves it is sufficiently distinguished from every other species".

The magnificent *Hedychium thyrsiforme* is, indeed, immediately distinguishable from all other species, combining luxuriant and very broad dark green foliage with a unique inflorescence. This generally unscented, though highly unusual, flower spike is wider than it is tall and comprises a large mass of small flowers, each with two short, linear, curling white lateral staminodes and a narrow, trumpet-shaped white labellum with a cream throat. The petals are much longer, but exceedingly narrow, and form contorted shapes as they twist downwards. The most distinctive feature of the flowers is their massively exerted creamy white stamens, seemingly out of proportion to the rest of the flower. It is the stamens that give the plant its entirely appropriate common name of pincushion ginger. Plants have also been marketed in the United States as *Hedychium* "Frilly White", but this is an intended description rather than a named variety. *Hedychium* 'Kahili White', meaning "white ginger", is, unfortunately also a U.S. nursery synonym for *H. thyrsiforme*.

Hedychium thyrsiforme is a native of the Indian Himalayan foothills at elevations of 600 to 1800 m (2000–5900 feet) from Kumaon to western Nepal, east through Nepal itself to Sikkim, Bhutan, and Assam. James Edward Smith named the plants, following the collection of material in 1802 from Narainhetty in Nepal, by a Dr. Buchanan. By 1822 plants were flowering in cultivation at the Liverpool Botanic Gardens, under William Roscoe. Following this, however the species appears to have become lost to cultivation in the West until its reintroduction in 1966, when Tony Schilling made collections from hills to the south of Kathmandu, where he found the plants to be "locally common in the mixed warm temperate forest at an altitude of 1800 m (5900 feet)".

Writing in 1982 Schilling regarded *Hedychium thyrsiforme* as "without a doubt a plant to be included under the tender heading", but luckily, that has proven not to be the case. Plants have successfully overwintered in Europe and the United States at surprisingly low temperatures. The matter of hardiness, however, has one proviso. *Hedychium thyrsiforme* flowers late in the season, rarely starting before late September, and often not until October-November or even December. In practice, therefore, the species will be a sporadic and reluctant flowerer when grown outside in gardens that experience cold snaps in early autumn. Despite this disadvantage, its superb foliage alone makes it worthy of trial in any possible site.

In its native climes the species is never entirely deciduous, although the old stems eventually wither in spring with the emergence of new growth. In temperate cultivation the plants will lose their foliage with the first frosts, although this doesn't prevent them from growing away successfully the following year. Experience with plants grown outdoors in the United Kingdom shows that the species is typically much shorter in stature even when blooming—to 120 cm (48 inches)—than is reported from the wild, or than is achieved when plants are grown under glass.

Hedychium thyrsiforme naturally arches very strongly and has no strong inclination to straight upward growth. This habit is probably an adaptation to growing on slopes. The plants can be staked upright if required or allowed to arch, in which case the flower spikes will automatically form in a fully vertical position and look highly pleasing against the glossy dark leaves. In outdoor cultivation in the southern United States *H. thyrsiforme* readily produces bright red seeds in (unusually) green pods, but the species is unlikely to produce seed when grown outdoors in the United Kingdom. This species is easily grown, well established in cultivation, and readily available from a number of nurseries. (Plate 38)

Hedychium villosum

Minimum temperature: -7°C (20°F) ?
Height: to 120 to 210 cm (48–83 inches)

Nathaniel Wallich named this species in 1820. It has a natural geographical territory that ranges from the Nepalese Himalaya in the west, through Bangladesh, Assam, Myanmar, Thailand, and Vietnam to the southeast, and on into the Guangdong, Guangxi, Hainan, and Yunnan provinces of China to the northeast. It can also be found at altitudes of 100 to 3400 m (330–10,800 feet).

Hedychium villosum is closely related to *H. forrestii*, *H. spicatum*, and *H. yunnanense*, and shares with those species a basic floral makeup. The plants produce strongly fragrant, medium-sized flowers. The narrow, white labellum is 2.5 cm (1 inch) wide, has a small salmon-coloured throat, and resembles a forked white tongue. The labellum is complemented by two delicately arching, narrow white lateral staminodes and an exerted, 4.5-cm (1³/4-inch) long, pale red to purplish filament.

Horticulturally *Hedychium villosum* differs most from its close relatives by having a larger flowering spike up to 25 cm (10 inches) tall with a showier and denser array of flowers than the other three species. In addition, the bracts and the calyces that bear the flowers are covered with silky (villous) hairs. *Hedychium villosum* has attractive, paddle-shaped leaves and readily forms good sized clumps of plants in cultivation, although the hardiness of the cultivated form(s) remains untested.

With such a diverse geographical range, particularly at the altitudes at which the species naturally grows, it is expected that divergent forms are likely to have evolved. One variety (or subspecies, depending on the botanist), var. *tenuiflorum*, has been recognized. It is also likely, if not certain, that forms from different localities will display very different habits and cold tolerances in cultivation. At present, however, although the species is established and available for gardeners, there have been very few different introductions of *Hedychium villosum*, and its full potential and diversity has yet to be explored. To put this in context, the highest natural limits of *H. villosum*, at 3400 m (10,800 feet), are some 200 m (650 feet) higher than those at which *H. spicatum* (the hardiest *Hedychium* species) occur.

In temperate cultivation *Hedychium villosum* generally flowers in August and September, but the flowering season in the wild is reportedly March and April (December for var. *tenuiflorum*). Plants will flower in April and May under glass, which would suggest a subtropical origin for the cultivated forms. After all, it seems highly unlikely that any *Hedychium* species will be found flowering in spring at 3400 m (10,800 feet) above sea level.

Hedychium villosum var. *tenuiflorum*
Minimum temperature: -5ºC (22ºF) ?
Height: to 90 to 120 cm (36–48 inches)

Nathaniel Wallich originally named this *Hedychium* in 1832; however, while it was referred to as *H. villosum* var. *tenuiflorum* for the following 60 years, Wallich failed to furnish a full and valid description of the plant and so it was left to Karl Schumann to officially publish the name in 1892. Shumann considered it to be, and published it as, a separate species named *H. tenuiflorum*. It remained thus until a new study was undertaken by the Indian botanists A. S. Rao and D. M. Verma in 1972, when they described the plant as *H. villosum* subsp. *tenuiflorum*, before it was reverted to varietal status in *Flora of China* (Wu and Larsen 2000).

Var. *tenuiflorum* is readily referable to the species, but is separated by having smaller flower bracts—1.5 cm (2/3 inch) long versus 1.8–2.5 cm (3/4–1 inch)—and a smaller labellum—1.5 cm (2/3 inch) versus 2.5 cm (1 inch). Indeed it is naturally smaller than var. *villosum* in all of its parts, with narrow, rather delicate pseudostems, and equally narrow, lance-shaped leaves.

Var. *tenuiflorum* was originally identified from plants located in India, but also occurs at 800 to 900 m (2600–3000 feet) alongside limestone streams and gorges in Yunnan. The plants naturally grow at least partly as epiphytes, and will, if freely watered, readily thrive in, or on, a rock or bark substrate. Material of var. *tenuiflorum* that was collected in 1998 from Yunnan by Tom Wood and is in cultivation in the United States is notable for having very striking stems that are stained deep purple-red. This colour extends to the flower spike, making a beautiful contrast with the strongly perfumed white flowers. In the wild this variety blooms in December, and in cultivation the plants will also not begin to flower until November or December. Thus, while var. *tenuiflorum* may well be moderately hardy—it has been tested to -5°C (22°F), but some forms may be hardier still—its use will always be restricted to those gardens that do not experience frosts until late December.

Hedychium ximengense

Minimum temperature: -10°C (15°F) ?
Height: 60–150 cm (24–60 inches)

Yi Yong Qian published the original description of this Chinese species in 1994. Native to forests of Zizhi county in southern Yunnan, *Hedychium ximengense* is a white-flowered species that, in July, produces a flowering spike of up to 30 cm (12 inches) tall, with groups of three to five flowers emerging from each bract on the spike. The flowers are white with a bilobed labellum that reaches approximately 3 cm (1 1/4 inches) long by 2 cm (3/4 inch) wide. The lateral staminodes are less than 2 cm (3/4 inch) long, and the filament is short and does not protrude in the dramatic manner of many species. Nevertheless, this species may hold considerable horticultural potential. Although not currently in cultivation, *H. ximengense* combines a short stature with presumed hardiness and a fairly good flowering display for the size of the plant. The future possibilities for short, hardier hedychiums, with good-sized flowering spikes (both new species and their hybrids) are indeed exciting. Currently, those shorter species that are in reasonably wide cultivation are generally too tender to thrive in frosty gardens.

Hedychium yungiiangense

Minimum temperature: -5°C (22°F) ?
Height: 60–80 cm (24–31 inches)

This dwarf and presumed epiphytic species is another of the newly described Chinese species. Shao Quan Tong named the plant in 1986, following examination of plants collected at 1200 m (3900 feet) from Yingjiang county in southwestern Yunnan. In September *Hedychium yungiiangense* bears small flowering spikes no more than 10 cm (4 inches) tall by 7 cm (2³/₄ inches) across. These are very densely packed with white flowers. The small labellum, 1 cm (¹/₂ inch) in diameter, is rounded and deeply notched. The lateral staminodes are from 1.5 cm to 4 cm (²/₃–1¹/₂ inches) long.

The late flowering season, coupled with the plant's natural distribution in China along the border with northern Myanmar, suggests that this species is not likely to be particularly hardy or to flower successfully in colder gardens. It has not yet been introduced to cultivation.

Hedychium yunnanense

Minimum temperature: -12°C (10°F)
Height: 50–80 cm (20–31 inches)

This species is a native of southern China, in Guangxi and Yunnan provinces, as well as south into neighbouring Vietnam. It produces a few fragrant flowers that have creamy yellow, linear petals curled around white lateral staminodes, a bifurcated, narrow white labellum, plus an elongated, pale flesh-red filament and anther. As they age the white flower parts flush with the same cream to pale yellow colouration of the petals and the corolla tubes that hold each flower.

François Gagnepain named *Hedychium yunnanense* in 1907, but cultivated stocks have long been confused or rather displaced by close relative *H. spicatum*. Most plants in cultivation under the name "H. yunnanense" are

153

in fact referable to *H. spicatum*. The true species is generally much shorter and stockier than its relative, with notably broader leaves—10 cm (4 inches) wide as opposed to typically 3 to 5 cm (1¼–2 inches) in *H. spicatum*. The two also flower at different times, at least in the forms that are in cultivation, with *H. yunnanense* being one of the earliest hedychiums to bloom. In cultivation, *H. yunnanense* blooms in June; in its natural habitat it reportedly blooms in September. Since cultivated plants are from the most northerly reaches of the species's native terrain, perhaps more southerly populations typically bloom later. More importantly the floral structure of the two species differs significantly. The most obvious difference is in the length of the filament that bears the anther. In *H. spicatum* the filament is not prominent and at 1 or 2 cm (½–¾ inch) is always shorter than the labellum, whereas in *H. yunnanense* the filament is greatly extended and reaches 4 cm (1½ inches) long. *Hedychium yunnanense* also has wider lateral staminodes than the almost filamentous ones that appear on *H. spicatum*. Overall, the flowers of *H. yunnanense* make for a more attractive and colourful display.

It seems likely that all of the true plants of *Hedychium yunnanense* in Western cultivation derive from one single introduction, namely, *Hedychium* L633. Roy Lancaster originally collected this form in 1980 from the Western Hills, some 15 km (9 miles) west of Kunming in northern Yunnan, believing it to be *H. forrestii* var. *latebracteatum*. His material was transferred successfully to Wakehurst Place, Sussex, where it was cultivated under glass, and where, upon flowering in 1984, it was correctly identified as *H. yunnanense* by Jill Cowley. *Hedychium* L633 thrived in cultivation and is now available from nurseries in the United Kingdom. It is an easily grown, readily accommodated, and very hardy early flowering species of *Hedychium*, not as flamboyant as some, but extremely attractive when in full bloom, with the flowers a combination of bright white, and soft yellow and red contrasting effectively against handsome foliage. It can be thoroughly recommended to temperate gardeners, although, in common with the other cooler region species, plants will probably not tolerate too much heat or direct sunlight. (Plate 39)

Hedychium Hybrids

Hedychium 'Anne Bishop'
Synonym: *Hedychium* 'Anne S. Bishop
Minimum temperature: -12°C (10°F)
Height: to 150 cm (60 inches)

Originally bred in Hawaii, this cultivar was introduced into mainland U.S. nurseries in 1996. Plants produce broad flower spikes densely packed with strongly fragrant, dark golden to apricot coloured flowers with darker orange throats and protruding orange filaments. This *Hedychium* is best grown in full or partial sun.

Hedychium 'Apricot'
Minimum temperature: -15°C (5°F)
Height: to 180 cm (71 inches)

This American hybrid of *Hedychium coccineum* has a few large flowers on an open spike. Emerging from golden buds, the flowers are pale apricot orange, with deeper orange throats and filaments on a slender, narrow-leaved plant. Strongly fragrant, the plant is reputed to also have a perfume reminiscent of apricots.

Hedychium 'Ayo'
Minimum temperature: -7°C (20°F) ?
Height: to 120 cm (48 inches)

This robust and vigorous hybrid of *Hedychium coccineum* var. *angustifolium* was bred by a Mr. Ayo of Louisiana. Plants have dense growth and relatively short, sturdy pseudostems that, in September, bear large flowers of a soft pinky peach. Each flower bears a large, rounded labellum, a deep red-orange throat, elongated coral pink filaments, and a strong fragrance. The flowers can bleach out to near white as they age, particularly if grown in full sun (although the throat colour is retained), and for that reason are best accommodated in semi-shade. This cultivar is available in United Kingdom and the United States. It may well be hardier than so far indicated.

Hedychium **'Beni-Oran'**
Minimum temperature: -10°C (15°F)
Height: to 180 cm (71 inches)

This Japanese hybrid (presumably of *Hedychium gardnerianum*) was bred by a Mr. Koyama and originally introduced into U.S. cultivation by various growers in the 1960s. Plants have notably impressive foliage with heavily textured and very broad, deep green leaves and sturdy, arching pseudostems. Blooming in August and September, the substantial flowering spikes are 30 cm (12 inches) tall. The flowers are a rosy apricot orange with deeper orange throats and prominent red filaments.

Hedychium **'Betty Ho'**
Minimum temperature: -7°C (20°F) ?
Height: to 210 cm (83 inches)

This hybrid was bred and introduced by the Lyons Arboretum in Oahu, Hawaii. It is a large plant with dramatic flower spikes, 30 cm (12 inches) tall and wide, bearing powerfully fragrant primrose yellow flowers. The lateral staminodes are very broad, and the cleft labellum is large and circular, with a prominent burnt orange throat patch complemented by similarly coloured filaments.

Hedychium **'Brandy Saito'**
Minimum temperature: -10°C (15°F) ?
Height: to 270 cm (106 inches)

Available in the United States, 'Brandy Saito' is a hybrid (or possibly a form) of *Hedychium flavescens*. Plants are substantial, with very long foliage, but with relatively modest-sized, pinecone-shaped flower spikes and flowers of cream, with a large golden flare in the throat of the labellum. This form is slow to increase at the rhizome.

Hedychium **'Carnival'**
Minimum temperature: -10°C (15°F)
Height: to 120 cm (48 inches)

Bred by Tom Wood, this short, sturdy hybrid has thick, upright pseudostems and, in August and early September, very large flower spikes at 35 cm (14 inches) tall. The inflorescences produce a succession of flowers for five weeks. Each flower has a large, forked, arching labellum and a pair of erect lateral staminodes, all of which are coloured a pale peach, with a tiny flash of orange at the apex of the flower.

Hedychium 'Clown Suit'

This interesting hybrid developed by Tom Wood is notable for its unusual, twisting flower segments. The narrow lateral staminodes turn through 180 degrees along their length, and the labellum is bifurcated to its centre with the two halves curling down upon themselves to form open tube shapes. The strongly fragrant flowers are primarily white, with orange-red staining at their centres, and with scarlet filaments. 'Clown Suit' flowers very early in the season, with the first spikes appearing in early June, and can also repeat flower in autumn where conditions allow.

Hedychium 'Coronata Cream'
Height: to 180 cm (71 inches)

This magnificent new American hybrid has large flower spikes that bear huge flowers. The labellum is almost circular and is notched at the tip. The lateral staminodes are, unusually for an *Hedychium*, very broad. In bloom continuously from June to September, the flowers have a base colour of pale peach, fading to white. A very large salmon-coloured blotch extends out from the throat and the filament is flesh red.

Hedychium 'C. P. Raffill'
Synonyms: *Hedychium* 'Raffilii', *H.* 'Raffilli'
Minimum temperature: -10ºC (15ºF)
Height: to 180 cm (71 inches)

One of the few older hybrids to have survived into modern cultivation, this cross between *Hedychium gardnerianum* and *H. coccineum* occurred at the Royal Botanic Gardens, Kew, and was named in honour of Charles Raffill, assistant curator of the gardens and also a noted breeder of magnolias there. Plants have waxy, stiff, blue foliage inherited from the *H. coccineum* parent. In August and September this hybrid produces very large flower spikes, heavily laden with dozens of individual flowers that have a rounded labellum and narrow flaring lateral staminodes. These are dark apricot in colour, with a large deep orange blotch extending out from the throat to colour much of the labellum. The greatly extended stamen filaments, inherited from the *H. gardnerianum* parent, are flame red. The name is often misspelled.

Hedychium 'Daniel Weeks'
Minimum temperature: -15°C (5°F)
Height: to 180 cm (71 inches)

This hybrid of *Hedychium flavescens* and *H. gardnerianum* was introduced to cultivation in 1992 by Gainesville Tree Farm of Florida. A popular variety, it is notable for several features. Under cultivation in the United States it has proven hardier than either parent and consolidates this by being among the earliest *Hedychium* to bloom. The flower spikes first emerge from mid-June and often continue until late August or even September. In appearance the flowers combine the strengths of the two parents, with spikes that are almost as large as those of *H. gardnerianum*, but which bear flowers that are close to *H. flavescens*. The flowers have a rounded, pale yellow labellum that has a prominent golden throat blotch, lateral staminodes of pale yellow, and a golden filament. The flowers are very powerfully fragrant, particularly in the evening, and the plants are vigorous and easily grown.

Hedychium 'Dave Case'
Minimum temperature: -15°C (5°F)
Height: to 210 cm (83 inches)

This robust hybrid from Tom Wood has broad, 25-cm (10-inch) tall flower spikes, heavily laden with pale orange flowers, each with a deeper orange throat. It is said to flower from August in the southern United States, but is much later to bloom in the United Kingdom, generally not until October, by which time plants will typically abort their flower spikes unless the season is unusually mild. The inflorescence is strongly scented. Plants require partial sun to flower well.

Hedychium 'Double Eagle'
Minimum temperature: -15°C (5°F)
Height: to 180 cm (71 inches)

This popular hybrid from Tom Wood has open, lax 15-cm (6-inch) tall flower spikes that produce large flowers of a pale peachy orange colour. Each flower has a broad labellum with a contrasting, darker peachy gold throat. 'Double Eagle' flowers in August and September and has a strong and rather unusual, spicy fragrance. It is available in Europe and the United States.

Hedychium 'Dr. Moy'

Synonyms: *Hedychium* 'Brush Strokes', *H.* 'Shooting Star', *H.* 'Robusta Variegated'
Minimum temperature: -15ºC (5ºF)
Height: to 120 cm (48 inches)

Bred by Ying Doon Moy of the San Antonio Botanical Garden, this highly regarded hybrid of *Hedychium flavum* and *H. coccineum* is semi-dwarf in habit, certainly much shorter than either parent, with stout pseudostems that remain erect and that can flower at 90 cm (36 cm). The short habit is due to the crowding of the foliage, with a very short interspace between each leaf. *Hedychium* 'Dr. Moy' blooms heavily, producing impressive flower spikes throughout August and September. The tangerine-coloured buds open to reveal peachy pale orange flowers, each with a deep orange throat and filament, plus dark golden petals. This hybrid is most notable, however, for its foliage, which is variegated with irregular cream-coloured slashes and smaller stripes. The variegation is generally not heavy, although plants may occasionally produce leaves with one large cream variegation covering nearly half the leaf surface.

This hybrid was the only seedling with variegation to result from this cross, and it is still the only variegated cultivar available. Add to this the plant's ease of cultivation, stout habit, and large fragrant flowers, and *Hedychium* 'Dr. Moy' ranks among the finest and most distinctive hybrids yet produced. (Plates 40 and 41)

Hedychium 'Edison Home'

This hybrid of *Hedychium coccineum* was originally found growing on the Thomas Edison estate in Fort Myers, Florida. Flowering in July and August, plants produce large spikes bearing a dense mass of large, peachy pink flowers with darker, salmon to red throats and petals.

Hedychium 'Elizabeth'

Minimum temperature: -15ºC (5ºF)
Height: to 270 cm (106 inches)

Bred in the mid 1980s by Tom Wood, this hybrid is the most popular and widely available one at present. Large numbers of plants are produced each year in the United States by micropropagation. 'Elizabeth' is a highly distinctive ginger that has flowers of a unique, bright raspberry pink with a

159

reddish patch on the large rounded labellum. The flowers are very different from the numerous peachy pink *Hedychium* hybrids that have been introduced. Produced throughout August and September, flowering spikes are well furnished with the strongly fragrant flowers. 'Elizabeth' was originally listed as growing to no more than 150 cm (60 inches) tall, but many specimens planted in open ground have considerably exceeded this height.

Hedychium 'Filigree'
Synonym: *Hedychium* 'Filagree'
Minimum temperature: -15°C (5°F)
Height: to 180 cm (71 inches)

This hybrid from Tom Wood was introduced as a dwarf plant with pseudostems to no more than 90 cm (36 inches); however, many plants in cultivation have considerably exceeded this height. Flowering continually from August to October, where conditions allow, plants have lax, open spikes with dark golden buds that open to reveal medium or small flowers of pale cream with a prominent dark golden flare in the throat. The slender stems invariably form an arching habit with narrow, lance-shaped leaves. 'Filigree' is available in Europe and the United States.

Hedychium 'Fireflies'

'Fireflies' is a distinctive hybrid from Tom Wood. The small white flowers have narrow, linear lateral staminodes splaying out at 90 degrees from the labellum which is arching with the two sides folded towards one another. Flowers also have greatly extended red filaments and orange petals. This hybrid is not currently available in the trade.

Hedychium 'Fireworks'
Minimum temperature: -10°C (15°F)
Height: to 150 cm (60 inches)

This short and strongly upright hybrid from Tom Wood has stiff, waxy leaves that are infused with red on their undersides. The flower spikes are 15 cm (6 inches) tall and appear from June to October, bearing flowers in which the labellum and lateral staminodes have been reduced to narrow orange-red filaments. 'Fireworks' grows best in full sun.

Hedychium 'Full Moon'
Height: to 120 cm (48 inches)

'Full Moon' is one of the shorter hybrids that Tom Wood has been developing to encourage a more diverse use of *Hedychium* in the garden. It is a stout and vigorous cultivar with bright lemon yellow flowers. The strongly fragrant flowers are said to emit one perfume at night and another in daylight.

Hedychium 'Gahili'
Minimum temperature: -10°C (15°F)
Height: to 150 cm (60 inches)

'Gahili' produces flowers of a strong peach pink colour in August and September from 20-cm (8-inch) tall spikes. The labellum is large, rounded, and very prominent with a salmon red blotch in the throat. The extended scarlet filaments display well against the paler background colour. This hybrid is best grown in full or part sun.

Hedychium 'Giant Yellow'
Minimum temperature: -10°C (15°F)
Height: to 280 cm (112 inches)

'Giant Yellow' is offered in the United States and is possibly no more than a large-flowered form of *Hedychium maximum*. The very robust pseudostems produce 30-cm (12-inch) tall flower spikes late in the season, generally starting in October. Individual flowers are very large—10 cm (4 inches) across—with a broad labellum and wide lateral staminodes. The fragrant flowers are creamy yellow with a darker gold patch on the labellum. (Plate 42)

Hedychium 'Golden'
Minimum temperature: -7°C (20°F)
Height: to 150 cm (60 inches)

Originating from Mercer Arboretum and Botanical Garden in Humble, Texas, this cultivar somewhat resembles its presumed parent, *Hedychium gardnerianum*, with large spikes appearing in August and September. The inflorescences have many small flowers with wide lateral staminodes and a comparatively small, cup-shaped labellum. The filament is flame red. Unlike *H. gardnerianum*, all the other flower parts of the hybrid are a bright, clear orange.

Hedychium 'Golden Butterflies'
Minimum temperature: -15°C (5°F)
Height: to 210 cm (83 inches)

Bred by John Banta, this hybrid of *Hedychium gardnerianum* and *H. flavescens* flowers in August and September. The 15-cm (6-inch) tall spikes bear fragrant, medium-sized flowers of pale copper orange. Each flower has a narrow labellum with a small darker red throat, and a brick red filament. 'Golden Butterflies' is also notable for having lush, broad and glossy foliage.

Hedychium 'Golden Glow'
Minimum temperature: -10°C (15°F)
Height: to 120 cm (48 inches)

This hybrid from Tom Wood has short, sturdy, upright pseudostems that start to bloom freely early in the season. The 20-cm (8-inch) tall spikes appear in succession from July to October and bear a dense arrangement of medium-sized flowers that open together to form a good display. The flowers are gold in colour with red filaments.

Hedychium 'Gold Flame'
Minimum temperature: -15°C (5°F)
Height: to 240 cm (96 inches)

One of the most widely distributed hybrids from Tom Wood, this easily grown and very vigorous *Hedychium* has a lax inflorescence with strongly perfumed and large, well-displayed flowers. The lateral staminodes are white and fairly broad, and the labellum is heart-shaped and white with a prominent golden orange patch. The petals and filaments are of a paler orange. The narrow stems invariably tend to arch over as they grow taller and heavier. Plants will flower in succession from July to October and are widely available in Europe and the United States. (Plate 43)

Hedychium 'Gold Spot'
Minimum temperature: -10°C (15°F)
Height: to 180 cm (71 inches)

The origin of this hybrid of *Hedychium coronarium* is unknown. The plant was introduced to cultivation by the Indian nursery of Ganesh Mani Pradhan and Son. Plants are similar in habit and appearance to *H. coronarium*, with large, fragrant white flowers produced in August and September, but differ in the labellum, which has a large golden orange patch. The filament is also orange, and the flowers have paler, creamy apricot petals. 'Gold Spot' is now available in the United Kingdom.

Hedychium 'Hardy Exotics 1'
Minimum temperature: -10°C (15°F)
Height: to 100 cm (39 inches)

This hybrid resulted from a chance seedling of *Hedychium gardnerianum* found at the Hardy Exotics nursery in Cornwall, England. From August, plants produce large flower spikes that have a very intense fragrance. The flowers are individually large and cream in colour with darker yellow throats and extended filaments.

Hedychium 'Kahili Ann'
Minimum temperature: -7°C (20°F)
Height: to 210 cm (83 inches)

Like *Hedychium* 'Betty Ho', this hybrid was developed and introduced by the Lyons Arboretum of Hawaii. In August and September plants produce large, lax flower spikes that bear wide flowers of a pale apricot orange with a deeper orange throat. 'Kahili Ann' is available in the United States and was introduced into Europe.

Hedychium 'Kai Yang'
Minimum temperature: -10°C (15°F)
Height: to 180 cm (71 inches)

Distributed by the now-defunct Southern Perennials & Herbs nursery of Tylerton, Mississippi, this hybrid produces cream-coloured flowers, with a coconut fragrance, in August and September. The plant is reportedly reluctant to flower until it is well established.

Hedychium 'Kanes Pink'
Minimum temperature: -10°C (15°F)
Height: to 180 cm (71 inches)

Named for a Mrs. Kane of Houston (or possibly San Antonio), this cultivar is very similar, and possibly synonymous with *Hedychium* 'Pink V'. The pseudostems carry stiffly upright, narrow leaves. In July and August, 20-cm (8-inch) tall flower spikes are densely clothed with medium-sized, faintly scented flowers of pale rose pink, with a salmon red flare in the throat, and with elongated, flesh red filaments.

Hedychium 'Kewense'
Minimum temperature: -15°C (5°F)
Height: to 210 cm (83 inches)

The name "Kewense" has, somehow, become applied to two separate plants. The original *Hedychium* ×*kewense* was supposedly a hybrid between *H. coccineum* and *H. gardnerianum* and was believed to have been selected by Charles Raffill. After examining the plants, Tony Schilling concluded that *H.* ×*kewense* is likely to be no more than a form of the widely variable species *H. coccineum*. While still cultivated, the original plant is not widely circulated.

The plant in common circulation under the name *Hedychium* 'Kewense' is quite different, with 30-cm (12-inch) tall spikes of large, well-displayed flowers of a soft raspberry pink—a similar though much lighter pigment than that of *H.* 'Elizabeth'. While only very mildly fragrant, on large plants the showy flowers are produced continuously from July to September. Whatever its origins, *H.* 'Kewense' is a distinctive, very hardy, and valuable ginger, vigorous and easily grown, with attractive, ladder-like narrow foliage held at 90 degrees from the pseudostems.

Hedychium 'Kinkaku'
Minimum temperature: -15°C (5°F)
Height: to 210 cm (83 inches)

Developed by the Japanese breeder Mr. Koyama and introduced into the United States by Gardner Waters in the 1960s, this robust and very hardy hybrid is now widely available and justifiably popular in Europe and the United States. Blooming from late July to September, plants produce 20-cm (8-inch) tall spikes with very fragrant flowers of a pale peach colour. The labellum is large and very showy with a small orange throat patch. Plants have attractive, upright stiff leaves. 'Kinkaku' is a vigorous grower and flowers reliably once well established.

Hedychium 'Lava Dome'
Height: to 90 cm (36 inches)

This Tom Wood hybrid is not yet in nursery circulation but is a highly promising plant for the future. It has a short, upright growth habit. The densely packed inflorescence bears flowers that age from yellow to orange.

Hedychium 'Lemon Beauty'
Minimum temperature: -15ºC (5ºF)
Height: to 180 cm (71 inches)

Flowering from August to October, this cultivar requires a sunny position where it will produce many good-sized flower spikes. The fragrant flowers are pale yellow with a golden orange labellum patch and reddish pink filaments.

Hedychium 'Lemon Sherbet'
Minimum temperature: -10ºC (15ºF)
Height: to 240 cm (96 inches)

This hybrid from Tom Wood is notable for flowering from early June. Plants have thick, robust pseudostems with 30-cm (12-inch) tall flower spikes bearing many strongly fragrant, densely packed, large flowers. These are apricot yellow to pale gold and have a broad, rounded, and "ruffled" labellum with contrasting coral pink stamens. This vigorous and impressive *Hedychium* is available in the United States and the United Kingdom. (Plate 44)

Hedychium 'Luna Moth'
Minimum temperature: -10ºC (15ºF)
Height: to 150 cm (60 inches)

This popular ginger has proven very easy to grow in the United Kingdom but appears to be less successful in warmer locations in the southern United States. From Tom Wood, this hybrid of the epiphytic *Hedychium hasseltii* (presumably with *H. cononarium* or hybrid thereof as the other parent) produces many densely packed stems clothed with notably broad, glossy leaves. The flowers are produced in small numbers in succession from July to October or beyond. They are large—12 cm (5 inches) across—and almost pure white with the merest hint of yellow at the axis of the labellum and with a pale coral filament. The labellum and lateral staminodes curl slightly. The very strongly fragrant flowers are held poised on long, arching corolla tubes.

It was originally suggested that, due to its epiphytic parentage, 'Luna Moth' should be maintained in pot-bound conditions with copious water and limited nutrition. The plants have, however, proven to be far more adaptable than that and will thrive, and indeed grow much larger, in the ground in any reasonable *Hedychium* soil. In the United Kingdom the plants will tolerate and probably flower better in sun, but, like any *Hedychium*, they should not be allowed to overheat or to dry out. 'Luna Moth' has a strongly upright habit and is vigorous, although its tight growth habit means that it never spreads far by rhizome. (Plate 45)

Hedychium 'Maiko'
Minimum temperature: -10ºC (15ºF)
Height: to 180 cm (71 inches)

This Japanese hybrid produces sturdy pseudostems with narrow, upright leaves that are slightly purple flushed beneath. From early July to September spikes of very fragrant flowers appear. Each flower has a large, undivided labellum and broad lateral staminodes, all of which are white, with a lime green patch on the labellum. The filaments are creamy white and somewhat extended.

Hedychium 'Molton Gold'
Height: to 45 cm (18 inches)

This new hybrid from Tom Wood is exceedingly dwarf and has been bred for patio or container culture. The flowers are deep gold and said to be long lasting. 'Molton Gold' is not yet in nursery cultivation.

Hedychium 'Moy Giant'
Synonym: *Hedychium* 'Giant'
Minimum temperature: -15ºC (5ºF)
Height: to 210 cm (83 inches)

Like *Hedychium* 'Dr. Moy', this hybrid was introduced and named after Ying Doon Moy, of the San Antonio Botanical Garden. 'Moy Giant' is a cross between *H. coccineum* and *H. coronarium*. Plants are notable for their good foliage, with leaves 43 cm (17 inches) long by 14 cm (5½ inches) wide, and for their large flower spikes that emerge from July to September. The flowers are strongly fragrant and similar in shape to those of the *H. coronarium* parent, with a large, notched labellum and lateral staminodes that flare out at 90 degrees. Both are cream to pale yellow with a large pale golden orange patch at the base of the labellum. The petals and filament are gold coloured. This hybrid is vigorous and easily grown.

Hedychium 'Multiflora White'
Minimum temperature: -15°C (5°F)
Height: to 150 cm (60 inches)

This interesting American hybrid of *Hedychium coronarium*, possibly with *H. thyrsiforme*, has short stems with large, strongly arching strap-shaped leaves. The plants are vigorous, rapidly increasing at the rhizome. Produced from August to the first frosts, the fragrant flowers are small and clear white, with a labellum that is folded over to produce an open funnel shape, tubular towards the axis. The formation of the labellum makes the wing-like, narrow lateral staminodes appear to be held discretely away from the rest of the flower, with the filamentous petals curling below, and a very greatly extended white stamen filament. Overall the flowers are unlike those of any other *Hedychium*.

Hedychium 'Mutant'
Minimum temperature: -15°C (5°F)
Height: to 120 cm (48 inches)

This unusual, semi-dwarf hybrid from Tom Wood produces a mass of exceeding congested, short pseudostems that are held stiffly upright. The flowers are pale cream, with a very narrow and somewhat contorted labellum that has a golden marked throat, looking more like an iris than an *Hedychium*. The flowers are powerfully fragrant, although the plants are rather shy to bloom, and spikes are rarely formed before September. Despite this late flowering, 'Mutant' has been demonstrated to be very hardy and is now available in the United States and the United Kingdom.

Hedychium 'Neon'
Height: to 90 cm (36 inches)

This new hybrid from Tom Wood combines large, ribbed leaves with a dwarf habit. Bright salmon orange flowers are held on elongated corolla tubes. A narrow labellum and lateral staminodes cascade downwards, with the flesh red filament held upright, away from the rest of the flower. Although very distinctive, this plant is of unknown hardiness. Tom Wood intends to acquire a plant patent and have 'Neon' reproduced by micro-propagation.

Hedychium 'Orange Crush'
Minimum temperature: -10°C (15°F)
Height: to 180 cm (71 inches)

This exceedingly fine hybrid is capable of blooming from late June to October, producing a succession of large flower spikes held above narrow and strongly upright foliage. The flowers are very large and rounded, with broad, paddle-shaped lateral staminodes and a circular labellum that is just notched at the tip. These flowers are fragrant, and of the palest apricot orange, deepening to a prominent dark orange patch on the labellum with a modest-sized pinkish red filament.

Hedychium 'Orchidesque'
Minimum temperature: -10°C (15°F)
Height: to 180 cm (71 inches)

Tom Wood describes this hybrid as being like a large *Hedychium* 'Luna Moth'. Plants have broad, heavily ribbed almost banana-like leaves and large maroon red spikes that bear unusual flowers each with a long, but rather narrow labellum that is strongly bilobed, each lobe ending in a sharply pointed tip. The lateral staminodes are arching and held aloft, and resemble bird wings. The flowers are essentially white, but all parts are stained gold at the flower apex. The reverse of the labellum is also flushed gold, and the stamens are of a similar deep gold.

Hedychium 'Oto Himi'
Height: to 180 cm (71 inches)

This Japanese hybrid is now available in the United States. The sturdy, thick pseudostems carry long, narrow leaves. In August and September large spikes are formed that bear very large flowers of palest pink opening from coral buds. The labellum is rounded and broad with a darker red patch, and the filament is orange-red.

Hedychium 'Palani'
Minimum temperature: -10°C (15°F)
Height: to 180 cm (71 inches)

This newly introduced hybrid was bred in Hawaii and is now being distributed throughout the United States. Produced in August and September, the spikes are densely clothed with fragrant, medium-sized flowers of deep, terracotta orange with an unusual purple-bronze throat marking and extended red filaments. The broad, glossy foliage is also flushed with red when newly unfurled.

Hedychium 'Peach Delight'
Minimum temperature: -15°C (5°F)
Height: to 260 cm (102 inches)

This hybrid was introduced by Plant Delights Nursery, of Raleigh, North Carolina. It is a big, robust ginger with long, stiffly upright leaves and a large inflorescence—both tall and broad—with the well-presented flowers held on long corolla tubes. The strongly fragrant flowers are produced from August to October, and the colour is the palest pinky peach with a salmon red flare at the centre of the labellum, pale gold petals, and a dark salmon red filament. The lateral staminodes are particularly broad, and the floral display looks very "full". (Plate 46)

Hedychium 'Pink Flame'
Minimum temperature: -15°C (5°F)
Height: to 150 cm (60 inches)

One of the best-known and most widely distributed hybrids from Tom Wood, this medium-sized ginger has a short spike 15 cm (6 inches) tall. The spike is broader than tall once the flowers have opened. Opening from pale golden buds the intensely fragrant flowers are white or very pale blush pink, with a dark, reddish labellum patch and a similarly coloured filament. The labellum is circular, notched at the tip, and held away from the medium-broad lateral staminodes. The blooming season runs from July to October. Plants prefer a position in semi-shade where they are easily grown and undemanding, if rather slow to increase.

Hedychium 'Pink Hybrid'
Minimum temperature: -15°C (5°F)
Height: to 180 cm (71 inches)

This ginger is possibly a pink form of *Hedychium coronarium* or certainly a hybrid of that species. Plants have 15- to 20-cm (6- to 8-inch) tall, upright spikes of large, pale rose coloured flowers with narrow arching lateral staminodes and a wide labellum. The flowers emerge from orange buds and have a faint citric fragrance. This hardy and robust variety is now widely available in the United Kingdom. (Plate 47)

Hedychium 'Pink Sparks'
Minimum temperature: -15°C (5°F)
Height: to 180 cm (71 inches)

This very fine, medium-sized hybrid of *Hedychium thyrsiforme* comes from Tom Wood. The foliage opens with a red-bronze flush. The flower spikes emerge from August to October and bear a dense array of mildly fragrant, medium or small shrimp pink flowers with dark rose pink throats and hugely exerted stamen filaments. The overall effect is essentially like a pink *H. thyrsifome*, although the individual flowers are larger, and the plants are taller.

Hedychium 'Pink V'
Minimum temperature: -15°C (5°F)
Height: to 150 cm (60 inches)

Bred by Tom Wood in the early 1980s, this hybrid is notable for a very long flowering season, starting in June and continuing until frost in autumn or winter. The medium-sized flowers are pleasantly, though not strongly, fragrant and are produced in large numbers on 20- to 25-cm (8- to 10-inch) spikes. Opening from gold buds the base colour of the flowers is a pale peachy pink, though this colour is darker than that of many similar hybrids and, even when grown in sun, does not bleach out to white. The labellum, which is broad with a large salmon to red throat, often has two lobes folded somewhat towards one another, in a winged formation. The filament is extended and is also red.

Hedychium 'Pradhanii'

Synonym: *Hedychium* 'Pradhamii'
Minimum temperature: -10ºC (15ºF)
Height: to 270 cm (106 inches)

This large, robust plant was originally bred at the Chandra Nursery in Sikkim, from where material was imported to the United States in the early 1950s. It produces very thick stems and handsome large leaves. Flowering from August to October, plants bear 25-cm (10-inch) tall spikes of large, fragrant creamy champagne-coloured flowers with a peachy yellow labellum patch and an elongated, coral-pink filament. Despite the plants' large stature, the robust pseudostems remain strongly upright and do not arch over. This hybrid is widely available in Europe and the United States. (Plate 48)

Hedychium 'Rayna'

Height: to 120 cm (48 inches)

This unusual American hybrid has short, slightly arching pseudostems clothed with attractive, glossy narrow leaves. Flowering from August to October plants produce relatively short but very broad spikes with very well displayed clusters of large white flowers. The labellum is heart shaped and entire, or sometimes notched at the tip, and the lateral staminodes are exceptionally broad and very showy; all three have a small, dark peach blotch at the throat. The peach-coloured filaments are exceptionally long and end in orange anthers.

Hedychium 'Salmon'

Minimum temperature: -10ºC (15ºF)
Height: to 210 cm (83 inches)

This uncommon hybrid of *Hedychium coccineum* (presumably with *H. gardnerianum* or one of its hybrids) has tall, strongly upright stems that produce large, densely clothed spikes of medium-sized, fragrant flowers in June and July. The flowers are coloured a bright salmon orange and have a labellum that is cupped, or partially folded, very much in the manner of *H. gardnerianum*, and a dark orange throat. The reddish orange filaments are much extended from the flowers. Where climate allows, the plants will repeat bloom in autumn.

Hedychium 'Samsheri'
Minimum temperature: -7°C (20°F)
Height: to 210 cm (83 inches)

This hybrid was developed by the Chandra Nursery in Sikkim and was introduced into the United States in the 1950s by the U.S. Department of Agriculture. It has been confused with *H.* 'Kinkaku' but is a separate and legitimately named plant. Flowering begins in August and continues to October with tall spikes producing many large flowers of palest pink with darker pink throats. (Plate 49)

Hedychium 'Sherry Baby'
Minimum temperature: -10°C (15°F)
Height: to 180 cm (71 inches)

This hybrid was introduced by Larry Shatzer of Our Kids Tropicals nursery in Orlando, Florida, using *Hedychium* 'Gardner Waters' as a parent. It is a robust plant with upright pseudostems well clothed with numerous long, narrow leaves. While not fragrant, the floral display is extremely impressive, with profuse spikes emerging from June to September. The inflorescence is often as wide as it is tall, with many large pale apricot flowers emerging from golden buds. The labellum is heart shaped and can be entire or notched at the tip, with a small, deep orange flare in the throat. The filaments are orange, although not greatly extended. This vigorous hybrid is easily grown in light sun.

Hedychium 'Shurei'

This Japanese hybrid was introduced to culture in the United States. The medium-sized spikes produce large coral-pink flowers with an orange labellum flare.

Hedychium 'Stepladder'
Minimum temperature: -7°C (20°F)
Height: to 90 cm (36 inches)

This introduction from Tom Wood has very short, rigidly upright pseudostems with unusually small internodes (the spaces on the stem between the leaves). The result is a dense arrangement of the broad leaves that in turn gives the plant its name. The flower spikes are 20 cm (8 inches) tall and bear many medium-sized gold flowers with extended orange filaments.

Hedychium 'Tac Moto'
Minimum temperature: -10ºC (15ºF)
Height: to 180 cm (71 inches)

This Hawaiian hybrid was bred by a Mr. Moto and was introduced into mainland U.S. cultivation in 1995. The large flowers are powerfully fragrant and a bright canary yellow with a darker golden labellum patch. The lateral staminodes are paddle shaped and the rounded labellum has a notched tip. The stamens are moderately extended and golden yellow.

Hedychium 'Tai Alpha'
Synonym: *Hedychium* 'Dees Alpha'
Height: to 180 cm (71 inches)

The Tai hybrids (formerly known as the Dees hybrids) are a newly introduced group of hedychiums developed by a retired scientist, formerly of the University of Georgia, and selected for their floral impact. Currently being distributed in the United States by James Scoggins of Clermont, Florida, the group has not been tested for hardiness nor has it been tried in Europe. It includes several unusual and distinctive plants.
Flowering from July to September, 'Tai Alpha' bears 20- to 30-cm (8- to 12-inch) tall spikes that hold up to 60 large cream flowers. The labellum is rounded and has a golden flare, and the filaments are pale red.

Hedychium 'Tai Conch Pink'
Height: to 180 cm (71 inches)

This robust grower has stiff, upright foliage and a short inflorescence only 15–20 cm (6–8 inches) tall. The inflorescence is broad, more or less globe shaped, and bears 50–70 near-white to blush-pink flowers with a broad labellum and narrow lateral staminodes. The labellum has a deep rose-pink flare, and the greatly extended filaments are also rose pink.

Hedychium 'Tai Emperor'
Height: to 180 cm (71 inches)

This hybrid reaches 30 cm (12 inches) tall and produces narrow and stiffly upright spikes in September and October. The spikes bear up to 60 medium-sized flowers 5 cm (2 inches) across and of a good, strong pink. The labellum is strongly bilobed and has a large, dark pink throat blotch. The filaments are extremely prominent and are also deep pink.

Hedychium 'Tai Empress'
Height: to 180 cm (71 inches)

This extremely distinctive hybrid has robust stems clothed with stiffly upright glaucous, blue-green leaves. The flowering spike is short at 12 to 18 cm (5–7 inches) tall but up to 20 cm (8 inches) wide, and produces between 40 and 50 large flowers. The labellum is large, but narrow waisted, and is slightly cupped, and the lateral staminodes are also narrow waisted towards the axis of the flower. The base colour for the flower is pale pink, deepening to a large throat patch that is a strong red with salmon orange overtones. Both the labellum and the lateral staminodes are also stained deep red to pink at the flower axis. The petals are tangerine orange, the filaments dark pink, and the unopened buds are golden orange, making for a multi-coloured inflorescence. (Plate 50)

Hedychium 'Tai Golden Goddess'
Height: to 180 cm (71 inches)

This robust hybrid has narrow, upright foliage and large spikes that are 35 cm (14 inches) tall. The lax and airy spikes bear up to 70 medium-sized flowers 5 cm (2 inches) across and coloured deep gold. The labellum is marked with a maroon red blotch, and the filaments, also maroon red in colour, are extended.

Hedychium 'Tai Mammoth'
Height: to 180 cm (71 inches)

Derived from *Hedychium coronarium*, this early flowering ginger produces spikes in succession from June to October. The inflorescence is very large, 30–40 cm (12–16 inches) tall by 20 cm (8 inches) or more wide, and can bear up to 125 large bright white flowers. The cream-coloured filament is extended and held upright, and the labellum is narrowed at the axis, separating it from the broad, arching lateral staminodes.

Hedychium 'Tai Monarch'
Synonym: *Hedychium* 'Dees Monarch'
Height: to 150 cm (60 inches)

This hybrid of *Hedychium gardnerianum* has short, upright pseudostems that produce large flower spikes from September onwards. The spikes are

25–35 cm (10–14 inches) tall and extremely densely packed with medium-sized, pale yellow flowers. Each flower has a narrow-waisted labellum with a darker yellow throat, arching lateral staminodes, and extended, upright-pointing stamens with pale apricot filaments. The overall floral effect is strongly reminiscent of *H. gardnerianum*, but with larger and much paler flowers.

Hedychium 'Tai Pink Princess'
Height: to 180 cm (71 inches)

This hybrid has a wide and very open inflorescence that is 20–25 cm (8–10 inches) tall. It bears 60–70 medium-sized flowers on long, flaring bracts. The flowers are shell pink, with a dark red flare at the axis of the heart-shaped labellum, and with extended pink stamens.

Hedychium 'Tai Pink Profusion'
Height: to 150 cm (60 inches)

This short, robust, and highly unusual hybrid presumably involves *Hedychium densiflorum* and *H. coccineum*, or hybrids thereof. The short flower spikes are 15 cm (6 inches) tall and are well clothed with medium or small flowers. These are bright pink with a narrow labellum that has a darker reddish flare and an extended, upwards-arching filament that is also deep pink.

Hedychium 'Tai Savannah'
Synonym: *Hedychium* 'Dees Savannah'
Height: to 180 cm (71 inches)

This dramatic hybrid shows strong evidence of *Hedychium gardnerianum* in its makeup. Plants have glossy broad leaves and produce flowers from July to October. The narrow but very tall spikes, to 37 cm (15 inches) in height, bear up to 130 medium-sized, cream-coloured flowers with widely flaring lateral stamens and extended, pale orange filaments.

Hedychium 'Tai Sunlight'
Height: to 150 cm (60 inches)

This hybrid blooms from July to autumn. The open spikes are 20–30 cm (8–12 inches) tall, each bearing 50–75 flowers. The individual flowers are medium sized and pale yellow with a large golden flare on the labellum and a coral orange filament.

Hedychium 'Tangerine'
Minimum temperature: -7ºC (20ºF)
Height: to 180 cm (71 inches)

This introduction produces flowers from August to October on large, open spikes. The strongly fragrant flowers are salmon coloured (that is, bright orange with an evident pink overtone). The broad bilobed labellum and the lateral staminodes tend to arch downwards, leaving the orange-red stamens fully exposed and strongly upright.

Hedychium 'Tara'
Synonyms: *Hedychium coccineum* 'Tara', *H. gardnerianum* 'Tara'
Minimum temperature: -15ºC (5ºF)
Height: to 200 cm (79 inches)

This *Hedychium* was collected as seed in November 1972 by Tony Schilling at 2280 m (about 7200 feet) from the Nagarot ridge on the eastern edge of the Kathmandu valley. The seed was germinated at Wakehurst Place, Sussex, and when the subsequent seedlings flowered outdoors in the garden, they were identified as an unusual form of the variable *Hedychium coccineum*.

The tall, sturdy pseudostems are clothed in glaucous, blue-green leaves. From July to October, the plant produces 20-cm (8-inch) tall spikes of vivid orange flowers. These are fragrant and medium sized with narrow lateral staminodes and long scarlet stamens. Both the notched labellum and the lateral staminodes are also scarlet at their axis.

Schilling named the clone in honour of his daughter Tara, whose name is Nepalese for "star". The plant was subsequently given an RHS award in September 1978. Plants of *H.* 'Tara' were gradually distributed throughout various gardens of southern England and proved to be both vigorous and extremely hardy.

With the passage of time it has become apparent that 'Tara' is almost certainly not a form of *Hedychium coccineum* but is rather a natural hybrid between that species and *H. gardnerianum*. 'Tara' bears close resemblance to *H.* 'C. P. Raffill', a hybrid known to be of this parentage. In addition, like *H. gardnerianum*, 'Tara' produces only two flowers from each bract, both of which open together, whereas *H. coccineum* has three to five flowers per bract, opening in succession. Finally 'Tara' has a strong fragrance, a feature unknown in any other form of *H. coccineum*. Tom Wood has proposed 'Tara' as a clone of *H. gardnerianum*, but since this species has never been recorded as having anything other than yellow flowers, the hybrid parentage seems the most likely. (Plate 51)

Hedychium 'Tarissima'
Height: to 210 cm (83 inches)

This larger hybrid from Tom Wood was selected for having very large and extremely fragrant flowers that are a deep orange.

Hedychium 'Telstar 4'
Minimum temperature: -10°C (15°F)
Height: to 180 cm (71 inches)

This British hybrid has 40-cm (16-inch) long, lance-shaped leaves. It bears open spikes of salmon-coloured flowers starting in August.

Hedychium 'Thai Spirit'
Minimum temperature: -5°C (22°F) ?
Height: to 120 cm (48 inches)

Collected in northern Thailand, this *Hedychium* may well be an unknown species cultivar rather than a hybrid. It has very glaucous, stiff, and waxy blue-green foliage and produces large flowering spikes that are 30 cm (12 inches) tall. The spikes bear a dense arrangement of medium or small, highly fragrant vivid orange flowers with deep orange throats and elongated stamens.

Hedychium Tresco 1
Minimum temperature: -10°C (15°F)
Height: to 180 cm (71 inches)

This presumed hybrid between *Hedychium gardnerianum* and *H. coronarium* occurred on Tresco in the Isles of Scilly and has never been formally named. A robust plant, it bears large flowering spikes in August and September. The strongly fragrant, creamy white flowers have a ruffled labellum with two small notches at the tip. The lateral staminodes are paddle shaped, and the labellum is heavily flushed with pale lemon yellow, this colour extending to the filament that darkens to strong orange along its length.

Hedychium 'Tropic Bird'
Minimum temperature: -10°C (15°F)
Height: to 60 cm (24 inches)

This hardy dwarf hybrid was bred by Tom Wood for patio or pot culture. It forms dense clusters of short, stout, rigidly upright pseudostems with 30-cm (12-inch) long, waxy leaves. Very floriferous, it produces from September until frosts many spikes that bear bracts covered with golden "fur". The flowers are strongly scented of cloves and are unusual for being long-lived, each persisting for up to five days. The lateral staminodes are narrow and linear, and the labellum is strongly divided, almost to the axis, giving two, ribbon-like, rippled narrow lobes. When newly opened the flowers are white (with orange red filamentous petals), but as they age they darken to cream and eventually become a deep butter yellow. The labellum and lateral staminodes all reflex downwards to fully expose the upright-facing stamens.

'Tropic Bird' was envisaged as a cut-flower crop plant and will bloom freely throughout winter if maintained as a conservatory or greenhouse plant. Nonetheless, it is reasonably hardy in the garden, although it will probably have a very limited period of flowering in temperate zones.

Hedychium 'UK-2'
Minimum temperature: -10°C (15°F)
Height: to 180 cm (71 inches)

This presumed hybrid of *Hedychium coronarium* was originally collected by the Indian nursery of Ganesh Mani Pradhan and Son. Produced from July onwards, the flower spikes are considerably taller and more elongated than those of *H. coronarium*. The individual flowers are similar in shape, though somewhat more narrow, and are produced in much greater numbers than is the case in the species. The flower colour is white, with a large but faint pinkish cream patch on the labellum. The blush pink stamen is greatly extended, unlike that of the presumed parent.

Hedychium 'White Starburst'
Minimum temperature: -15ºC (5ºF)
Height: to 210 cm (83 inches)

This hybrid of *Hedychium coronarium* was bred by Tom Wood in the mid-1980s. It is notable for producing flowers in a circular, wheel-like arrangement around the small spikes, the feature that gives the plant its name. Where climate allows, plants bloom from September to November. Although the flowers are not produced in large numbers, they are of a good size and are well formed, each with a circular, unlobed labellum and very broad lateral staminodes. The flowers are fragrant and almost entirely white, with the merest touch of yellow-green in the throat.

Hedychium 'Yellow'
Minimum temperature: -10ºC (15ºF)
Height: to 210 cm (83 inches)

A hybrid of H*edychium gardnerianum*, possibly with *H. coronarium* as the other parent, this plant was introduced into cultivation by Stokes Tropicals of Louisiana. It was originally found growing on a building site in Hawaii. Plants produce thick stems clothed with very large, glossy, and slightly undulating leaves. The flower spikes appear from September and bear a loose, open arrangement of medium-sized pale golden yellow flowers, with arching lateral staminodes and a rather narrow labellum. The filament is extended and flame red. Plants require sun to bloom effectively.

Hedychium 'Yellow Spot'
Minimum temperature: -10ºC (15ºF)
Height: to 120 cm (48 inches)

This slow-growing, semi-dwarf selection is derived from *Hedychium coronarium*. It has narrow, long leaves and short flowering spikes from July to October. Each spike bears a small number of large, very rounded fragrant flowers held on long corolla tubes. The labellum is circular and slightly lobed, and the lateral staminodes are broad and lightly cupped at the margins. The flowers are white, with a large golden patch on the labellum, this colour also just touching the staminodes at their axis. The petals are butter yellow, and the filament is cream coloured and not extended.

Hemiorchis

Contained within the tribe *Globbaea*, the genus *Hemiorchis* comprises three species: two rarely cultivated members, *H. burmanica* and *H. rhodorrhachis*, both native to northern Thailand and neighbouring countries, plus the more easterly situated and more frequently encountered *H. pantlingii*. Wilhelm Kurz first described the genus in 1873, choosing a generic name that literally means "half orchid", referring to the appearance of the flowers. *Hemiorchis* species produce their inflorescence on a short stem separate from the foliage; this stem arises directly from the rhizome to form a loose spike of bracts from which the flowers emerge. The emerging flower stems are the first sign that the plants have broken into growth, and some month or so later the foliage appears, with groups of up to six leaves clasped together at the petiole to form a short pseudostem.

Plants of *Hemiorchis* are small with archetypal, if rather small and non-descript, *Zingiberaceae* foliage, but with exceedingly appealing flowers. In the open garden the beauty of the flowers is likely to get lost. From an ornamental point of view, the plants are perhaps better suited to pot culture where their features may be appreciated at eye level. Furthermore, because the flowering season lasts for only a month or so at best and the plants are not particularly noteworthy for the rest of the year, pot culture might allow for the plants to be displayed only when at their best.

Hemiorchis species are not difficult to cultivate and may be maintained in a gritty, or woodland mix, with plenty of nutrition and moisture when in growth. The plants develop from elongated, narrow white rhizomes that branch and form irregular contortions depending upon what they meet in the soil. When well grown these rhizomes can bulk up considerably during the course of a season and are easily divided simply by cutting them at their narrowest points, allowing for two or three buds on each length of separated rhizome. When container grown, *Hemiorchis* species are perhaps best maintained in a shallow, wide pot that will force the rhizomes outwards rather than into an impenetrable, downwards tangle. During dormancy the medium should be kept less moist, although *H. pantlingii*, at least, is far less prone to rotting in winter than are many of the small, semi-tropical gingers. Plants are equally successful in the open ground in a shady position given a well-drained, humus-rich soil.

Hemiorchis pantlingii

Minimum temperature: -7°C (20°F) ?
Height: to 30 cm (12 inches)

Named, like a number of southern Asian plants, for botanist Robert Pantling, this species is a native of northern Thailand, west into the Indian Himalaya. The plant emerges early from dormancy, with the flowering spikes appearing in April and May. These reach approximately 10–15 cm (4–6 inches) tall and bear a cluster of up to 20 flowers which open in succession, each persisting for four or five days. The flowers open from dusky fawn-coloured bracts to reveal three petal-like lobes that are pale, coppery fawn. The lobes surround a 2.5-cm (1-inch) labellum that is golden yellow, heavily patterned with deep red. Although small, this arrangement is extremely attractive. In flower, the species resembles a terrestrial orchid, all the more so for its precocious habit. The foliage emerges after the flowers have finished, and the broadly lanceolate, glossy leaves reach 15 cm (6 inches) long by 5 cm (2 inches) wide.

Hedychium pantlingii is now widely available in Europe, although it is currently something of a rarity in the United States. The species has not been extensively tested for cold tolerance, but has proven to be easy to cultivate in the United Kingdom and requires no special treatment (over and above that afforded to any small, shade-loving ginger) to succeed.

Kaempferia

Named by Carl Linnaeus in 1753 to commemorate Englebert Kaempfer, an eminent German botanist of the seventeenth and early eighteenth centuries, the genus *Kaempferia* consists of approximately 50 species of low-growing, often prostrate gingers. Unusually among the family *Zingiberaceae*, *Kaempferia* species are grown primarily for their ornamental foliage rather than for their flowers. In addition, several species have long been cultivated for their medicinal properties. In fact, *K. galanga* and *K. rotunda* are now widely grown for this purpose throughout the tropical world, although the genus is probably originally native only to Southeast Asia and southern China.

Collectively, *Kaempferia* species are often dubbed peacock gingers, a reference to their generally beautifully patterned and coloured foliage. The leaves of the smaller, flatter-growing species resemble those of the ginger relatives *Maranta* (the so-called prayer plants) and their close cousins *Calathea*. The large-leaved forms bear a superficial resemblance to *Hosta*, and the upright varieties have a look that is all their own.

Kaempferia leaves are produced directly from the rhizome and are held on short pseudostems. The leaves are fairly uniform in shape throughout the genus and are almost always ovate, varying from nearly circular to more elongate. The foliage may be held erect, as in *K. rotunda*, but is usually held flat at or upon the ground. Virtually all species have heavily ribbed foliage, patterned with a variety of greys, greens, silvers, and purple-blacks, the colours running along, or separated into blocks along, the ribbed veining.

The *Kaempferia* inflorescence is borne in one of two ways. Most species produce a short pseudostem at the centre of the leaf rosette, this being largely or entirely enclosed by the leaf sheaths. From this the flowers appear, generally one at a time, often for a prolonged period through summer and early autumn. Other species, notably *K. rotunda*, produce a separate inflorescence stem that arises directly from the rhizome, up to a month before the first leaves emerge. The flowers are not large, varying from a few centimetres (about 1 inch) across in some to 8 cm (3 inches) across in *K.* 'Grande', but can be extremely pretty, and have a pair of broad, generally rounded lateral staminodes and a large labellum. In many species, such as *K. pulchra* and its kin, the labellum is fully divided into two halves, and together with the lateral staminodes this gives the distinct impression of four "petals" (see Figure 3). Other species have a labellum that is only partially divided, generally with a dark throat patch as a guide for pollinators. Behind these "petals" are the three corolla lobes, which in species such as *K. galanga* and *K. rotunda*, are white, narrowly linear, and unusually elongated, forming an important and ornamental element of the flower.

Despite their principally tropical origins, *Kaempferia* species are generally far hardier than might be supposed, due primarily to that fact that most of them have a natural period of dormancy when they become deciduous. In the wild this dormancy is aligned with the monsoon season, so that the plants are only in growth when sufficient humidity and ground moisture can sustain them. In temperate gardens this same dormancy occurs then temperatures drop in autumn. The plants can tolerate surprisingly low winter temperatures so long as they are not waterlogged.

The rhizomes of kaempferias bear roots upon which small, globular or elongated tubers occur. These tubers offer the plants a further method of food and water storage, deeper within the soil than the rhizomes, and so

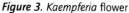

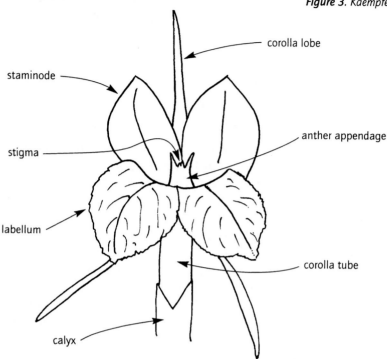

Figure 3. Kaempferia flower

corolla lobe

staminode

anther appendage

stigma

labellum

corolla tube

calyx

perhaps prevent desiccation when plants are dormant. The plants cannot be reproduced from these tubers alone, however, as the growing points occur solely on the rhizomes. When well grown, most varieties readily form new outgrowths, and these may be separated, or the main rhizome divided at the end of the growing season.

Nurseries often refer to *Kaempferia* as a potential garden substitute for *Hosta*. Like hostas, kaempferias are primarily, although not exclusively, plants of the shady forest floor, and most will take well to woodland or shade-garden conditions, where they require a well-drained, open-growing medium that will prevent winter rotting. They are also substantially less hardy than *Hosta*, or to be more accurate, they have a substantially shorter growing season in temperate regions, with many species plants not emerging from dormancy until June, and disappearing again in October.

As with all the neo-tropical gingers, the successful cultivation of kaempferias depends on understanding their natural wild patterns and adapting conditions for the plants accordingly. Aside from the basic prerequisites of shade, shelter, and a free-draining soil, kaempferias are generally trouble-free and highly rewarding plants to grow and should be more widely used in temperate European gardens.

Kaempferia angustifolia

Minimum temperature: -10°C (15°F)
Height: to 20 cm (8 inches)

Named by William Roscoe, this unusual species has (as the specific name suggests) atypically narrow foliage. Each lanceolate leaf reaches about 15 cm (6 inches) long by 3 cm (1¼ inches) wide, with markedly undulating edges and a prominent "fold" around the midvein. The leaves tend to be a pale green with darker veining. *Kaempferia angustifolia* blooms in July and August with the inflorescence forming at the axis of the leaves. At about 2.5 cm (1 inch) across the flowers are small, but certainly pretty upon close inspection. Each flower has a pair of white staminodes held above a partially divided lavender labellum with a large, darker violet throat.

    Kaempferia angustifolia is fairly widely available and has proven to be easily grown in a shady, moist location, provided with some protection from winter wet. Under these conditions plants will increase well and can form good-sized colonies.

Kaempferia atrovirens

Synonym: *Kaempferia pulchra* 'Silverspot'
Minimum temperature: -10°C (15°F)
Height: to 15 cm (6 inches)

Somewhat confused in cultivation, due to the attachment of the name "Silver Spot", and the presumption that the plant was a variety of *Kaempferia pulchra*, *K. atrovirens* was named from a specimen collected from Indonesian Borneo in 1886. The species is also present in Australia, where it was probably introduced, and it is now listed as a naturalized weed in Japan.

    Plants have beautiful, broad, ovate leaves, approximately 15 cm (6 inches) long, and heavily infused with blackish purple, the colour essentially covering all of the green on the upper leaf surface. The leaf margins have interveinal silver patches, and a further set of silver patches appears either side of the central vein. The small flowers occur in June and July at the centre of the leaf junctions and have a narrowly ovate, undivided purple labellum with paler edges and white throat, coupled with narrow, lanceolate white staminodes. The flowers have reduced parts and are not showy.

Kaempferia atrovirens is slow to establish and does not bulk up as readily as some other species in the genus, this doubtless being a consequence of its tropical origins. Nevertheless, the natural dormancy of *Kaempferia* allows species such as this to be cultivated in a wide variety of climates. *Kaempferia atrovirens* has proven to be surprisingly hardy. Plants require a fiercely drained medium that is seasonally moist. They may also be pot grown for more control over the watering regime.

Kaempferia elegans

Minimum temperature: -10°C (15°F)
Height: to 20 cm (8 inches)

Considered by some botanists to be synonymous with *Kaempferia atrovirens*, this species is native to Sichuan province in China, as well as northern India, Myanmar, Thailand, and peninsular Malaysia, with a further population present in the Philippines. Nathaniel Wallich named the species as *Monolophus elegans* in 1830, and it was absorbed into *Kaempferia* some 60 years later.

Kaempferia elegans bears groups of between two and four ovate leaves, each around 10 cm (4 inches) long; these are generally unpatterned green and are held more or less prostrate. The flowers are produced in June and July from the centre of the foliage and appear to have four pink or pale lavender petals. These "petals" are actually made up of the two lateral staminodes, plus the labellum, which is divided to its base, producing two distinct lobes. The flowers are approximately 4 cm (1½ inches) across, but they are held facing upright and are relatively conspicuous against the foliage. The species is available in cultivation, but the unpatterned foliage makes it less desirable than many kaempferias.

Kaempferia elegans 'Satin Cheeks'

This well-established cultivar has undulate, heavily ribbed leaves that reach 18 cm (7 inches) long. The base colour is pale green as the leaves open and gradually flushes darker until the leaves mature to a deep, velvety green with purple overtones. Laid upon this are even purple marks, in bands adjacent to the leaf edges and also in separate bands running the length of the leaf, either side of the central vein, giving a distinctive, checkerboard pattern. 'Satin Cheeks' is easily grown and multiplies well at the rhizome.

Kaempferia elegans 'Shazam'

'Shazam' is similar to 'Satin Cheeks' with leaves that reach 20 cm (8 inches) long. The leaves are paler, with more of a silvery overtone, and have a strong, almost black variegation that runs in four or six bands along the length of the leaf. The blocks of colour are less distinctively margined and are more irregular than those of 'Satin Cheeks' but the effect is at least as beautiful. The flower colour is pale lavender.

Kaempferia galanga

Minimum temperature: -10ºC (15ºF)
Height: to 10 cm (4 inches)

Named by Carl Linnaeus in 1753 and almost certainly the type species of the genus, *Kaempferia galanga* is a native of Guangdong, Guangxi, and Yunnan provinces of China, as well as Taiwan and India. The species is very widely cultivated across Southeast Asia, where the rhizomes are harvested and used for a variety of internal and external medicinal purposes, as well as for the commercial production of an essential oil. *Kaempferia galanga* is also occasionally used as a spice, primarily in Thailand, but is not to be confused with the spice galangal, which is derived from *Alpinia galanga*. The specific name for both plants refers to the aromatic water plant *Cyperus longus*—the original galangal.

Kaempferia galanga produces pairs of very handsome, fleshy, glabrous, circular leaves, plain green with conspicuous veins. These can reach around 20 cm (8 inches) across and are followed in July, August, or September by the flowers, which appear at the centre of the leaf axis. Though not large, the flowers are highly attractive, with broad, white lateral staminodes and a bicleft labellum, also white, but with a violet purple blotch at the throat of each lobe. Three linear, white corolla lobes complete the floral display.

Though not widely grown as an ornamental, *Kaempferia galanga* possesses rather impressive, *Hosta*-like foliage that looks all the more interesting for being held flat against the ground. The foliage has the added advantage of displaying the pretty flowers well. The species is readily grown in shady woodland conditions, and plants of Chinese origin are reasonably hardy in temperate gardens. (Plate 52)

Kaempferia gilbertii

Minimum temperature: -10ºC (15ºF)
Height: to 30 cm (12 inches)

This unusual species from Myanmar and northern Thailand is closely related to, and possibly comes within, *Kaempferia angustiflolia*—in which case the name *K. gilbertii* would have priority. Plants have relatively narrow, lanceolate, and generally arching, upright foliage, the individual leaves reaching 30 cm (12 inches) long. The species is represented in cultivation by two specific variegated clones. The one that is distributed under the species name (that is, without a cultivar name) has a narrow creamy white band running along the leaf margins and fairly showy flowers. Each flower has a pair of ovate, white lateral staminodes and a broad, *Roscoea*-like, bilobed labellum that is dark lavender with the inner half coloured a deep violet. This species is widely available in the United States, but largely untried in the United Kingdom.

Kaempferia gilbertii '3D'

This sport of the "species" form was selected by Tom Wood for its foliage. The leaves are broader and much more heavily variegated than those of the species, each with wide, irregular bands of pale creamy white running to the leaf tip, as well as more narrow bands of deep green concentrated at the midvein. The remaining 20% to 40% or so of the leaf is mid-green, and the combination of the three colours is quite remarkable. Flowers are as for the typical species. Of the two cultivated forms of *Kaempferia gilbertii*, '3D' is slower growing, as might be expected given the heavy variegation. The plant has been micropropagated and is widely available in the United States. (Plate 53)

Kaempferia laotica 'Brush Strokes'

Minimum temperature: -10ºC (15ºF)
Height: to 20 cm (8 inches)

Named by François Gagnepain in 1907, *Kaempferia laotica* is a scarce species represented in cultivation by one clone. 'Brush Strokes' has broad, ovate leaves that reach 18 cm (7 inches) long by 10 cm (4 inches) across and are held nearly prostrate. The leaf colour is a dark, velvety green, but this is largely covered by a nearly solid block of dark, blackish purple, leaving just the veins picked out in narrow bands of green, together with a broader green leaf margin. The flowers can appear from July or August, and are small and lavender in colour. Each spike bears four nearly equal pale lavender flowers, made up of the two lateral staminodes and a fully cleft labellum.

Kaempferia marginata

Minimum temperature: -10ºC (15ºF)
Height: to 30 cm (12 inches)

Native to grassland and scrubland in Yunnan province of China, northeastern India, Myanmar, and Thailand, this species was named by William Carey in 1824 for its purple-brown margined leaves. These handsome leaves appear in pairs and are fleshy, largely circular or broadly ovate, to 25 cm (10 inches) in diameter, and held flat to the ground. The leaf colour is variable but generally dark green, infused to various degrees with purple. The very narrow margin is dark purple margin. Flowers appear in July and August from the centre of the leaf axis and can be pale lavender or white, with two broad lateral staminodes and a fully divided labellum that has small violet and white markings in the throat. *Kaempferia marginata* is not a vigorous grower, but the magnificent foliage makes it well worth growing whenever possible. It is best in a shady, sheltered position grown in an open, woodland soil.

Kaempferia pulchra

Synonym: *Kaempferia pulchra* 'Bronze Leaf'
Minimum temperature: -10ºC (15ºF)
Height: to 10 cm (4 inches)

This species is a native of the forests of much of Thailand, south into Malaysia and Indonesia, where plants grow to form a groundcover among the leaf-litter. *Kaempferia pulchra* is highly variable, particularly in its leaf patterning. It has hybridized with neighbouring species to form intermediate plants that have yet to be properly identified.

The basic form of *Kaempferia pulchra* has velvety textured, ovate to nearly circular leaves, around 15 cm (6 inches) long, and coloured almost entirely deep inky purple. This nearly black base (generally though inaccurately referred to as bronze) is overlaid by various patterns and markings of silver, generally with a green central midvein. A number of cultivars have been selected for their leaf variegation. In most cases the leaves are held flat, just above the ground, although the precise arrangement is variable—possibly because not all forms that are being grown are true cultivars of the species.

Kaempferia pulchra can flower at any time from June to October, depending upon local conditions, the flowering stems appearing from the centre of the leaves. While the flowers are small and not as interesting in construction as those of many *Kaempferia* species, they are well displayed against the nearly flat foliage. The plants are also rather floriferous with a long succession of flowers appearing through the season.

Kaempferia pulchra is often grown as a conservatory plant and can be induced to remain evergreen by keeping temperatures above 18ºC (65ºF). In the wild, however, the plants are naturally dormant. The dormancy is timed to combine with inter-monsoonal dry periods, and thus the plants can be grown successfully in temperate gardens, where they will typically emerge into growth in early June, with flowering commencing approximately a month later.

As with all kaempferias, *Kaempferia pulchra* must not be allowed to get too wet while dormant. Appropriate protective measures should be taken in autumn, when the leaves are still visible. In the right site, this species will readily form a good, fairly solid groundcover for shady, sheltered gardens. Provided the plants are not overwhelmed by larger or more vigorous plants, colonies can form and allow the attractive flowers and striking foliage to be displayed to their best advantage.

Kaempferia pulchra 'Alva'

Ginger aficionado John Banta of Alva, Florida, created 'Alva' by hybridizing a white-flowered cultivar with a lavender-flowered form of the species. The superb plant that resulted has unusually large flowers of very pale pinkish lavender with a large central creamy white eye. The flowers are extremely well displayed against the foliage. The 30-cm (12-inch) long leaves have very distinctly separated bands of blackish purple and pale, silvery green—a pattern very similar to 'Silver Spot'. (Plate 54)

Kaempferia pulchra 'Bicolor'

Many kaempferias look very like marantas, but this cultivar is all but indistinguishable unless in flower. The leaves have a base colour of pale green, overlaid by alternating, irregular broken bands of pale silvery green and blocks of pale, charcoal purple. Each leaf has a slightly different combination, but they are always symmetrical on either side of the midvein, looking like a floral Rorschach ink blot. The flowers are typical for the species, but of a very pale lavender.

Kaempferia pulchra 'Manson'
Synonyms: *Kaempferia pulchra* var. *mansonii, K. mansonii*

This plant of slightly mysterious origins was supposedly purchased by a Mr. Manson from a market stall in the Philippines and is generally (but wrongly, since it has never been described or formally named) referred to as *K. pulchra* var. *mansonii.* It may yet prove to be a separate variety of the species. 'Manson' is a valuable and now widespread garden plant with heavily ridged leaves about 20 cm (8 inches) long by 10 cm (4 inches) wide. Although very different in shape and bearing, the leaves have a pattern similar to that commonly seen on *K. rotunda,* with a base colour of dark, purple-green, overlaid by a symmetrical radiating pattern of silver speckles with a prominent, flame-shaped central zone of purple. The flowers are pale lavender and typical for the species. 'Manson' is easily grown and more vigorous than *K. pulchra* itself.

Kaempferia pulchra 'Roscoe'
Synonyms: *Kaempferia roscoeana* hort., *K.* sp. 'Mottled Leaf'

A large-growing form of the species, 'Roscoe' has handsome leaves about 25 cm (10 inches) long by 20 cm (8 inches) across. Leaf variegation consists of alternating bands of silver and greenish deep purple radiating out from the axis. The lavender flowers are freely produced throughout summer and are also somewhat larger than those of the typical species. Note that there is much confusion surrounding the name *K. roscoeana* and various Anglicized permutations thereof.

Kaempferia pulchra 'Silver Spot'

This widely distributed cultivar is typical for the species, except for the leaf variegations, which display wide, jagged bands of pale, greenish silver over a deep, blackish purple base colour. The cultivar name is misleading, since there are no "spots" to speak of. This very beautiful and easily grown form of the species is well worth seeking out. (Plate 55)

Kaempferia pulchra 'Silverspeck'

Introduced by David Peterson of Texas, this cultivar is very similar to the better-known 'Silver Spot', but with somewhat smaller leaves.

Kaempferia pulchra–white
Synonym: *Kaempferia roscoeana*—white

A white-flowered form of *Kaempferia pulchra* has been distributed, largely (and wrongly) under the name *K. roscoeana*. This form is lacking in pigment overall. The generally velvety green leaves have only faint or occasional purple banding, and the pure white flowers have only the merest hint of pale yellow at the centre.

Kaempferia roscoeana

Minimum temperature: -7ºC (20ºF)
Height: to 4 cm (1½ inches)

Originally described by Nathaniel Wallich in 1829 and seemingly the subject of much confusion ever since, the true species is a rare native of Thailand and Myanmar and is infrequently seen in cultivation. Plants may be distinguished from various forms of *Kaempferia pulcha* bearing the same name by their entirely white flowers that are produced in an almost continuous succession from June to September, and which measure approximately 3 cm (1¼ inches) across, with a fully subdivided labellum. More significantly, each stem bears just two leaves and these are held entirely prostrate to the soil, whereas in white forms of *K. pulchra* the leaves are held in a more upright position. The leaves are large—12 cm (about 5 inches) long in the type description but 35 cm (14 inches) on plants in cultivation—and mottled with dark green. (Plate 56)

Kaempferia rotunda

Minimum temperature: -10°C (15°F)
Height: to 60 cm (24 inches)

This highly distinctive species is probably the finest ornamental member of the genus, unusual for being erect in growth and large of flower. Carl Linnaeus named it *Kaempferia rotunda* in 1753 for its rounded rhizome. Most likely it originally was a native of the Indian Himalaya, southern China, and Thailand. It has long been widely cultivated throughout tropical Asia for its medicinal properties.

Kaempferia rotunda is naturally deciduous and produces spear-like pseudostems in late spring to early summer. The pseudostems bear two to four erect, broadly lanceolate leaves, which typically are 20–25 cm (8–10 inches) long by 9 cm (3½ inches) wide and strongly ribbed. On their upper surface the leaves have silver and deep green variegations, the degree of variegation depending on the plant and the light levels, but generally consisting of a deep green central patch that runs the length of the leaf, surrounded by silver that dissipates to pale green at the leaf margins. The leaf under surface is usually deep maroon red as the leaves open, generally fading as the leaves mature. The inflorescence occurs on a separate flowering stem that generally appears in May (April in the wild and in warmer gardens), before the leaves emerge. Each stem carries between four and six flowers, which open in succession to reveal a pair of sharply tipped, upright, pure white, 5-cm (2-inch) long lanceolate lateral staminodes. The flamboyant, arching labellum is divided to the base, creating two broad lobes each 4 cm (1½ inches) long by 2 cm (¾ inch) wide and coloured pale violet with deeper purple veining and a darker throat. The three white corolla lobes are extremely long and narrow, but form an important part of the "look" of the flower as they surround and create a counterpoint to the petaloid parts.

Kaempferia rotunda has acquired a number of common names, as befits a species so widely cultivated, including resurrection lily or Asian crocus, both referring to the precocious flowering habit. This plant is easy to grow and seems to thrive in a various locations, but not in bright, direct sunlight. The plants readily increase at the rhizome but, since *K. rotunda* is an erect species, it is unsuitable for use as groundcover. Instead, it will form highly appealing small stands where kept free of competition from more vigorous plants. (Plate 57)

Kaempferia rotunda 'Dreamcatcher'

Florida-based collector and ginger enthusiast David Petersen selected this showy cultivar. The foliage has irregular, long, block-like silver variegations, arranged in four rows—two on either side of the midvein.

Kaempferia rotunda 'Frost'

This cultivar from Tom Wood has leaves with much of their surface covered in a light dusting of silver. There is a central area of dark green, radiating out from the midvein along each interveinal section. Each of these sections terminates in a small silver block, before giving way to the dusted silver that continues to the leaf margins.

Kaempferia rotunda 'Raven'

This fine foliage selection has more upright and narrow leaves that have a deep green centre and strongly contrasting silver bands. The silver variegations appear to have been painted on with a brush, the colour giving way to fine lines towards the deep green leaf margin.

Kaempferia rotunda 'Red Leaf'

This form was introduced by Naga Gardens of Houston, Texas, and is typical for the species but with the underside of the leaf remaining more persistently red.

Kaempferia rotunda 'Silver Diamonds'

This spectacular new selection was named and introduced by Tim Chapman of Gingerwood Nursery, St. Gabriel, Louisiana. Plants have twin rows of large, diamond-shaped silver variegations, with a row running up the centre of each side of the leaf blade. The leaf margins are also slightly undulate. This cultivar is said to be very slow to increase at the rhizome, although in other respects it is no more demanding than the usual species.

Kaempferia rotunda 'Titan'
Height: to 90 cm (36 inches)

Selected by John Banta and under cultivation by Tim Chapman, this cultivar is larger in stature than the usual forms, or indeed the existing records for the species, with leaves up to 45 cm (18 inches) long.

Kaempferia simaoensis

Minimum temperature: -7°C (20°F)
Height: to 40 cm (16 inches)

Named by Yi Yong Qian as recently as 1995, this Chinese species is endemic to the Simao prefecture of southern Yunnan, where plants were found growing in forest at 900 m (3000 feet). *Kaempferia simaoensis* bears four to seven narrowly ovate leaves up to 27 cm (11 inches) long by 10 cm (4 inches) wide. The leaves have a deep green upper surface and a grey-green underside, sometimes infused with purple. The inflorescence appears on a separate stem arising directly from the rhizome before the foliage appears. Each flowering spike carries up to nine flowers, and these have a pair of obovate lateral staminodes that are white nearest the centre, becoming purple towards their tips. The labellum is bilobed but not fully divided, and is purple with a deep violet centre. In Yunnan province, China, the plants flower very early—in April and May. The species has not yet been introduced to cultivation, so it is not known if the species would also bloom early in gardens.

Kaempferia sp. 'Red Leaf'

Minimum temperature: -10°C (15°F) ?
Height: to 10 cm (4 inches)

Not to be confused with *Kaempferia rotunda* 'Red Leaf', this *Kaempferia* cultivar was distributed by Stokes Tropicals of Louisiana from material originally sourced in northern Thailand. The leaves are 15 cm (6 inches) long, ovate, leathery, and held entirely prostrate. The upper surface leaf colour is variable from deep maroon red to green, with an overtone of red. Flowers are reported to be white with bluish purple markings.

Kaempferia sp. 'Ribbed Leaf'

Synonym: *Kaempferia parishii*
Minimum temperature: -10°C (15°F) ?
Height: to 45 cm (18 inches)

Introduced and distributed by the nursery of Ganesh Mani Pradhan and Son of West Bengal, this kaempferia is of unknown origin and uncertain identity. Plants are upright, with unmarked, rather *Hosta*-like, ovate green leaves that reach to 20 cm (8 inches) long by 10 cm (4 inches) wide, and have very prominent "ribbed" veining. The flowers are produced in succession throughout summer on a stem borne at the centre of the leaves, and are strongly four-lobed, with an entirely divided labellum. The four "petals" are lavender-purple, with a central small white "eye".

Ganesh reports that the plant responds very differently to different light conditions, remaining dwarfed in bright light, but growing much taller, with the flower stems considerably elongated, in shade. The plants do not suffer from leaf scorch in full sun, strongly suggesting that this is not a forest species. 'Ribbed Leaf' is now available in Europe and is proving relatively easy to cultivate, although slow to break dormancy, with growth often not emerging until June.

Kaempferia Hybrids

Kaempferia 'Grande'
Synonym: *Kaempferia rotunda* 'Grande'
Minimum temperature: -10°C (15°F) ?
Height: to 60 cm

Possibly a form of *Kaempferia rotunda*, or alternatively a hybrid that clearly involves that species, or maybe a new species altogether, this extremely distinctive and impressive plant has long, ovate, slightly arching upright leaves up to nearly 60 cm (24 inches) long by 20 cm (8 inches) wide. The upper surface has a deep blackish purple tone, which is bisected by four jagged silver lines—two on either side of the midvein—running the length of the leaf. On the outside of the furthest line (that is, towards the leaf margin), the leaf colour changes to dark green. The lower leaf surface is entirely deep burgundy red.

In addition to the beautiful and substantial leaves, 'Grande' has the largest flowers in the genus. These are produced in late spring, before the foliage, on a separate flowering stem and comprise a pair of ovate lateral staminodes and a large, heart-shaped labellum with a notched tip. All parts of the flower are coloured pale blush-pink, with small, darker pink and pastel yellow markings in the throat, quite different from *Kaempferia rotunda*.

Hardiness is largely untested, and will clearly depend upon the precise origins and parentage of the plant, but it would be hard to imagine a more spectacular *Kaempferia*. 'Grande' is scarce but now available from a handful of specialist nurseries in the United States.

Kaempferia 'Neutron Star'
Minimum temperature: -10ºC (15ºF)
Height: to 25 cm (10 inches)

This hybrid from Tom Wood has deep blackish green, shiny leaves patterned with large, elliptical silver variegations. It is apparently highly floriferous. The flowers are said to be deep violet in colour.

Roscoea

The genus *Roscoea* was named in honour of William Roscoe, a founder of the Liverpool Botanic Garden and a man with an early passion for gingers. James Edward Smith described the type species, *R. purpurea*, in 1804, and since then a further 18 species have been discovered, the most recent coming from China, where there is doubtless the possibility, or even the likelihood, that further species await discovery and description.

All *Roscoea* species are native to eastern Asia, with two main areas of natural distribution. The first reaches from Kashmir, eastwards through the Himalayas, and on into the Indian province of Assam. The second is primarily centred on the botanically fantastically rich area of southern China contained within Sichuan and Yunnan provinces, with populations spreading on into northern Vietnam.

Taken as a group *Roscoea* species are not only the most northerly situated of the gingers geographically, but, having been collected from locations between 1200 and 4850 m (3,900–15,600 feet) elevation, are also found to naturally occur at the highest elevations of any members of the family. Several species fall into the broad and ill-defined category of alpine plants. From a horticultural point of view, this classification makes them certainly the hardiest gingers, and therefore, although they are dwarfed in number by several other genera, they are among the most important for the hardy gardener. Indeed this is the only genus within the order *Zingiberales* all of whose members can be considered to be truly and fully hardy, certainly for cultivation within British gardens.

Roscoeas are relatively small plants with pseudostems typically reaching 30–60 cm (12–24 inches) tall. Up to five leaves are produced together and these are clasped to the stems by tubular sheaths. The leaves are relatively uniform throughout the genus and are invariably upright and more or less lanceolate, narrow and almost grass-like in *R. scillifolia*, broader in the largest species. The inflorescence is produced at the centre of the leaves, at the terminus of the stem, and contains flowers that are arranged spirally in a loose grouping of bracts. The flowers open in succession over two or three weeks and are similar in overall structure throughout the genus, with a very large, showy labellum that generally reflexes downwards, coupled with a pair of lateral petals. *Roscoea* is one of the few genera of the family *Zingiberaceae* in which the petals play a significant ornamental role. Above the laterals petals is a single dorsal petal held in a cupped, hood shape that also contains the staminodes and the single stamen (see Figure 4).

As a result of their hardiness and general amenability to cultivation, roscoeas are now the most frequently encountered gingers in European gardens. A wealth of new forms and some new hybrids have been introduced in Europe since 1990, and they are now proliferating out of the realms of the specialist nursery and the collector's gardens, into garden centres, and thus on into the hands of the general gardening public. As such

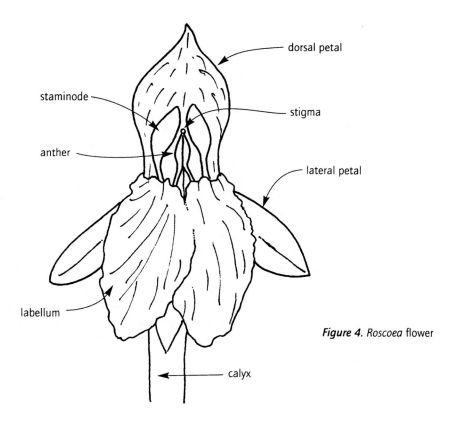

Figure 4. Roscoea flower

roscoeas are among the vanguard of the new interest in gingers. It is hoped that those gardeners initially tempted to try roscoeas in the garden will soon be smitten by the charms of their plants and yearn to venture into the realms of the other ginger genera. This popularity in Europe makes it all the more surprising that the plants are, up to now, relatively unknown in general cultivation in North America. They are certainly eminently suitable for use in a wide array of garden situations and it is hoped that their acceptance and popularity on that continent will not be long in coming.

In cultivation, *Roscoea* species have traditionally been grown as woodland plants with shade-loving perennials, or, in the case of the smaller species, they have been used for alpine, rock, and scree garden plantings. In many respects this latter use is closest to the natural setting in which most species are found growing in relatively exposed, often very steep meadows, frequently in highly inaccessible locations where the plants are more protected from the depredation of grazing animals. In practice, however, many of the species and their forms are tolerant of a wide range of garden conditions and present far fewer problems for the gardener than, say, *Meconopsis* or high altitude *Primula*, both of which share some of the gingers' natural habitat. With a few exceptions these are easy plants that will grow well and proliferate in any good garden soil that is not allowed to become parched in summer or waterlogged in winter.

Several growers have noted that while most species will indeed thrive in a woodland garden setting, they do not always colour so fully in such conditions. The pigment in the flowers and in the coloured stems (where present) seems to be somewhat dependent on light levels. Temperature at flowering time and/or possibly at the time of bud development is also presumed to have an effect upon the ultimate pigmentation of the flowers: plants in cooler locations seem to produce stronger colouration in their flowers. Certainly I have observed substantially different flower colouration on specific, identified plants from year to year, but more study needs to be done to determine the exact significance of the various factors that are playing a role in this. Within the order *Zingiberales* this phenomenon seems to be restricted to *Roscoea* and appears not to have been noted in any other genera of ginger. Of course, given that most *Roscoea* species originate from high-altitude (cool) and open, exposed (bright) sites, it shouldn't be too surprising that many flower most colourfully when those two factors are offered to them in cultivation.

I have attempted to incorporate and describe, if only in brief, all the species and named forms of *Roscoea* currently in nursery cultivation. There will doubtless be many future additions to this listing, particularly as various hybridization programmes start to bear fruit.

Roscoea alpina

Minimum temperature: -20ºC (-4ºF)
Height: 12–20 cm (5–8 inches)

The species is widespread throughout the Indian Himalaya, ranging from Kashmir in the west through Nepal to Bhutan and Yunnan in the east and Xizang (Tibetan Autonomous Region) in the north. It occurs fairly commonly at altitudes of 2000 to 4300 m (6,600–14,100 feet) throughout its range. Despite its specific name, it is primarily a denizen of open woodland characterized by the presence of *Betula*, *Juniperus*, and *Rhododendron*, although populations also occur in more exposed grasslands and rock crevices.

Roscoea alpina bears comparatively large (for the overall stature of the species) and fairly showy flowers of a typically mauve purple, generally without any prominent streaking. These flowers are in a characteristic arrangement for the genus, with a hooded dorsal petal and a pair of recurved lateral petals surrounding a prominent labellum, which is divided to form a "split lip". Given the range of habits, it is not surprising that there is natural diversity in the flower colour of wild populations. Forms with darker, violet purple and paler, pinkish white flowers have been recorded, although unfortunately none of these have been introduced into cultivation as yet. In their native habitat the plants produce flowers variously from the end of May to mid-August, but in the garden flowering is concentrated in June and early July.

Although not as showy as some of the larger species, *Roscoea alpina* is certainly a delightful sight when well grown as a colony, and the short, stocky stature of the plants makes them quite distinctive alongside other *Roscoea* species. First described and named by John Royle in 1839, *R. alpina* has been regularly collected and brought into cultivation ever since, with numerous introductions in the late 1800s and again since 1990. Despite this, the plant has never been widespread in cultivation. In fact, it has been saddled with a reputation that it is hard to grow. While it is true that early introductions did not persist in cultivation for very long, modern collections have proven to be fairly straightforward to please. Because the species is so naturally widespread, previous problems may have been due to the source material having been collected from extreme localities. Generally speaking, however, *R. alpina* seems to resent excessive heat in the garden and should ideally be grown in cool, dappled or open shade where it will increase successfully to form good clumps of plants.

There has traditionally been much confusion between cultivated stocks of this species and *Roscoea scillifolia*, although any similarities between the two are slight, and side by side it would be impossible to mistake one for the other. Nevertheless, many stocks of the pink form of *R. scillifolia* have been labelled as *R. alpina*, a practice that unfortunately still persists in some nurseries.

Despite the variability of the species, and the comparatively large number of introductions into cultivation, there are no named forms currently known, nor have any hybrids been produced. Recent collections include BBMS 2 and BBMS 14, two pale purple forms, collected on expedition lead by William Baker to Ganesh Himal in Nepal in 1992; BBMS 3, a darker purple flowered form collected by the same expedition; and CC1820, a mid-purple form collected by Chris Chadwell from the Almora Hills, Uttar Pradesh. (Plate 58)

Roscoea auriculata

Minimum temperature: -20°C (-4°F)
Height: 25–40 cm (10–16 inches)

The true species is a native of Nepal, Sikkim, and Xizang (Tibetan Autonomous Region), where plants grow in generally open situations on rough, stony ground and along roadside margins at altitudes of 2100 to 4900 m (6,900–16,100 feet). This showy and highly desirable species bears large flowers of a good, strong violet purple and a contrasting white throat. The flowers are held above appealing, large, lance-shaped leaves.

Natural populations vary, with bicoloured- and white-flowered forms having been reported, but since *Roscoea auriculata* is not as frequently encountered as some other *Roscoea* species, plants introduced to cultivation are fairly consistent in flower colour and shape, with the exception of the two named forms (which see). In their natural habitats plants flower from May to September, cultivated plants from mid-June to early August, notably before *R. purpurea*, although later than *R. cautleyoides*.

Roscoea auriculata has long been confused in cultivation with *R. purpurea*. All of the initial introductions of this species were indeed labelled as *R. purpurea* and are presumed to have originated from plants collected in Sikkim under Joseph Hooker in the mid-1800s. Subsequently these collections were distributed to British growers and botanical gardens. When Karl Schumann first described and named *R. auriculata* in 1904, it became clear that a proportion of the plants then being grown as *R. purpurea* were in fact referable to this species instead, and a painfully slow process of recognizing and separating the species began. Although the two are certainly similar, they can best be separated by examination of the leaves, all of which are clearly and consistently auriculate (eared) in specimens of *R. auriculata*. Further, this species flowers earlier and has deeper coloured flowers (certainly in cultivated populations) than does *R. purpurea*, and the flowers also have a strongly downward-facing labellum (lip), whereas in *R. purpurea* the labellum is held closer to the horizontal.

This species is essentially problem-free and is easily cultivated in a bright location. It thrives and increases well in a rich, peaty soil, although it also takes to general garden cultivation without problem.

Roscoea auriculata 'Floriade'

Originating in Holland, this named form of the species is quite a star and substantially larger in all of its parts than the normal species. Each violet-purple flower has a large, partially divided lip of around 5 cm (2 inches) wide and seated beneath white staminodes. The stems and foliage are also notably larger, to 60 cm (24 inches) tall, than in typical cultivated *R. auriculata* and give the plant much distinction even when not in flower. This form was introduced to cultivation in the late 1990s and is rapidly gaining in popularity after having been commended by the Royal General Bulbgrowers' Association of Holland (KAVB), which acts as the international registration authority for the genus. (Plate 59)

Roscoea auriculata 'White Cap'

'White Cap' is the first bicoloured form to be named. The plant bears flowers typical for the species, but, as its name suggests, with a white dorsal petal "cap" that creates a pleasing contrast with the purple labellum and lateral petals.

Roscoea australis

Minimum temperature: -10ºC (14ºF) ?
Height: 25–40 cm (10–16 inches)

This species was finally described and named in 1982 by Jill Cowley, based on the accounts of and material collected by Frank Kingdon-Ward in 1956. The latter first encountered large colonies of the plants in Myanmar, in fruit, growing at 2210 m (about 7200 feet) on the harsh southern-facing Mindat ridge of Mt. Victoria, the highest of the Chin Hills mountain range, which forms the southernmost outpost of a southward extension of the Himalayas into Southeast Asia. When first seen, in April, the plants had overwintered with heavy quantities of seed, despite the fact that many had somehow worked themselves free of the soil and were "drifting freely on the hillside, having been snapped off below ground level, the ovary still intact". The harsh climate, combining heavy frost with strong winds, was presumed to account for the strange state in which the plants were found, and the fruiting bodies were generally protected from damage by the plant leaves that encircled them. Returning to the same location that June, Kingdon-Ward found the plant life of the mountain to be spectacularly abundant, with the *Roscoea* population in full flower and no worse off for the harsh winter.

This species most closely resembles the (slightly) more familiar *Roscoea tibetica*, with short, stout stems holding a rosette of two or three shiny green leaves. Each bicoloured purple and white flower has a hooded dorsal petal that is noticeably wider than in *R. tibetica*.

Roscoea australis occurs as an isolated population 3 to 4 degrees south of its closest geographical relatives and seemingly indigenous only to the Chin Hills. The genus is absent from the more northerly, neighbouring mountains of Manipur but reoccurs again in the Himalayas. This distribution indicates that *R. australis* has evolved from a now-disappeared common *Roscoea* ancestor, in isolation from its cousins, to suit its Burmese environment.

Given this geographical information, it is perhaps hardly surprising that *Roscoea australis* is one of the trickier member of the genus in cultivation, requiring a very harshly drained substrate to succeed. It is particularly intolerant of wet soil during winter. While perfectly hardy, it is perhaps best grown in containers where plants can be dried off when dormant and their overall water supply monitored more carefully. This species is also very reluctant to increase vegetatively, which is unusual in this genus. Seed is the only reliable means of propagation.

Roscoea australis is rare in cultivation and has been infrequently collected from the wild. Its habitat is now designated a national park, so despite its very limited natural distribution the species may be safe for now. No forms of *R. australis* have been selected or named, nor hybrids introduced.

Roscoea brandisii

Minimum temperature: -15°C (5°F)
Height: 25–35 cm (10–14 inches)

Endemic to the highlands of the Khasia Hills in Assam, this plant was originally named as a variety of *Roscoea purpurea*, although it is botanically and geographically closest to *R. auriculata*, and in some respects represents a dwarf form of that species. Aside from overall stature, the two species can be separated by their foliage: that of *R. brandisii* is narrow and falcate (sickle-shaped), with most leaves also lacking the distinctive auricles of *R. auriculata*. In addition, the flowers of *R. brandisii* are smaller with a distinctive elongated corolla visibly extending from the calyx.

Roscoea brandisii has been collected on several occasions. The plants were found growing in small numbers in grasslands, rocky ground, and on cliffs in open locations and also in semi-shade. The species is seemingly not in cultivation. One form apparently originated at the Royal Botanic Gardens, Kew, where it was named 'Purple Giant'. It was distributed more widely in the late 1990s and subsequently found to be referable to *R. tumjensis*.

Roscoea capitata

Minimum temperature: -10°C (14°F) ?
Height: 18–30 cm (7–12 inches)

This interesting and distinctive species is endemic to a small, restricted area of northwestern Nepal where it is fairly common among open meadows and shadier gullies, and particularly on rough, rocky areas at altitudes of 1200 to 2600 m (3900–8500 feet). When in flower *Roscoea capitata* cannot be mistaken for any other species in the genus: it produces a highly distinctive, pinecone-shaped collection of bracts that, uniquely, are held well above the foliage. The individual flowers are smaller than might be expected for the stature of the plant, but are typically produced in succession, in opposite-facing pairs from hairy calyces. Flowering occurs in July and

August in cultivation, June to September in the wild. Although wild plants in Nepal reportedly have flowers coloured magenta through mauve to white, cultivated specimens are of a fairly uniform violet purple colour.

Nathaniel Wallich described *Roscoea capitata* in 1822, but despite various attempts to bring the species into cultivation, it only became established in 1992, following the introduction of material by the Oxford University expedition to Ganesh Himal. William Baker, who led that expedition, described finding specimens growing in "vertical, grassy banks" and the "rubble of terrace walls". This latter habit gives rise to the idea that the plants are early colonizers of disturbed and previously cultivated ground, seeding, as they do, into suitable crevices among stone walls. Due to the failures of previous collections of this species to survive, those plants now in cultivation are being treated with kid gloves. They are kept in a very harshly drained medium (which is probably necessary) and maintained frost-free (which is almost certainly not necessary, given their natural climes).

Roscoea capitata is yet another *Roscoea* with a horribly confused history of naming in cultivation. The primary reason for this confusion is that plants originating in southwestern China were described or named as forms of this species, when they are, in fact, colour variants of *R. cautleyoides*. At the time of writing, the true *R. capitata* is not yet available in the nursery trade, but plants from the 1992 expedition are now well established in cultivation and it is hoped that they will soon receive a wider distribution. No hybrids or forms have been selected or named. Plants deriving from the 1992 introductions have the collection numbers BBMS 13, 55, and 56 (for Baker, Burkitt, Miller, and Shrestha). (Plate 60)

Roscoea cautleyoides

Minimum temperature: -25°C (-13°F)
Height: 18–45 cm (7–18 inches)

Roscoea cautleyoides is the best-known and most widely encountered *Roscoea* species in cultivation. It is also an easily grown and fine, if rather variable, garden plant. Typically, plants have strongly upright, narrow, lance-shaped or linear foliage, with single or small groups of beautiful flowers produced from pinkish or brown bracts. Blooming from May to July, *R. cautleyoides* is the first species in the genus to flower. Most plants in cultivation have flowers coloured pale lemon to primrose yellow, but purple and white forms also exist, and a rare pink-flowered form has been reported.

Cultivars with larger or non-yellow coloured flowers have been selected, and the best of these greatly enhance the appeal of the plant.

The species is a native of Yunnan and Sichuan provinces in southwestern China, where it occurs commonly at 2000 to 3500 m (6,600–11,500 feet) in a variety of habitats from open, sunny meadows, through rocky cliffs, to shady *Pinus* forest, and at the margins of *Quercus* and *Rhododendron* woodland. This multitude of habits suggests that the species tolerates different conditions, as has indeed proven to be the case in cultivation, where plants will thrive in woodland, alpine, or normal border conditions, especially if given a free-draining, but moisture-retentive, rich soil. When given appropriate growing conditions, *Roscoea cautleyoides* increases more rapidly than any other species of *Roscoea*, and fine, showy clumps can soon be achieved.

The species was twice named and described by François Gagnepain in 1902. Using material collected from the same site in Yunnan by Pierre Delavay in 1883, Gagnepain named one plant *R. chamaeleon* and the other *R. cautleyoides*. This slightly bizarre state of affairs arose because Delavay found material in May, when the plants were just beginning to flower, and again in July, when flowering was coming to a finish. Some 19 years later the collections were seen as being sufficiently different to appear to be two species, and this perhaps serves as a cautionary tale about the problems of identifying plants purely from dried material. (Plates 61 and 62)

Roscoea cautleyoides Blackthorn strain

Developed by Robin White of Blackthorn Nursery, Hampshire, Blackthorn seemingly is an intermediate seed strain "hybrid" between the purple and the pale yellow colour forms of the species. Plants are robust with large, showy flowers that display a wide and very variable array of patterning and streaking, always with purple overlaying a near white base. This strain also produces occasion mutations that display fused flowers with multiplied flower parts. (Plate 63)

Roscoea cautleyoides 'Early Purple'
'Early Purple' produces medium-sized, mid-purple flowers that are typical for the species. The flowers appear before those of any other *Roscoea*, with flowering commencing from late April.

Roscoea cautleyoides 'Jeffrey Thomas'

One of the best forms of the species, 'Jeffrey Thomas' has flowers with an enlarged labellum that opens primrose yellow and fades to creamy white. The hood retains a deeper, yellow colour. The end result is a pleasing bicoloured effect that is further enhanced by the overall larger flower size. This form is now available in the trade. (Plate 64)

Roscoea cautleyoides 'Kew Beauty'

After growing most forms of *Roscoea cautleyoides* alongside one another for comparison, I have found that 'Kew Beauty' consistently appears the most eye-catching. The flowers are of a good, strong lemon yellow and are substantially larger than those of the typical species. Overall plant stature is also larger. (Plate 65)

Roscoea cautleyoides var. pubescens

This variety is endemic to grasslands at approximately 2000 m (6600 feet) in Xichang county, southwestern Sichuan province. Originally described in 1988 by Zheng Yin Zhu as a separate species, *R. pubescens*, it was, after further study, proven to be indistinguishable from *R. cautleyoides*, apart from having pubescent sheaths, abaxial leaf surfaces, and slightly longer fruits.

Roscoea cautleyoides 'Purple Giant'

While the purple-flowered forms of the species are less distinctive than the yellow-flowered forms, this selection represents the best of that colour. It produces large flowers, in May and early June, broadly equivalent to those of 'Kew Beauty' but in a dark mauve-purple.

Roscoea cautleyoides 'Reinier'

This form, too, was selected for larger-than-typical flowers. The labellum is broader than that of the species. The flowers are a good solid colour of deep primrose.

Roscoea cautleyoides 'Yeti'

The Dutch breeder Rene Zijerveld selected this delightfully named cultivar. Plants bear large, pale yellow flowers with particularly extended lateral petals that are said to resemble a (bearded) Yeti.

Roscoea debilis

Minimum temperature: -10ºC (14ºF) ?
Height: 18–25 cm (7–10 inches)

Native on southern Yunnan, where plants grow among grasslands and forest margins at comparatively low altitudes of between 1600 and 2400 m (5200–7900 feet), this species is similar to *Roscoea capitata*, with medium-sized flowers of blue-purple or occasionally white, produced in succession, in groups of up to three in July and August. Unlike *R. capitata*, however, *R. debilis* has inflorescences generally nestled among the leaves or held on short flowering stems. Furthermore, the flowers are also variable, depending upon the moisture levels present in the location.

Little is known about the requirements of this species, but since Yunnan is now the subject of regular seed-collecting expeditions, it is hoped that new material will soon be established in cultivation. In the wild the plants have often been located in fairly dry situations. This habitat suggests that in cultivation the plants would be best grown under alpine conditions, with strong drainage and some winter protection.

Two separate names have been applied to this taxon due to flowering and morphological variations. *Roscoea debilis* itself was described by François Gagnepain in 1904, while *R. blanda* was named two years later by Karl Schumann. The two are now regarded as being synonymous, with the earlier name given preference.

Roscoea debilis var. *limprichtii*

This variety was recognized as separate from the typical species in 1923 (published as *Roscoea blanda* var. *limprichtii*). Plants are known only from the grasslands of Dali prefecture in western Yunnan at 1900 to 2000 m (6200–6600 feet). This variety is distinguished from the main variety (var. *debilis*) in two ways: the leaf underside is densely pubescent, and the plant is larger is stature and flower. This variety, although being even more sparsely distributed in the wild than var. *debilis*, would undoubtedly make a finer plant in cultivation.

Roscoea forrestii

Minimum temperature: -20°C (-4°F)
Height: 20–30 cm (8–12 inches)

This species was named by Jill Cowley in 1982 in memory of George Forrest, who collected the original material in 1913. A native of western Yunnan, *Roscoea forrestii* inhabits shrubland and growths of dwarf bamboo, as well as crevices and cliff ledges, in open, sunny positions at altitudes of 2000 to 3400 m (6,600–10,800 feet).

The species is very similar to *Roscoea humeana* and grows in the same locations, but can be separated from that plant by having less showy flowers, with considerably smaller petals and calyces. The flowers are also generally produced when the foliage is fully developed, unlike the near-precocious-flowering *R. humeana*. Like its close relative, *R. forrestii* occurs in both yellow- and purple-flowered forms, although only the latter is presently in cultivation.

Roscoea forrestii is relatively straightforward in its requirements, given a sunny, well-drained but fertile soil. The species is seldom offered for sale. As with so many roscoeas, confusion over the identity of some specimens does not help. No forms have been named nor hybrids produced.

Roscoea ganeshensis

Minimum temperature: -15°C (5°F) ?
Height: 12–15 cm (5–6 inches)

Roscoea ganeshensis was discovered in 1992 in central Nepal by Baker, Burkitt, Miller, and Shrestha, on the same Oxford University expedition that introduced *Roscoea purpurea* 'Red Gurkha', as well as various forms of *R. alpina*. The species has only been found in a single valley location, at Buri Gandaki, in the Ganesh Himal. It may prove to be endemic to that spot, where four other *Roscoea* species are also found in relative abundance. The plants were first spotted growing as a single colony in typical *Roscoea* ground—rough, disturbed, and rocky, amid terrestrial orchids, ferns, and grasses at 1900 m (6200 feet) on a steep bank beside a path. When compared with nearby specimens of *R. purpurea*, the new plants were soon confirmed to be distinctive.

Indeed, *Roscoea ganeshensis* is unusual in a number of ways. First, the species is rather dwarf. Second, although its leaves are broad, they are produced in a very congested manner on a short stem. Third, it is the sole

Indo-Himalayan species to bear hairy leaves, bracts, and calyces, a characteristic shared only with a few of the Chinese species of *Roscoea*. More distinctive from a gardener's point of view are the flowers. They appear in August and, at first sight, closely resemble the flowers of *Kaempferia rotunda* in shape, having a large, dark purple labellum with a texture of crumpled tissue paper. The labellum, which is held well apart from the predominantly white dorsal hood and petals, emerges facing upright, rather than horizontally, as is typical for the genus. Further floral differences involve the stamen structure and the enclosure of immature flower buds within a "sealed" calyx, which the emerging flowers must break through before they can unfold. Yet another interesting characteristic is that plants produce offsets at the base of the stems and leaves, where they contact the soil, a phenomenon not seen in any other species of *Roscoea*.

Roscoea ganshenensis has proven to be easy to cultivate under conditions similar to those of its native neighbours, *R. alpina* and *R. purpurea*. Although most specimens are currently maintained under glass, plants should certainly prove to be perfectly hardy and, given a gritty, open soil, quite robust. Overall, *R. ganshenensis* is a highly distinctive and very attractive plant, and it is hoped that the living collections well established at the Royal Botanic Gardens, Kew, and elsewhere will soon be given a wider distribution so that gardeners can enjoy the charms of these very special plants. No forms have been named or hybrids attempted.

Roscoea humeana

Minimum temperature: -20°C (-4°F)
Height: 10–35 cm (4–14 inches)

This relatively well-known species is native to Yunnan and Sichuan provinces of southwestern China. Within its territory it is rather widespread and can be found growing in natural alpine meadows and yak-grazed pastures, at the margins of scrubby conifer forest, and on rocky slopes and the faces of dry limestone cliffs, all at 2900 to 3800 m (9,500–12,500 feet).

After examining plants grown at the Royal Botanic Garden, Edinburgh, from seed collected by George Forrest, Isaac Balfour and William Wright Smith first described the species as *Roscoea humeana* in 1926. Previously it had been identified as part of *R. chamaeleon* (now a synonym of *R. cautleyoides*). Balfour and Smith were much taken by Forrest's plants and pronounced *R. humeana* as "the finest species yet known in the genus".

In its best forms *Roscoea humeana* is indeed magnificent. The flowers are typically large and showy, coloured pale to mid-purple, white, or some combination of the two. The dorsal petals are unusually large in both breadth and length, which makes the flowers distinct from those of other species, particularly the closely related *R. cautleyoides*. A further difference, which also add to the plant's appeal, is that the flowers are produced precociously, before the foliage, so that the display on a large clump of the plants is considerably enhanced. The leaves, produced typically in pairs, but up to six in a group, are handsome when they emerge, being up to 30 cm (12 inches) long by 6 cm (2½ inches) wide with a glossy, bright green appearance. The purple-flowered forms have red-stained stems.

Although most plants in cultivation are of the typical form (f. *humeana*), the flower colour and indeed the entire plant is variable, and some of the best bicoloured clones are now being named. Flowers occur in June and July in cultivation, considerably later than those of f. *lutea* (which see), so it is not surprising that the two forms do not appear to have interbred in the wild. Pure white-flowered forms of the species occur among wild purple-flowered populations, but have yet to be seen in cultivation. Violet-red and rose-purple forms have also been recorded in Sichuan province.

This species is fairly easy to cultivate and will succeed in several garden situations, but does best in a rich, moist soil that is well drained during winter. Plants prefer a bright position, but away from strong sun. A partially shaded or westerly facing location tends to suit them best. *Roscoea humeana* is not as vigorous as some species in cultivation, but it will increase at the rhizome to form good clumps over time. (Plate 66)

Roscoea humeana f. *lutea*

Specimens that agree with *Roscoeae humeana* f. *humeana* in all respects but which have pale yellow flowers are now given the designation f. *lutea*. Named by Jill Cowley in 2000, this beautiful colour form is a rarity among native populations of the species in Yunnan, although it does occur there spontaneously among the purple- and white-flowered stands. It is, however, the most common form in neighbouring Sichuan province. George Forrest recorded and collected plants from Yungning in Sichuan with deep yellow to orange flowers. Unfortunately, plants with these thrilling sounding flower colours are not yet in cultivation.

One interesting aspect of f. *lutea* is that it flowers very early in the *Roscoea* season, generally in mid-April, in conjunction with the similar and also yellow-flowered species *R. cautleyoides*. Perhaps the early flowering of the yellow-flowered plants indicates a successful relationship with a specific pollinator?

Forma *lutea* had its own, albeit brief, life as a species, namely, *Roscoea sichuanensis*. Miau, who used as the type specimen a plant collected by Joseph Rock, published this name in 1995, only for it to be sunk into *R. humeana* five years later upon the publication of the *Zingiberaceae* in the *Flora of China* (Wu and Larsen 2000). This form is now becoming available in the trade from stock having originated from seed collected by a Western expedition to Sichuan in 1992. Plants are proving no more troublesome to grow or maintain in the garden than those of the type, *R. humeana* f. *humeana*.

Roscoea humeana 'Purple Streaker'

This form, now reasonably well established in cultivation, bears flowers in June and July. The are pale to mid-purple in colour with striking longitudinal white stripes on the labellum and dorsal petals.

Roscoea humeana 'Rosemoor Plum'

A selection from the Royal Horticultural Society Garden at Rosemoor, north Devon, which has flowers of a uniform, dark plum purple together with a more vigorous habit than the usual species.

Roscoea humeana 'Snowy Owl'

Named and introduced by Nigel Rowland of Long Acre Nursery in Somerse, this cultivar was derived from stock that originated at the Royal Botanic Garden, Edinburgh. Plants bear unusually large flowers of pure white and to date represent the only named, white-flowered selection of the species.

Roscoea humeana f. tyria

Like f. *lutea*, this form was named by Jill Cowley in 2000. It differs from f. *humeana* in having showy flowers of a deep blackish, or Tyrian purple.

Roscoea humeana f. tyria 'Inkling'

This selection of f. *tyria* was exhibited at the Alpine Garden Society Summer Show South in 1997, from where it went on to be named. In June

1998 it received a Certificate of Preliminary Commendation from the Royal Horticultural Society. It is a magnificent plant, chosen for its large flowers that are a particularly intense, deep violet.

Roscoea kunmingensis

Minimum temperature: -20ºC (-4ºF)
Height: 8–12 cm (3–5 inches)

The two varieties of this species were named in 1992, having been first collected from Kunming in Yunnan province, China. The plants were discovered at adjacent sites, both growing in the understorey of *Pinus* forests above 2100 m (6900 feet). They are plants for the collector rather than the general gardener. Certainly from the material introduced to cultivation, neither variety has great horticultural appeal. At present, this species appears to be one of the least showy roscoeas, with plants producing relatively small, white-striped, mauve to purple flowers in May. Several new collections have been made in recent years and this species is now available in cultivation, at least within Great Britain. No forms have been named or hybrids produced.

Var. *kunmingensis*, the typical variety, has leaves 2.5–3 cm (1–1 1/4 inches) long. The very short bracts extend to just 5 mm (1/5 inch) when in full flower.

Roscoea kunmingensis var. *elongatobractea*

This variety was originally located at 2200 m (7200 feet) in Kunming and differs from var. *kunmingensis* in having broader leaves around 4 cm (1 1/2 inches) wide, a later flowering season, generally June, at least in its native habitats, and, most significantly, substantially larger flowering bracts. These bracts not only give the plant its varietal name, but are most distinctive, extending to around 8 cm (3 inches) when in full flower. The bracts are so long they almost cover the small flowers, at least in cultivated specimens that I have observed, and the flowers often remain only partially open. It is interesting to posit what evolutionary stimulus has caused this plant to develop its unusual bracts. Perhaps they are a weather protection mechanism. They certainly seem to do little to enhance the flowers' chances of being insect pollinated.

Roscoea nepalensis

Minimum temperature: -25ºC (-13ºF)
Height: 10–25 cm (4–10 inches)

First seen and collected in 1952 by O. Polunin, W. R. Sykes, and L. H. J. Williams, at 3050 m (10,000 feet) near Jumla in northwestern Nepal, this species was finally named by Jill Cowley in 1980. It is seemingly endemic to that corner of Nepal, and native plants grow at high altitude on rocky ground and grassland, as well as at the margins of coniferous forest. Relatively little is known about the requirements of *Roscoea nepalensis* as it has seldom been collected and is not presently known to be in cultivation. Florally it is said to be closest to the Chinese species, *R. debilis*; however, it is certainly distinctive, being the only *Roscoea* species to consistently bear all-white flowers. Coupled with this, the flowers of *R. nepalensis* are also rather showy, each with a very large, bilobed labellum and comparatively small, narrow dorsal and lateral petals. It is hoped that plants of this desirable species will soon be introduced into cultivation.

Roscoea praecox

Minimum temperature: -10ºC (14ºF) ?
Height: 7–30 cm (2³/₄–12 inches)

Native to shady shrubland, grassland pastures, and stream banks of Yunnan province, at 2200 to 2300 m (7200–7500 feet), this distinctive *Roscoea* species is the only truly precocious one: it always bears flowers before the leaves have emerged. These flowers are borne in groups of up to three on a short stem that is produced from the midst of the undeveloped leaf sheaths. The flowers are white, purple, or darker violet and of a relatively good size, with a labellum of up to 4 cm (1½ inches) long and 2.5 cm (1 inch) wide. On darker flowered plants this lip is also marked with white at the junction of the limb and claw. In China flowering occurs from late April to June.

Roscoea praecox in found in a small area of southern Yunnan, where the only other native *Roscoea* is *R. debilis*. Both species grow at similar, comparatively low altitudes. In her 1982 revision of the genus *Roscoea*, Jill Cowley suggested that the two taxa may in fact be varieties of the same species, but this is based solely upon examination of dry specimens. The precocious flowering habit and much earlier flowering season of this species would seem to mitigate against that. As the only two species in their habitat, clearly however they share a common ancestor at least. (Plate 67)

Roscoea purpurea

Minimum temperature: -25°C (-13°F)
Height: 15–40 cm (6–16 inches)

Roscoea purpurea is the second most widely cultivated species in the genus. It is also the type species for the genus and the first to be named, by James Edward Smith in 1806. In the wild *R. purpurea* occurs commonly throughout its large range, which extends from Himachal Pradesh in the Indian Himalaya, eastwards though the length of Nepal and on to Bhutan. The natural success of the species is undoubtedly due to its tolerance of a wide range of habitats, from moist, shady woodland margins to open alpine grassland and dry, south-facing cliff faces. Its success as a garden plant mirrors this, and, if provided with a reasonable garden soil, in neither too dry nor too wet a location, *R. purpurea* will thrive and will increase to form fine, handsome clumps of plants.

The wide range of natural habitats has resulted in a variety of natural forms. Short, compact plants occur in dry, exposed locations, and much taller and generally bulkier plants are found in more benign positions. The size and colouration of the flowers, stems, and foliage vary widely too, both from location to location and within specific populations. The most frequently seen form bears pale lavender to lilac-purple flowers, typically with a large, showy, and bilobed labellum and with a variety of white markings in the throat. Some forms, however, have an undivided lip, and white-flowered plants occur, most frequently in eastern Nepal, although they are more rare than is the case in some other species. Pink- and red-flowered forms have also been discovered, this last colour now being well established in cultivation.

Most *Roscoea* species have at one time or another been mixed up with at least one other. *Roscoea purpurea* is no exception, with a certain amount of confusion surrounding the separation of this plant from *R. auriculata*. The latter is a native of Sikkim, further east than any population of *R. purpurea*. Although the two are certainly closely related, they are also distinct from one another. *Roscoea auriculata* has darker, true purple (or pure white) flowers, a more strongly deflexed flower lip, and leaves that are uniformly auriculate (eared).

The natural variety of *Roscoea purpurea* combined with its frequency in the wild and the fact that it is a native of relatively accessible regions has led to many introductions being made. A larger number of forms have been named than in any other species, some from wild-collected material and others derived from breeding programmes. (Plate 68)

Roscoea purpurea 'Brown Peacock'

Selected in Holland, 'Brown Peacock' is one of the finest named forms. The leaves are longer and broader than those of the typical species. The stems are taller, reaching 50 cm (20 inches), and are very heavily flushed with deep mahogany red for their entire height. The flowers are very large and pale purple, providing a striking contrast with the dark stems. (Plate 70)

Roscoea purpurea 'Nico'

This much shorter, stocky growing form is devoid of all reddish brown colouration in the stems and leaves, but has exceptionally large flowers. The labellum in particular is enlarged at approximately 4 cm (1½ inches) wide by 6 cm (2½ inches) deep. The flower colour is pale to mid-lilac or purple.

Roscoea purpurea 'Peacock'

From the same Dutch stable as 'Brown Peacock' and 'Peacock Eye', this cultivar is probably the tallest of the named selections, with stems reaching around 70 cm (28 inches). The plant has a very sturdy and substantial look to it, with thick apple green stems and large lavender to purple flowers. (Plate 71)

Roscoea purpurea 'Peacock Eye'

The stem colour of this selection has some of the same deep reddish brown pigmentation as 'Brown Peacock', but it is not as dark or as striking. The flower is larger, and the lip is approximately 4.5 cm (1¾ inches) deep by 4 cm (1½ inches) wide and is mid-purple with a contrasting white throat. (Plate 72)

Roscoea purpurea 'Polaris'

This form was selected and named at The Europa Nursery as the best and most distinctive of a large batch of seed-grown plants. It is short and stocky with stems to around 20–25 cm (8–10 inches) long. The pseudostems are of a bright red colour, very similar to the colouration found in 'Red Gurkha'. The flowers, however, are very different, being exceptionally pale lavender to white in colour. Frustratingly, the flower colour is inconsistent and changes season by season, depending on the temperature at flowering time. At its best the plant displays flowers that are almost entirely white, with just the slightest touch of lavender on the labellum. (Plate 73)

Roscoea purpurea 'Red Cap'

This selected form has large flowers in the same colour range as 'Red Gurkha', although the colour is neither as bright, nor as clear as in that form.

Roscoea purpurea 'Red Gurkha'

This truly extraordinary form must rank as one of the most sought after and desirable hardy garden plants. Most wild plants of *Roscoea purpurea* have flowers in the purple to white range, but 'Red Gurkha' has stems and flowers that are a true, bright scarlet, without any hint of blue-purple pigmentation.

The red-flowered form of the species was discovered in the Buri Gandaki river valley in central Nepal. An expedition from Oxford University found the plants in August 1992 growing at 1990 m (6500 feet) in one isolated village location where the plants had spread among rough, ungrazed banks and rocky agricultural terraces. No other *Roscoea* taxa were found anywhere in the vicinity, suggesting that this small and highly vulnerable community of *R. purpurea* had evolved in isolation. Living plants were collected and brought back to the Royal Botanic Gardens, Kew, where they have been cultivated in pots under moist, shaded conditions in a cool glasshouse. Given such conditions 'Red Gurkha' has thrived and bulked up rapidly to form large clumps. Plants have been introduced into the nursery trade, allowing this spectacular ginger to finally be grown as a garden plant.

Flowers occur late in the season, even for *Roscoea purpurea*, with flowering commencing in August and continuing to September, depending on temperatures. Considering the extreme terrain where the wild plants are forced to survive (the more hospitable ground being either grazed or cultivated for agriculture), it is fair to say that 'Red Gurkha' should prove to be as easy in cultivation as the is normal species. Overall this plant should have a considerable impact on the popularity of hardy gingers in the garden, as well as providing a mouth-watering array of hybridizing possibilities. (Plate 74)

Roscoea purpurea 'Vincent'

This form was selected for its size. The tall, robust stems reach 60 cm (24 inches) or more and bear very large flowers of mid-purple.

Roscoea purpurea 'White Amethyst'

This striking form was found at the Royal Horticultural Gardens at Wisley and was named to commemorate the RHS's bicentenary collection of plants. The flowers are bicoloured, each with white dorsal and lateral petals, and with a broad labellum that is also predominantly white, particularly at the margins, but which shades to mid-purple at the centre. A clear white-striped midvein runs down each side of the divided lip. A similar form was distributed under the name *Roscoea purpurea* Striped Form in the late 1990s by Buckland Plants nursery, Kirkcudbright, Scotland. (Plate 69)

Roscoea schneideriana

Minimum temperature: -20°C (-4°F)
Height: 30–40 cm (12–16 inches)

This Chinese species is native to rocky slopes and mixed woodland at 2600 to 3400 m (8,500–10,800 feet) in Sichuan and Yunnan provinces, where plants are typically located in fairly moist, shady habitats. The habitat contrasts with the sunny, open meadowland that many roscoeas inhabit and suggests that, under garden conditions, *Roscoea schneideriana* is best treated as a shade lover.

This species is a close relative of *Roscoea debilis* and *R. praecox*, but occurs at considerably higher altitudes and also more northerly latitudes within China. *Roscoea schneideriana* is also distinct from these species in its flowers, which are uniformly purple, lacking the white striping that is typically found in the throat of many *Roscoea* flowers. Pure white-flowered examples have been reported but have yet to be seen in cultivation.

The most unusual feature of this species, however, is its foliage. Produced in a rosette, typically four to six very narrow, elongated leaves are held at the top of the relatively tall pseudostem. Each leaf is up to 23 cm (9 inches) long by as little as 5 mm (¹/₅ inch) wide. The flowers do not protrude greatly from this rosette and can be somewhat obscured by it, but the plants are, nevertheless, large and striking.

This species was originally described by Ludwig Eduard Theodor

Loesener in 1923 and named as *Roscoea yunnanensis*. Loesener identified two varieties, var. *schneideriana*, and var. *dielsiana*, separated by their leaf width and the length of the flower stem, but these differences are deemed to be inconsistent, and too minor to warrant separation. As with so many other roscoeas, Jill Cowley unravelled and corrected the naming of this species, publishing the name R. *schneideriana* in 1982.

Although still very rare as a garden plant, *Roscoea schneideriana* has become established in cultivation following the collection of seed by various expeditions to southwestern China in the 1990s. No forms or hybrids have been named.

Roscoea scillifolia

Minimum temperature: -20°C (-4°F)

Roscoea scillifolia grows in open, stony mountain grasslands at altitudes of 2700 to 3400 m (8,900–10,800 feet) in Yunnan province. It has variously (and bizarrely in the first instance) been described as a form of R. *capitata* and R. *yunnanensis*. Jill Cowley gave it full and much-deserved specific status in 1982.

The species is a very contentious one for two reasons. First, it has for many years invariably been confused with *Roscoea alpinia* in cultivation, and until the 1980s most collections of R. *scillifolia* were labelled as R. *alpina*. The two species bear almost no resemblance to one another and could not possibly be confused with one another in cultivation, but the misunderstanding arose from the lack of a proper name for this species. It is hoped that this issue is now largely resolved, although doubtless some plants are still mislabelled.

The second and still ongoing issue for *Roscoea scillifolia* is that, from a gardener's point of view, it is actually two very different "species". Not only is it distinct from all other *Roscoea* species, but also the two forms which represent it in cultivation are distinct from one another. To unravel this problem we need to look at the history of the plant. Pierre Delavay first collected the species in 1887, from a site in Dali prefecture in Yunnan, where he encountered a group of plants consisting of two very different forms. Specimens of one form had pale rose pink to white flowers, and those of the second form had deep violet flowers. Delavay collected and maintained the two forms separately. Because the plants were found together, they were subsequently treated as variants of the same species. Those two collections have largely given rise to the plants now in cultivation, although recently various new introductions of the pink form (not, to my knowledge, the dark form) have occurred.

In her 1978 treatment of the genus Jill Cowley stated that the two forms cannot be separated, even as varieties of the species, as there are many intermediate stages in colour and habit; however, no such intermediate forms have been introduced to cultivation, nor have they arisen from crossings between cultivated plants. The two forms also differ in far more than just flower colour. The morphology of the flowers is different, as is the plant stature, leaf shape and size, flowering time, vigour, seed production habit, seed germination success, and propensity to hybridize.

As new introductions of *Roscoea scillifolia* are made, these differences appear to be remarkably consistent, and it seems possible, at least, that the two are separate species, or, more likely, evolving or coexisting forms of one species, sharing adjacent territory and potentially hybridizing to produce intermediate forms. Other *Roscoea* taxa, such as *R. humeana* f. *lutea*, have been given separate designation from the species on seemingly less botanical difference. From a horticultural and commonsense point of view it is essential to have some means of separating the two plants which are fundamentally different in so many respects. They are discussed separately here.

Roscoea scillifolia dark-flowered
Height: 20–30 cm (8–12 inches)

The darker-flowered form of *Roscoea scillifolia* is the scarcer, seemingly both in cultivation and in the wild. In June plants bear few, narrow, almost grass-like leaves that are typically held firmly upright, while the flowers are produced on an elongated flower stem and are held well above the foliage. These flowers—and those of the pink form—are the smallest in the genus, being just a few centimetres (about 1 inch) across, but they are beautifully shaped and have a unique, intense violet colouration with contrasting yellow anther appendages. The flowers appear black at even the slightest distance, a characteristic enhanced by the shiny surface of the petals.

This form of *Roscoea scillifolia* does not readily self-seed (perhaps the unusual colour limits the number of pollinators that are attracted to the flowers?), although it is certainly fertile and can be successfully hand-pollinated to produce viable seed. The plants are also much slower to increase vegetatively, with relatively few new rhizomes forming each year.

This form seems to do best in a well-drained, fairly bright location, away from the competition of more vigorous plants that would swamp it. While its features are small, the plant is quite exquisite and also adapts well to container cultivation where its delights can be more readily appreciated at eye level. (Plate 75)

Roscoea scillifolia pink-flowered
Synonym: *Roscoea longifolia*
Height: 5–20 cm (2–8 inches)

Often encountered as *Roscoea alpina* 'Pink' or 'Rose' or even 'White', this plant has also recently been introduced and circulated under the invalid name *R. longifolia*. All these names are referable to *R. scillifolia* pink-flowered.

Plants bear small flowers (marginally larger than the dark form) of white, with minute stippling of rose red, giving an overall pale pink appearance. The amount of pigment varies, and some flowers can appear nearly white. Unlike flowers of the dark form, flowers of this variety have white anther appendages. This trait is a significant factor in determining whether this is a separate botanical variety of the species. Plants produce a rosette of thin, papery leaves that are typically broader than those of the dark form at 3 cm (1¼ inches) wide. The flowers are held on very short stems just above or in the midst of the foliage.

The pink form of *Roscoea scillifolia* is the easiest *Roscoea* to grow, thriving in almost any garden soil and in shade or sun, damp or dry. Clumps of plants regularly bear copious amounts of seed and will readily self-seed, so much so that if pampered they can start to get out of hand with innumerable seedlings sprouting in dense clumps. If left as they grow, these will generally be too close and competing to allow flowers to form, but if thinned out they will typically flower the year after germination. Even when not allowed to self-seed, plants will vigorously increase at the rhizome, although never enough to be a nuisance.

In cultivation *Roscoea scillifolia* pink-flowered produces flowers much later than the dark form. Indeed the two rarely overlap their flowering times, with the pink form bearing flowers from July to September. Crosses that I have attempted between *R. cautleyoides* and *R. scillifolia* pink-flowered have failed to produce seed, although this maybe due to pollen viability, since the pollen from the *R. cautleyoides* parent needs to be cold-stored for some time before the flowering of *R. scillifolia* pink-flowered allows pollination to be attempted. (Plate 76)

Roscoea tibetica

Minimum temperature: -25°C (-13°F)
Height: 10–20 cm (4–8 inches)

This species is probably the most misidentified and mislabelled *Roscoea* in cultivation. Most nursery stock in distribution labelled as *Roscoea tibetica* is not true to name, such plants most commonly proving to be *R. alpina*. Having said that, the true species is very variable (possibly comprising several subspecies) and correct identification is not always easy.

Roscoea tibetica nudges up against the eastern distribution limits of *R. alpina*, and the two are doubtless closely related; however, in its best forms, *R. tibetica* is perhaps the more appealing garden plant with (typically) larger flowers of bluish purple produced in June and July, and seated upon an attractive rosette of broad leaves, with each leaf up to 20 cm (8 inches) long. Wild variants are said to have flowers varying from violet through rose to white, but such forms have not yet been introduced to cultivation.

Roscoea tibetica has a very wide distribution, with populations occurring in Assam, Bhutan, Myanmar, Xizang (Tibetan Autonomous Region), and Sichuan and Yunnan provinces in China. The plants typically frequent areas of sunny grassland close to the edge of the permanent snowline at altitudes up to 4300 m (14,100 feet). *Roscoea tibetica* has also been found at lower altitudes, down to 2100 m (6900 feet), among moist, open pine forest and on scrubby cliff sides.

As is true for several other species, a wider natural distribution goes hand in hand with a less-specific habitat requirement, which in turn indicates a tolerance that should translate into ease of cultivation in the garden. That theory doesn't always work out in practice, but is justified in the case of *Roscoea tibetica*. It is among the easiest roscoeas in cultivation, particularly when given a bright, open location in the garden. No forms or hybrids have been named. (Plate 77)

Roscoea tumjensis

Minimum temperature: -20°C (-4°F)
Height: 20–60 cm (8–24 inches)

Jill Cowley named this species in 1982. The epithet refers to Tumje, Nepal, where the original type material was collected in 1953. Plants are endemic to grassland on rock-strewn slopes at 2700 to 3000 m (8900–9800 feet) in central Nepal.

This handsome species closely resembles *Roscoea humeana* but has a labellum that is much larger than the dorsal petals, whereas in *R. humeana* the dorsal petals form the most striking part of the flower. The large flowers are produced in May and June, and are, in cultivated stock, a bright lilac to purple. *Roscoea tumjensis* is almost certainly the largest of all *Roscoea* species. In her 1982 revision of the genus Jill Cowley gave the maximum height of the plant as 25 cm (10 inches); however, this was based on dried, wild-collected material. When fully grown, cultivated plants have very large rhizomes and are almost always substantially taller than 25 cm; in addition the flowers are generally produced before the leaves emerge, producing a more prominent display than in many other *Roscoea* species.

Cultivation requirements are similar to other, longer established species, such as *Roscoea humeana* and *R. purpurea*. *Roscoea tumjensis* seems to be more susceptible to rot caused by winter wet while the rhizomes are dormant. Bearing this in mind, a bright, well-drained spot should suit the plants well.

Even by the standards of *Roscoea*, this species has a confused history in cultivation. The earliest specimens were labelled as *R. humeana*, which is a strictly Chinese species, and *R. chamaeleon*, which is a synonym of *R. cautleyoides*. Much of the material in cultivation in Europe derives from a collection grown at the Royal Botanic Gardens, Kew, that was distributed under the name *R. brandisii* 'Purple Giant' or 'Purple King'. Other private collections of material from Nepal have also been identified as this species, and a wider distribution is now well underway. None of these collections has been given a (legitimate) name. No hybrids have been produced, although the size of the species certainly lends itself to use in a future breeding programme. (Plate 78)

Roscoea tumjensis 'Himalaya'

'Himalaya' is a large-growing, white-flowered form of the species recently selected by the Dutch grower Rene Zijerveld.

Roscoea wardii

Minimum temperature: -20ºC (-4ºF)
Height: 15–30 cm (6–12 inches)

Roscoea wardii is a very handsome species. This close relative of *R. australis* and *R. tibetica* has flowers that are consistently coloured a deep, sometimes almost black purple, each with a large, somewhat ruffled and very showy labellum.

Jill Cowley named this species in 1982, although plants were originally discovered and collected by Frank Kingdon-Ward more than 50 years earlier. Kingdon-Ward saw the plant on his expedition to Myanmar in 1926 and was evidently much taken by its beauty, a factor that encouraged him to collect from further populations in Assam and Xizang (Tibetan Autonomous Region), and again in Myanmar throughout the late 1920s and early 1930s, at altitudes from 2400 to 3700 m (7,900–12,350 feet). The species is also a native of Yunnan province. This relatively wide distribution is perhaps due to the plants' adaptability.

In the wild, populations often frequent shady, moist forest margins and shrubland, but *Roscoea wardii* has also been found growing successfully in open grassland, scree, alpine pasture, and on muddy snowmelt slopes. This range suggests to the gardener that the species is tough and should be amenable to various garden situations. *Roscoea wardii* is currently rare in cultivation, due primarily to a lack of distributed material rather than any problems with the plants in the garden, where they seem to perform well. Cultivated plants have thus far been treated as alpines, but the species should certainly prove to be more adaptable than that.

Roscoea wardii is rather slow to increase vegetatively. It is best reproduced from seed taken from isolated or insect-protected plants. No forms have been named or hybrids produced. (Plate 79)

Roscoea Hybrids

Roscoea 'Beesiana'

Minimum temperature: -20ºC (-4ºF)
Height: 40–70 cm (16–28 inches)

Roscoea 'Beesiana' is a variable hybrid between *R. cautleyoides* and *R. auriculata*, generally intermediate between the two species, with slender stems bearing narrow leaves and, typically, tall and angular flowers. Two separate but unnamed variants of this cross are widely cultivated in Europe: a dark form and a pale form.

The dark form is a vigorous garden plant with rather striking flowers (Plate 81). These have a base colour of pale primrose overlaid by combinations of various streaks and speckles of purple. The best dark forms have very large, ruffled lips, heavily speckled with blackcurrant purple.

The pale form, also unfortunately known as the white form (an instance of wishful thinking on the part of some past nurseryman rather than an accurate description?), is much closer to the *Roscoea cautleyoides* parent (Plate 80). It has somewhat larger flowers than those of the species. They are a paler cream colour with only occasional faint purple flecking, this being concentrated upon the lip.

It is interesting to note that when hybrids like this one between *Roscoea cautleyoides* and *R. auriculata* occur within *Roscoea*, the colours do not combine to form an intermediate or blended colour (in this instance yellow and purple could combine to form red, or at least overlay to give the appearance of orange-red, as they do in some other genera). Instead either one colour or the other is expressed, cell by cell across the surface of the flower. While frustrating in some respects for the breeder, this colouring can lead to some highly attractive patterning and very bold bicoloured flowers for the gardener.

Both the dark and the pale forms are excellent garden plants. They are undemanding in their cultivation requirements and vigorous in their rate of increase.

These hybrids are currently given the overall designation of *Roscoea* 'Beesiana', which implies that they are a single, selected clonal form, and therefore from a gardener's point of view, consistent and stable. Unfortunately, this is not the case. The intended designation of these hybrids was *R. ×beesiana*, with the various forms then being given their own clonal "fancy" names. Because the rules of horticultural nomenclature state that a plant with a Latinized name must have its description and naming published in Latin for the name to be valid, these two forms are for now lumped together under the 'Beesiana' banner.

Roscoea 'Beesiana Monique'

This Dutch hybrid is an exceptional *Roscoea*, almost a holy grail of the genus, as the flowers are pure white, totally lacking any of the yellow genes of the *R. cautleyoides* parent, and with just an occasional and tiny fleck of purple in the lip from the *R. auriculata* parent. The flowers are in other respects similar to those of other forms of this cross. The plant benefits from the same ease of cultivation and hybrid vigour as other hybrids. While scare in cultivation, 'Beesiana Monique' is sure to become widely circulated over the coming years. (Plate 82)

Roscoea 'Gestreept'

This recently introduced Dutch hybrid of *Roscoea cautleyoides* has flowers that are streaked alternately yellow and reddish purple. The cultivar name is the Dutch word for "striped".

Roscoea 'Grandiflora'

This plant originated at the Royal Botanic Gardens, Kew, where a large clump grew in the Asiatic rock garden. The history of the form is unfortunately lost, but it was originally named as *Roscoea cautleyoides* 'Grandiflora' by G. Preston, the former assistant curator, although it is not referable to a wild source. It appears to be a cross between *R. cautleyoides* and *R. humeana*. Plants bear primrose yellow flowers, similar to *R. cautleyoides*, but larger than is typical for that species, together with much wider leaves and a considerably shorter peduncle. (Plate 83)

Roscoea scillifolia × R. cautleyoides

Minimum temperature: -20ºC (-4ºF) ?
Height: 20–30 cm (8–12 inches)

This hybrid was produced at The Europa Nursery using a hooded plant (to prevent pollen contamination) of *Roscoea scillifolia* as the seed parent. The plant was emasculated (the anthers removed before maturity, so as to avoid self-pollination) and crossed with cold-stored pollen that had been earlier taken from a large-flowered clone of *R. cautleyoides*. The seedlings flowered two years after germination and produced unexpected results, to say the least. Because *R.* 'Beesiana' expresses the colours of the parent flowers in stripes and stipples, a similar effect was expected with this cross. Instead, the seedlings carried the same intense blackcurrant colour from the seed parent, but in much larger flowers held on a much taller flowering stem. The flower shape is exactly the same as that of *R. cautleyoides*, but intermediate in size between the two parents.

I have high hopes for this cross, as it serves to carry the superb pigment from *Roscoea scillifolia* into a plant that produces a far better floral display—the effect is that of a deep violet *R. cautleyoides*. Given that the pollen parent is also an easy and vigorous garden plant, the hybrids should hopefully follow suit, and the seedlings are currently being monitored so that the best can be selected for propagation. The next stage is to attempt to backcross this hybrid with *R. cautleyoides* to see if a bicoloured flower can be produced. (Plate 84)

Siphonochilus

Named by John Medley Wood and Millicent Franks in 1911, this exclusively sub-Saharan African genus of perhaps twelve species derives its name from the Greek "siphono", meaning "tube", and "chilus", meaning "lip", a reference to the broadly trumpet-shaped flowers. Most of the species were originally named as members of the short-lived genus *Cienkowskya*, which was created by German botanist Hermann Maximilian C. L. F. zu Solms-Laubach. *Cienkowskya* was made a subgenus of *Kaempferia* in 1904 by Karl Schumann, and the species were duly absorbed into that genus before being transferred, one by one, to *Siphonochilus*.

Unlike most genera in the *Zingiberaceae*, the genus *Siphonochilus* is comprised of dioecious plants, with male and female reproductive organs produced on separate plants. The females tend to be somewhat smaller, but in other respects are horticulturally indistinguishable. All have very fine, showy, more or less trumpet-shaped flowers of a rather delicate, tissue-paper consistency. Like *Kaempferia* flowers, *Siphonochilus* flowers consist of four petal-like lobes that appear similar but are actually made up of a single, divided labellum, together with a pair of lateral staminodes.

All *Siphonochilus* species are naturally deciduous, and their dormancy habits can be adapted to temperate winters reasonably well, provided they are protected from winter wet. In some cases this means that the rhizomes must be kept barely moist when the plants are dormant, a condition generally unachievable in the open garden. *Siphonochilus decorus* and *S. kirkii* are far more tolerant than other members of the genus and will succeed in an open, free-draining soil without having to be cultivated in containers that are dried off for winter.

Siphonochilus aethiopicus

Minimum temperature: -7°C (20°F)
Height: to 40 cm (16 inches)

The Natal ginger was originally named as *Cienkowskya aethiopicus* before that genus was dissolved into *Kaempferia*, and finally arrived in *Siphonochilus* courtesy of Brian Burtt in 1982. The specific name means "of southern Africa" and the species is, or rather was, native to the forests of Zimbabwe and South Africa itself, where it is now believed to be extinct in the wild due to a combination of habitat loss and overcollecting for the traditional herbal medicine trade. Fortunately, before its wild demise, *S. aethiopicus* was placed into micropropagation in South Africa and is now available from specialist nurseries in the United States and Africa.

The species is naturally deciduous, with 15-cm (6-inch) long lanceolate leaves produced on short, narrow, arching stems that emerge in early summer. The lightly fragrant flowers appear before the foliage on separate, short stems in May and June in cultivation (October to February in the wild), and are held at ground level. The flowers are large and extremely showy, reminiscent of *Kaempferia*, with four petal-like lobes made up of the bifurcated labellum and twin lateral staminodes. Overall the flowers are about 10 cm (4 inches) across and are predominantly coloured pale lavender with a prominent golden flare at the centre of the labellum. The throat of the flower is white.

Siphonochilus aethiopicus is nominally hardy but requires an essentially dry winter dormancy to prevent winter rot. It might better be accommodated in a pot where the flowers may also be more clearly observed at eye level. In other respects it is fairly easy to grow in a well-drained woodland soil in semi-shade.

Siphonochilus brachystemon

Height: to 30 cm (12 inches)

This very rarely seen species has recently been introduced to cultivation in the United States. It has broad, ribbed and rippled upright foliage with 20-cm (8-inch) long leaves that emerge in late spring. These are followed in June and July by a long succession of extremely beautiful, open trumpet-shaped, blue-violet flowers, each with a bilobed circular labellum and smaller pair of lateral staminodes. The throat of the flower is white, with small golden markings on the labellum. The blue floral colouration is extremely unusual for a member of the *Zingiberaceae*. Athough the plants have not been extensively trialled, they are proving to be very free flowering and increase well at the rhizome. An exciting future seems assured.

Siphonochilus carsonii

Minimum temperature: -7°C (20°F)
Height: to 60 cm (24 inches)

Also native to southern Africa, this species is very similar to, if less well known than, *Siphonochilus aethiopicus*. In midsummer plants bear narrow, arching stems with lanceolate leaves. These are preceded in June by the large, fragrant flowers. The flowers are pink, with a prominent golden flare at the centre of the labellum, which is surrounded by fine, deep red veining. *Siphonochilus carsonii* should be cultivated in bright shade and given a free-draining soil that is kept barely moist through winter. The species is occasionally available in the United States. (Plate 85)

Siphonochilus decorus

Minimum temperature: -10°C (15°F)
Height: to 60 cm (24 inches)

First described as *Kaempferia decora* by Denise van Druten in 1955, this species was moved to *Siphonochilus* by John Michael Lock as recently as 1999. *Siphonochilus decorus* is distinct from the other *Siphonochilus* species in cultivation; it has much larger leaves, to 45 cm (18 inches) long, that are broad, glossy, and heavily ribbed, more closely resembling those of *Curcuma*. The leafy stems emerge in May and June, followed by the inflorescences shortly afterwards on separate peduncles that emerge direct from the rhizome in June and August, each bearing between five and ten trumpet-shaped flowers. The flowers are extremely beautiful; each has a huge, 7-cm ($2^3/_4$-inch) circular labellum and a pair of broad, ovate lateral staminodes, all of which are deep primrose to daffodil yellow, with a darker golden flare in the throat of the labellum. The plants often flower in two distinct seasons, separated by a month or so.

Siphonochilus decorus is the easiest and most vigorous member of the genus in cultivation. Plants may be readily grown in semi-shade or light sun, given a moist, free-draining medium. In common with the rest of the genus, *S. decorus* must be kept as dry as possible in winter, but this may be achieved by covering the plants while dormant in the garden. This species is much more amenable to cultivation in the open ground than its cousins and it has more prominently displayed flowers. (Plate 86)

Siphonochilus kirkii

Synonym: *Siphonochilus roseus*
Minimum temperature: -7°C (20°F)
Height: to 45 cm (18 inches)

Joseph Hooker originally described this species as *Cienkowskya kirkii* in 1872, but it was transferred to *Kaempferia* along with the rest of the genus in 1982. In 1980 botanist Y. K. Kam of the Royal Botanic Garden, Edinburgh, determined that the plant was not a *Kaempferia* and created a new genus, *Cienkowskiella*, to accommodate it. This genus proved to be even shorter lived than the one whose name it referenced, as Brian Burtt, another, more senior Edinburgh botanist, determined that the species was referrable to *Siphonochilus*. Thus *S. kirkii* was finally born.

The species combines elements of both *Siphonochilus decorus* and *S. aethiopicus*. It bears extremely handsome, heavily pleated, 40-cm (16-inch) long, broad leaves that appear in May and are held upright on very short stems. The inflorescences occur in June and July on 10-cm (4-inch) long stems that emerge directly from the rhizome. The flowers are essentially bowl-shaped, with a substantial, bilobed circular labellum and pair of broad lateral staminodes. All of these have a slightly crimped margin and are coloured a soft, lavender-pink with delicate white veins radiating out from a white throat and a prominent golden labellum patch.

Siphonochilus kirkii is more tender and also less robust than *S. decorus*. It requires a shady position with a well-drained, woodland soil. (Plate 87)

Siphonochilus Hybrids

Siphonochilus 'Big Spot'

Height: to 45 cm (18 inches)

This hybrid from Tom Wood is a cross between *Siphonochilus kirkii* and *S. decorus*. It is said to have 8-cm (3-inch) long trumpet-shaped flowers of bright pink with two maroon stripes in the labellum.

Siphonochilus 'Pale Face'
Height: to 45 cm (18 inches)

Another hybrid from Tom Wood, this plant has large trumpet-shaped flow-ers of creamy white.

Zingiber

The type genus for the family *Zingiberaceae*, *Zingiber* was first named as *Zinziber* in 1754 by Miller. The amended spelling was published some six years later by German botanist Georg Boehmer. Although the original der-ivation of the word is disputed, the familiar Latin word for the culinary gin-ger (*Z. officinale*) was always "zinziber", the plant having been known and used in Europe since Roman times. In late Latin "zinziber" became "gin-giber" and directly produced the English word "ginger", as well as, most appropriately, being adapted to form the family name.

Zingiber is a genus of up to 150 species, all native to southern and south-eastern Asia, with particular concentrations in Thailand and southern China. Almost all the species are tropical or subtropical in origin. Some outlying plants in more temperate zones may be readily cultivated in hardy gardens, along with some truly tropical species that are proving to be intriguingly adaptable in their cultivation requirements.

Zingibers are medium-sized gingers from 30 to 180 cm (12–71 inches) tall. They produce erect, often thick pseudostems that bear their generally lanceolate leaves. Almost all the species produce their inflorescences on short, separate flowering stems, or peduncles, that arise directly from the rhizomes a short distance away from the pseudostems. The inflorescences are conical, sometimes greatly elongated, other times short and indistinct. Most species have an assemblage of tightly clasped, overlapping bracts that often age to yellow, red, or chestnut brown. These are often extremely showy and very long-lived, leading to the cultivation of a number of species for the cut-flower trade.

The flowers have a large labellum with the lateral staminodes fused onto either side to produce a three-lobed appearance. Even more distinctive is the thick, tongue-like, elongated, arching anther crest that is seated above the labellum with the stigma at the tip and with the pollen-containing the-cae towards the base, in the throat of the flower. The corolla splits into three lobes as the flower expands, forming, respectively, a hood above the labellum and a narrower pair of lobes below the labellum. The flowers are generally extremely short-lived, sometimes no more than a matter of hours, but are produced in succession for a long season.

Naming in *Zingiber* is in a state of flux. Several wild-collected species in widespread cultivation were only recently formally examined and described. Others remain to be named, and undoubtedly many new plants will be introduced over the coming years. Many of these will not be hardy, but the 40 or so species from China, plus those naturally deciduous monsoonal species from Thailand, Vietnam, and Laos, are all potentially exciting prospects for the temperate garden.

It is difficult to generalize about cultivation requirements for the genus, since a widely disparate collection of species may be attempted by the hardy gardener. Most, if not all, zingibers are forest-dwelling species by nature and require a well-drained soil, particularly when dormant. In temperate gardens they do not necessarily require shade, since summer and autumn heat is often the most important factor for good growth. A number of the most spectacular species are exceedingly difficult to flower outside of semi-tropical locations, not because they are not hardy, but because they do not receive a long enough growing season. In this respect they are similar to many other gingers, but the extraordinary quality of their inflorescences (in particular those species with large flowering "cones") makes the zingibers worth every possible effort to cultivate them.

Zingiber atrorubens

Minimum temperature: unknown
Height: to 110 cm (43 inches)

François Gagnepain described this Chinese species in 1902, but it is not known to be in cultivation. It is mentioned here, if only briefly, because it is among the most northerly situated species of the genus. Discreet populations have been found in Guangxi province, bordering Vietnam, and in the much more northerly situated Sichuan province, from where large numbers of hardy garden plants have originated. The glaucous, lanceolate leaves are up to 25 cm (10 inches) long. An egg-shaped, green or pale purple inflorescence is held at ground level and bears 5-cm (2-inch) long purple flowers.

Zingiber cassumunar

Synonym: *Zingiber purpureum* Roscoe
Minimum temperature: -10°C (15°F) ?
Height: to 90 cm (36 inches)

William Roscoe described this species in 1807 as *Zingiber purpureum*, but the name had already been given to another plant by William Roxburgh. Roxburgh separately gave the name *Z. cassumunar* to this plant in 1810.

Zingiber cassumunar was originally native to Thailand and the Himalayan regions of northern India and Nepal but is now in widespread cultivation throughout the world, where it has been put to a bewildering and ever-increasing array of medicinal uses. With the possible exception of *Z. officinale* (the culinary ginger), *Z. cassumunar* is probably the most important member of the *Zingiberaceae* in respect of its usefulness to mankind. Unlike many gingers whose properties have been exploited more in the past than they are today, much of its potential is only now being investigated. Despite this, *Z. cassumunar* is very rarely grown as an ornamental plant.

The species produces narrow pseudostems heavily clothed in lanceolate leaves. The inflorescence arises from an adjoining stem (peduncle) 20 cm (8 inches) tall and comprising a tight, pinecone-shaped arrangement of bracts that start out green and quickly age to a dark, bronzy brown. The flowers are cream to palest yellow with a prominent, ruffled labellum and are produced in a long succession throughout early autumn.

Zingiber cassumunar will succeed in mild, temperate conditions. It is naturally winter dormant in the wild and thus better able to cope with temperate conditions than are many zingibers. As is true for all zingibers, this one requires a free-draining medium in winter. (Plate 88)

Zingiber chrysanthum

Minimum temperature: -7°C (20°F) ?
Height: to 120 cm (48 inches)

First described by William Roscoe, *Zingiber chrysanthum* was named for the golden colour of parts of its flower. It is a fairly scarce native of Sikkim and northeastern India where plants are found growing in forest margins and clearings at elevations up to 1600 m (5200 feet).

The slender pseudostems emerge in late spring or (in cultivation) early summer and are clothed with 20- to 25-cm (8- to 10-inch) long, lanceolate leaves. The inflorescence appears in September on a separate, extremely short stem that emerges directly from the rhizome. The flowers are essentially held at ground level. *Zingiber chrysanthum* lacks the typical *Zingiber* cone-shaped inflorescence. Instead, the flowers emerge from a partially buried, loose arrangement of bracts. Individual flowers are produced for as long as the plants remain sufficiently warm, which in temperate gardens may be only a few weeks. The most decorative element of the flower is the large labellum, with a base colour of cream, heavily impregnated with purple-red or rusty orange stippling and veining, and with a large, centrally seated golden anther crest arching across the surface.

If conditions remain warm enough after flowering, then dark scarlet seed capsules will form in a tight mass at ground level, each eventually splitting to reveal a vivid red interior with seeds contained in contrasting white pulp (aril). This persistent fruiting display is undoubtedly the most ornamental aspect of this species, and plants should be positioned to allow for maximum autumn warmth to encourage their fruiting potential.

Zingiber chrysanthum is a naturally deciduous species and adapts to temperate cultivation reasonably well, although plants can be frustratingly slow to break dormancy and the small basal flowers are easily overlooked in the garden. Ultimately more satisfactory results may be obtained by container culture, with plants started into growth under heat in spring before transferring to a warm garden site. *Zingiber chrysanthum* is now available from a number of nurseries in Europe.

Zingiber citriodorum

Synonym: *Zingiber* 'Chiang Mai Princess'
Minimum temperature: -7ºC (20ºF)
Height: to 120 cm (48 inches)

John Mood found this deciduous species in the Chiang Mai province of northern Thailand in 1998. The plant was duly introduced into cultivation in the United States under the name *Zingiber* 'Chiang Mai Princess'. In 2002 Ida Theilade and John Mood published the plant as a new species under the name *Z. citriodorum*. The specific name refers to the strongly lemon scented rhizome.

Zingiber citriodorum is naturally winter dormant with new pseudostems emerging in May and June. In some plants the stems have a very unusual silvery grey appearance with similarly coloured foliage, but in others the foliage is a glossy green. In all cases the pseudostems are erect or slightly arching, and heavily clothed with upright-facing, lanceolate leaves. The inflorescence is borne on a separate 30-cm (12-inch) tall flowering stem and is also extremely unusual for a *Zingiber*, comprising a 15-cm (6-inch) tall, elongated open arrangement of tough, pointed bracts. These bracts emerge green, but age to a vivid red with tiny pure white flowers appearing from the bracts in succession for up to two months.

Zingiber citriodorum has not been fully tested for hardiness but might reasonably be expected to perform as do other deciduous gingers from the same region. Plants are strongly resentful of winter wet and when dormant must be protected with a solid, water-resistant covering if grown outdoors.

Zingiber clarkii

Synonym: *Zingiber clarkei*
Minimum temperature: -7°C (20°F)
Height: to 180 cm (71 inches)

Native to Himalayan forests of eastern Nepal, northeastern India, and Bhutan at elevations up to 1500 m (4900 feet), this unusual and large species produces thick, upright or gently arching pseudostems that bear substantial, narrowly ovate leaves. The leaves can attain 40 cm (16 inches) long and are glossy green on the upper surface with a silvery sheen beneath.

Unlike most zingibers, *Zingiber clarkii* bears its inflorescence at, or close to, the tip of the leafy pseudostem rather than on a separate flowering stem. The inflorescence is a semi-loose arrangement of pale green bracts up to 30 cm (12 inches) long. When it does reach its maximum length, the inflorescence invariably arches over, or becomes fully pendent under its own weight. Flowers emerge in small numbers in succession for three weeks or so and consist of a large labellum 8 cm (3 inches) long. The labellum is slightly frilled, arching, and golden yellow in colour stippled with deep red margins. A thick yellow anther crest reaches to the tip of the labellum and a narrow, pale yellow corolla lobe arcs away in the opposite direction.

Following flowering, fat green seed pods appear on the old flowering stems and hang like bunches of miniature bananas, before eventually turning red as they ripen. In the wild *Zingiber clarkii* flowers in July and August, but in cultivation it may not bloom until September, and seed is unlikely to be set under these circumstances.

This very spectacular, naturally deciduous species can be grown in temperate gardens when provided with a deep winter mulch and some protection from excess wet. A sunny, warm position will ensure that plants emerge as early as possible. Plants require copious food and water when in full growth.

Zingiber collinsii

Minimum temperature: -10°C (15°F)
Height: to 120 cm (48 inches)

Originally found in Vietnam in 1980 by Mark Collins, this spectacular species was finally named in 2000 by John Mood and Ida Theilade. The specific name honours the collector.

Zingiber collinsii is endemic to the forests of Vietnam. It has a naturally deciduous habit. Emerging in cultivation in May and June, the new leafy pseudostems are a deep burgundy red and are clothed with gorgeous, broad, ovate, gently nodding leaves coloured in alternating, symmetrical bands of pale silver and deep, purple-infused green, the colours appearing in a series of interconnected V shapes that span out from the midvein. The plants flower in autumn, and where temperatures allow for inflorescences to occur, these make a display that at least equals that of the foliage. Emerging directly from the rhizome on separate short stems each inflorescence consists of a very elongated, narrowed cone-shape arrangement of tightly clasped bracts. The bracts are a deep cherry red at the base of the stem, moving though deep orange at the centre to become rich sulphur yellow to apricot at the tip of the spike. The tiny flowers appear in ones and twos from the side of the bracts and are pale yellow with red netting on the throat of the labellum. The anther crest has a dark red tip.

No right-thinking gardener would conceive that such an ultra-tropical-looking plant could possibly be even remotely hardy, yet *Zingiber collinsii* has been successfully trialled at -10°C (15°F) in the United States. The rhizomes are exceptionally sensitive to wet while dormant, and the plants should certainly be mulched and fully covered with a rain-shelter for winter. *Zingiber collinsii* requires a position in bright shade, with enough warmth to promote growth but little direct sun that might result in foliar scorch. The species has been micropropagated in the United States and should soon become widely available to gardeners worldwide.

Zingiber ellipticum

Minimum temperature: -7°C (20°F) ?
Height: to 100 cm (39 inches)

Originally named as *Plagiostachys elliptica* by Shao Quan Tong and Yong Mei Xia in 1987, this species was transferred to the genus *Zingiber* by Qi Gen Wu and Te Lin(g) Wu in 1996. It is seemingly endemic to forests of Maguan county in southeastern Yunnan province.

This species is separated from other members of the genus by its inflorescence, which, although stemless and appearing on the leafy pseudostems, is not held at the terminus but rather breaks through the sheath at the base of the stem to be held parallel to the pseudostem. The robust pseudostems hold bold, elliptic leaves that are densely pubescent beneath and can reach 55 cm (22 inches) long by 15 cm (6 inches) wide. The inflorescences emerge in August and September and appear 20–50 cm (8–20 inches) above ground level. Each flowering spike is a narrow, torch-shaped arrangement of overlapping, pale cream bracts, up to 18 cm (7 inches) tall, bearing a succession of flowers. The labellum is 2.5 cm (1 inch) long, lined with purple and blotched with yellow.

Zingiber ellipticum has been successfully introduced to cultivation. Its hardiness has yet to be assessed.

Zingiber mioga

Minimum temperature: -23°C (-10°F)
Height: to 80 cm (31 inches)

Named *Amomum mioga* by Carl Thunberg in 1784, this species was transferred to *Zingiber* by William Roscoe in 1807. It remains something of an anomaly in the genus and is the only species that occurs in Japan, where it is widely grown for its culinary and medicinal uses. Although long naturalized there, the species may well have been introduced to Japan. It is native to almost all of southern China where the plants grow in shady, moist forested river and mountain valleys.

Zingiber mioga is naturally deciduous and emerges from dormancy in April, to produce pseudostems clad with narrow, pale green, lanceolate leaves up to 35 cm (14 inches) long by 5 cm (2 inches) wide. The inflorescence is borne on a separate, short stem that emerges direct from the rhizome from August to October. Each flowering spike consists of a number of loosely held reddish-purple veined green bracts that open in succession to reveal attractive flowers with a conspicuous 3-cm (1¼-inch) labellum. The flowers are seated more or less at ground level and are typically pale creamy yellow. Cornish grower Edward Needham has collected a notably darker, daffodil-yellow flowered form from China (Plate 89).

Zingiber mioga is the hardiest member of the genus, and indeed one of the hardiest gingers, on a par with the toughest *Roscoea* species. It may be readily cultivated in many temperate gardens where it enjoys a shady, moist location. Plants have been successfully overwintered to extremely low temperatures in Canada with the benefit of a protective and insulating layer of snow cover. They are correspondingly intolerant of too much summer heat and should be kept out of strong sunlight. *Zingiber mioga* is resentful of too much winter wet while dormant (although not to the same extent as the semi-tropical species). The growing medium should be suitably coarse to allow for good drainage. Otherwise this is an easy and vigorous ginger that should be far more widely grown as a hardy ornamental.

Zingiber mioga 'Dancing Crane'
Minimum temperature: -12°C (10°F)
Height: to 60 cm (24 inches)

This variegated form was selected by Japanese grower Masato Yokoi and is widely available in the United States and Europe. Compared to the typical species, 'Dancing Crane' produces shorter, stout, upright pseudostems with broad pale green leaves that have irregular, asymmetrical cream margins and occasional creamy white slashes across their surface. The plant is less hardy than the typical species, although in other respects it is it is just as easily grown, vigorous, and free flowering.

Zingiber neglectum

Minimum temperature: -10°C (15°F)
Height: to 180 cm (71 inches)

This spectacular species is a native of shady forest sites in Indonesia but is naturally deciduous and has been found to be remarkably hardy. Leafy shoots emerge in June and produce robust, upright pseudostems with long, 45-cm (18-inch), lanceolate leaves. Where temperatures allow, the flowering stems appear separately, directly from the rhizome in September and

October, and bear a 30-cm (12-inch) tall torch-like arrangement of cup-shaped, interlocking bracts. These bracts start out green but age to deep red at the lip, retaining the contrasting green beneath. The small white flower has a broad, reflexing labellum that is stippled and marked with purple. The inflorescence is extremely long-lived and flowers appear in succession for six weeks or so.

Although root hardy, this beautiful ginger is unlikely to bloom in most temperate locations, since it requires considerable heat in summer and an elongated balmy autumn. It can certainly be tried in the U.S. South, where it should succeed given a position in full shade, with a free-draining soil and protection from winter wet.

Zingiber niveum

Synonym: *Zingiber* 'Milky Way'
Minimum temperature: -10ºC (15ºF) ?
Height: to 90 cm (36 inches)

Another species named by John Mood and Ida Theilade in 2002, this plant was originally bought in 1995 from a Lao plant collector who had located a population growing at approximately 250 m (820 feet), near Savannakhet on the Laotian border with northern Thailand. The plant was first cultivated at the Nong Nooch Tropical Gardens, south of Bangkok, and from there material was introduced to the United States under the name 'Milky Way' by nurseryman Stephen Nowakowski of Houston, Texas.

Zingiber niveum is naturally deciduous, with silvery, glaucous new pseudostems emerging in May or June to bear numerous, narrowly lanceolate upright 30-cm (12-inch) long leaves. The inflorescence normally appears on a separate 30-cm (12-inch) stem (occasional terminal inflorescences can also occur on the leafy pseudostems) and consists of a short, club-shaped arrangement of tightly clasped pure white bracts that open in succession from August for up to two months, and eventually flush with pink as they age. The flowers are clear yellow, with a narrow, bicleft labellum and a large hood from the upper corolla lobe.

Zingiber niveum is best in a warm location with moderate sun and an open, free-draining soil. In such conditions, plants are reasonably hardy and fairly vigorous. This extremely striking *Zingiber* species has rapidly proven to be one of the best and most easily grown members of the genus for temperate gardens. It is now available in the United States.

Zingiber officinale

Minimum temperature: -10°C (15°F)
Height: to 180 cm (71 inches)

This is the familiar culinary ginger, in cultivation for at least 2000 years, and long the most commercially important member of the *Zingiberaceae*. While *Zingiber officinale* is cultivated as a spice throughout most of the tropical and subtropical world, it has limited value as an ornamental and ranks, perhaps, as an interesting curiosity more than anything.

Carl Linnaeus first described the species in 1753 as *Amomum zingiber*. In 1807 William Roscoe transferred it *Zingiber* under the name *Z. officinale*. The specific name means, literally, "useful plant". There are a variety of sterile commercial crop cultivars, although no named varieties are available as ornamentals.

Growing the plants from shop-bought rhizomes will produce variable results, with some forms no more than 60 cm (24 inches) tall and others 180 cm (71 inches) or more. In all cases *Zingiber officinale* has narrow arching leafy pseudostems clothed with 25-cm (10-inch) long, narrow, linear leaves. The overall impression is similar to a short, if rather lax, bamboo. Plants flower from a separate, 20-cm (8-inch) stem that arises directly from the rhizomes. The flowering spike bears a tight cone of green bracts from which emerge tiny, translucent pale yellow flowers, each with a purple and white labellum. The inflorescence is very rarely seen in cultivation, even in tropical areas, and will almost certainly never be produced in hardy gardens.

Zingiber officinale is not a naturally deciduous species and is therefore not best adapted to temperate cultivation. Nevertheless, the plants are relatively hardy and may be accommodated in a sunny location given a free-draining, but nutritious soil.

Zingiber rubens

Minimum temperature: -12°C (10°F)
Height: to 150 cm (60 inches)

Named by William Roxburgh in 1810, this deciduous species is native to the northeastern Himalaya from Nepal though Sikkim to India. The pseudostems appear in May or June and bear broad, lanceolate leaves that reach 40 cm (16 inches) long. Inflorescences occur in August on separate, very short true stems that arise directly from the rhizome, and are seated on or just above ground level, each consisting of a tight cluster of deep red, pointed bracts. The flowers open in succession for approximately three weeks and consist mainly of a large, showy labellum that has a base colour of pale yellow, very heavily speckled and lined with ox-blood red. A narrow, pinkish red corolla lobe arches away above the labellum and a prominent golden yellow anther crest emerges from its throat.

Zingiber rubens is among the hardiest zingibers and may be readily cultivated in a warm, sheltered location in semi-shade or partial sun. The species is available in the United States and fairly widely so in Europe.

Zingiber spectabile

Minimum temperature: -7°C (20°F)
Height: to 180 cm (71 inches)

Named by William Griffith as the "showy" (spectabile) *Zingiber*, the plant has also become known as the beehive ginger in reference to its magnificent inflorescences. *Zingiber spectabile* is native to southern Thailand, peninsular Malaysia, and Sumatra where plants grow in heavy shade of dense tropical forest. Amazingly they have proven tolerant of several degrees of frost, although they require a prolonged period of heat to bloom.

Sturdy thick, dark red pseudostems bear narrowly ovate, gently arching leaves that reach around 30 cm (12 inches) long. The famed inflorescences form on separate stems produced directly from the rhizome from July to October. They are the largest in the genus and among the most impressive flowering bodies in the gingers, with substantial flowering spikes 30 cm (12 inches) tall. The inflorescences consist of torch-shaped arrangements of dozens, in some cases hundreds, of pouch-shaped bracts. Newly emerged bracts are green in colour but slowly age to deep red at the outer margins, beginning from the base of the inflorescence. A typical display has the two colours merging into one another. The flowers are produced in small numbers in a long succession and have a tongue-like, deep mahogany-brown labellum, liberally scattered with golden yellow spots, and a dark brown central anther crest.

Coming as it does from non-seasonal, tropical regions, *Zingiber spectabile* is a naturally evergreen species. It will grow but not flower in temperate locations where it will become deciduous. The plant needs an early heat boost plus a prolonged, mild autumn to succeed in the long term or to bloom. Nevertheless, it can be expected to survive where protected in the southern United States and may be transferred to pot culture in the United Kingdom to allow for an extended growth season. In dormancy *Z. spectabile* must be protected from winter wet; it requires a full rain-proof covering to prevent rhizome rot. (Plate 90)

Zingiber zerumbet

Minimum temperature: -10°C (15°F)
Height: to 200 cm (79 inches)

Originally named as *Amomum zerumbet* in 1753 by Carl Linnaeus, this very well known ginger was transferred to *Zingiber* by William Roscoe in 1806. The wild origins of the species are unclear as it has long been cultivated as an ornamental and, to a lesser extent, as a medicinal plant. It is popularly known as the shampoo ginger, reflecting just one, albeit particularly unusual, purpose to which the species has been put; in this case it is the sticky, soapy residue that the flower bracts exude that is used as a shampoo. Naturalized populations can be found in Hawaii and Florida. The species also occurs across southern China, most of Southeast Asia, Myanmar, India, and Sri Lanka at altitudes of up to 1200 m (3900 feet).

Zingiber zerumbet produces robust, upright pseudostems that emerge in May or June, depending on local temperatures, and that are clothed by lanceolate leaves up to 40 cm (16 inches) long by 8 cm (3 inches) across. The inflorescence arises directly from the rhizome on a separate 10- to 30-cm (4- to 12-inch) peduncle. In tropical areas these are produced in July and August, but in temperate gardens, where the plants have been later to emerge from dormancy, the species produces flowers in September and continues into October if weather permits. The inflorescence takes the form of a 10- to 15-cm (4- to 6-inch) tall, pinecone-shaped arrangement of tightly clasped bracts that emerge green and slowly mature to bright red. The flowers appear in small numbers in a long succession and are uniformly cream to pale yellow with a ovate, three-lobed 3-cm (1?-inch) labellum, and three similarly coloured corolla lobes.

Zingiber zerumbet is naturally deciduous and has been extensively tested for hardiness. Like many other sub-tropical gingers, it can be slow to break dormancy and it requires a prolonged period of heat before emerging. In colder areas, this can mean that the plants do not have a long enough growing season to enable them to flower successfully, but in this respect they are no different than many *Hedychium* species and can reasonably be attempted wherever that genus succeeds. *Zingiber zerumbet* is suitable for a sunny, warm position. While not severely affected by overwintering problems, it should not be planted in heavy clay soil or allowed to overwinter in water-saturated conditions. In warmer areas *Z. zerumbet* is extremely vigorous and enjoys the dubious distinction of having been labelled a weed species in Hawaii and other Pacific islands.

As might be expected from such a wide-ranging species, *Zingiber zerumbet* has yielded different forms. Some of these have been collected, although relatively few have been properly named. Two are described here.

Zingiber zerumbet 'Darceyi'
Synonyms: *Zingiber zerumbet* 'Darcii', *Z. zerumbet* 'Darcyi', *Z. zerumbet* 'Variegata'
Height: to 90 cm (36 inches)

This well-known variegated cultivar was originally described as a new species (*Zingiber darceyi*) in 1890 but is readily referable to *Z. zerumbet*, differing only in its height and its foliage. The pseudostems are shorter than those of the typical species. The leaves reach approximately 20 cm (8 inches) in length and have narrow, irregular bands of creamy white at the margins, concentrated towards the leaf axis, with occasional slashes of cream across the main leaf surface. 'Darceyi' is as vigorous and as hardy as the typical species and is widely available worldwide.

Zingiber zerumbet 'Twice as Nice'
Height: to 60 cm (24 inches)

This dwarf cultivar originated with Tim Chapman of Gingerwood Nursery, St. Gabriel, Louisiana. It is named for its habit of flowering not just on basal stems, but also at the terminus of each of the leafy pseudostems. The inflorescences are somewhat smaller than those of the typical species, but colour in the same way. This cultivar is currently in micropropagation and may be expected to become widely available over the coming years.

Chapter 9
Tropical Gingers in Cultivation

Except for the alpine and sub-alpine species of gingers, that is, *Roscoea*, *Cautleya*, and high-altitude *Hedychium*, all the species and varieties listed in chapter 8 may also be grown as tropicals. Some genera, notably *Curcuma* and *Globba*, and most *Kaempferia* species have a deciduous habit, even when grown in tropical conditions, and a period of dormancy forms a natural part of their annual growth cycle. Many other gingers will remain evergreen when maintained in tropical conditions, even when this is not their natural habit.

For some escapees that have been introduced from temperate climates to tropical zones, this change in environment has allowed them to grow with unchecked vigour. Several genera (primarily *Hedychium*, but also *Zingiber*) that would naturally be deciduous have become serious weeds among the delicate flora of New Zealand, Hawaii, South Africa, and a number of Atlantic and Pacific islands, where there is no natural seasonal barrier, and plants remain in growth year-round. These, however, are very much the exceptions. Most members of the *Zingiberaceae* and the *Costaceae* are naturally fully evergreen and are truly tropical plants that can only be cultivated where temperatures consistently remain above 15°C (59°F).

Among the most popular tropical species, with many named cultivars, is the cone ginger, *Alpinia purpurata* (Plate 3). A substantial plant native to the islands of the South Pacific, it can grow to 360 cm (142 inches) tall and rather more across. This species is much used in the cut flower trade. It produces elongated, 30- to 45-cm (12- to 18-inch) tall spires of red or pink bracts that last for approximately three weeks. The leaves are 90 cm (36 inches) long, banana-like, and oblong.

Another noteworthy and widely available alpinia is *Alpinia vittata*, a native of New Guinea and probably the most dramatically variegated ginger (Plate 4). The plant rarely flowers in cultivation. Yet, its deep green,

60-cm (24-inch) long lanceolate leaves, each marked by large, asymmetrical splashes of bright white, are certainly reason enough to include it in any tropical collection.

Costus has a wealth of beautiful species to grow, and the best specialist nurseries now offer up to 20 varieties, most originating from South America. The 210-cm (83-inch) tall Costa Rican red tower ginger, *C. barbatus*, is among the best-established and most popular species (Plate 11). It produces 30-cm (12-inch) tall flower spikes of intensely red bracts, with contrasting, bright gold tubular flowers. Another species native to Costa Rica as well as neighbouring Panama is the magnificent *C. glaucus* whose stems can reach 500 cm (200 inches) in its native humid forest habitats, to be toped with ruffled white flowers that appear from May to August (Plate 13).

Costus amazonicus is a fine, variegated plant and has 240-cm (96-inch) stems, clothed by ovate leaves that are very heavily lined with creamy white. *Costus lateriflorus* is one of the African species represented in cultivation, and plants produce an abundance of narrow stems clothed with fleshy obovate leaves and beautiful trumpet-shaped, crepe-paper-textured daffodil yellow flowers throughout summer (Plate 14). As is true for many genera of gingers, renewed interest in cultivation of *Costus* has encouraged the introduction of many new forms. Most of these have yet to be formally identified and are currently offered as *Costus* sp., with an additional, descriptive, "fancy" name.

All members of the *Costaceae* are suitable for tropical cultivation, and indeed most can only be grown in this way. The pretty 60-cm (24-inch) tall, shade-loving *Monocostus uniflorus* bears large, trumpet-shaped, canary yellow flowers. With similar flowers, but on a much larger scale is *Dimerocostus strobilaceus*, a magnificent native of Central and South America. It produces cane-like stems that reach 360 cm (142 inches), topped by large racemes of flaring, yellow trumpet flowers.

While most *Hedychium* species are more or less temperate hardy, a few, generally epiphytic, tropical species have entered in cultivation. The most widely distributed of these is *H. phillipinensis* (more commonly, if incorrectly, known as *H. muluense*), a small species native to Malaysian Borneo that bears small, but pretty flowers with green petals, an orange stamen, and a twisted white labellum and lateral staminodes.

Zingiber probably has the most potential for the tropical gardener, with a plethora of new introductions arriving from Southeast Asia. As with *Costus*, many of these are not fully identified, may represent species new to science, and are generally offered without specific identification. Further species that are established in cultivation include *Z. gramineum*, the palm ginger, with highly distinctive narrow leaves arranged on the stem to resemble a feather palm, and the semi-dwarf, near-black-leafed *Z. malaysianum* 'Midnight', which bears beautiful pinkish apricot flower spikes. Species such as *Z. spectabile* will also perform much better and flower far more readily if grown under tropical conditions.

Without doubt the most spectacular genus in the *Zingiberaceae* and arguably among all flowering plants is *Etlingera*, a group of about 70 species, primarily native to Indonesia. These species produce tall, sometimes massively tall, cane-like leafy pseudostems and inflorescences on separate stems that emerge directly from the rhizome. The showy part of the inflorescence is the involucre of petal-like, sterile bracts. These are generally vivid red or pink, and are often beautifully sculpted and arranged in crown- or star-like shapes. In some species, such as *E. triorgyalis* and *E. littoralis*, the flowering stems are just a few centimetres (about 1 inch) tall, with the inflorescences held at ground level.

Etlingera corneri was introduced from Thailand and has much taller flowering stems that bear overlapping bracts arranged like rose petals. The most widely distributed species is the giant *E. elatior*, or torch ginger. This Indonesian native is grown in tropical gardens the world over, and many cultivars have been selected. The plants can reach 600 cm (236 inches) tall, with hugely thick stems and enormous 120-cm (48-inch) long, oblong leaves. The inflorescences are produced more or less at eye level and have a rim of broad, flaring sterile bracts at the base, supporting a cone of white-edged fertile bracts that peel open to reveal golden-lipped flowers.

Appendix 1
Where to See Gingers

United Kingdom

Birmingham Botanical Gardens and Glasshouses
Westbourne Road
Edgbaston
Birmingham, B15 3TR
www.birminghambotanicalgardens.org.uk

Bristol Zoo Gardens
Clifton
Bristol, BS8 3HA
http://bristolzoo.org.uk
Holder of the NCCPG (National Council for the Conservation of Plants and Gardens) collection of *Hedychium*.

Cruckmeole House
Cruckmeole
Shrewsbury
Shropshire, SY5 8JN
www.nccpg.com
Open by appointment only. Holder of the NCCPG collection of *Roscoea*.

Eden Project
Bodelva
St Austell
Cornwall, PL24 2SG
www.edenproject.com

Logan Botanic Garden
Port Logan
Stranraer
Wigtownshire, DG9 9ND
www.rbge.org.uk/rbge/web/visiting/lbg.jsp

Royal Botanic Garden, Edinburgh
20A Inverleith Row
Edinburgh, EH3 5LR
www.rbge.org.uk

Royal Botanic Gardens, Kew
Richmond
Surrey, TW9 3AB
www.rbg.kew.org.uk

Savill Garden
Windsor Great Park
Berkshire, SL4 2HT
www.savillgarden.co.uk

Wakehurst Place, Royal Botanic Gardens
Ardingly
Haywards Heath
West Sussex, RH17 6TN
www.rbg.kew.org.uk/visitor/visitwp.html

Wales, National Botanic Garden
Llanarthne
Carmarthenshire, SA32 8HG
www.gardenofwales.org.uk

United States

Fairchild Tropical Gardens
10901 Old Cutler Road
Miami, Florida 33156
www.fairchildgarden.org

Florida Botanical Gardens
12175 125th St North
Largo, Florida 33774
www.flbg.org

Fullerton Arboretum
1900 Associated Road
Fullerton, California 92831
www.arboretum.fullerton.edu

Mercer Arboretum and Botanical Gardens
22306 Aldine Westfield Road
Humble, Texas 77338
www.cp4.hctx.net/mercer

Missouri Botanical Garden
4344 Shaw Boulevard
St. Louis, Missouri 63166
www.mobot.org

Mitchell Park Horticultural Conservatory
("The Domes")
524 South Layton Boulevard
Milwaukee, Wisconsin 53215
www.countyparks.com/horticulture

New Orleans Botanical Garden
1 Palm Drive
New Orleans, Louisiana 70124
www.neworleanscitypark.com/nobg.php

New York Botanical Garden
Bronx River Parkway & Fordham Road
Bronx, New York 10458
www.nybg.org

Phipps Conservatory and Botanical Gardens
One Schenley Park
Pittsburgh, Pennsylvania 15213
www.phipps.conservatory.org/index1.html

San Antonio Botanical Garden
555 Funsten
San Antonio, Texas 78209
www.sabot.org

Waimea Arboretum and Botanical Garden
59-864 Kamehameha Highway
Haleiwa, Hawaii 96712
www.botanique.com/tours/ustoursp/HI/hi.wai
mea.html

Appendix 2

Where to Buy Gingers

There are numerous wholesale suppliers for gingers in the United States and Southeast Asia, but until very recently few retail nurseries were specializing in these plants. That situation is now changing, particularly in the United Kingdom. All of the following suppliers offer a good selection, with most also offering a mail-order service. Where a supplier offers only one genus of gingers on its list, that genus is noted beside the nursery name.

United Kingdom

Amulree Exotics
Tropical Wings
Wickford Road
South Woodham Ferrer
Essex, CM3 5QZ
www.turn-it-tropical.co.uk

Crûg Farm Plants
Griffith's Crossing
Caernarfon
Gwynedd, LL55 1TU
www.crug-farm.co.uk
Mail-order not available.

The Europa Nursery
P.O. Box 17589
London, E1 4YN
www.europa-nursery.co.uk
Address starting 2006: Woolleigh Cross, Beaford,
Winkleigh, Devon, EX19 8NS.

Fillan's Plants (*Hedychium*)
Tuckermarsh Gardens
Tamar Lane
Bere Alston, PL20 7HN
e-mail: filliansplants@yahoo.co.uk

Fir Tree Farm Nursery
Tresahor
Constantine
Falmouth
Cornwall, TR11 5PL
www.cornwallgardens.com

Hardy Exotics
Gilly Lane
Whitecross
Penzance
Cornwall, TR20 8BZ
www.hardyexotics.co.uk

Jungle Seeds and Gardens (*Hedychium*)
P.O. Box 45
Watlington SPDO
Oxon, OX49 5YR
www.junglegardens.co.uk

Kobakoba
2 High Street
Ashcott
Bridgewater
Somerset, TA7 9LP
www.kobakoba.co.uk

Long Acre Plants (*Roscoea*)
Charlton Musgrove
Somerset, BA9 8EX
www.longacreplants.co.uk

Mulu Nurseries
Longdon Hill
Wickhamford
Evesham, WR11 7RP
www.mulu.co.uk

Oakland Nurseries
147 Melton Road
Burton-on-the-Wolds
Loughborough, LE12 5TQ
www.oaklandnurseries.co.uk

Pan-Global Plants (*Hedychium*)
The Walled Garden
Frampton Court
Frampton-on-Severn GL2 7EU
www.panglobalplants.com

Paul Christian Rare Plants (*Roscoea*)
P.O. Box 468
Wrexham, LL13 9XR
www.rareplants.co.uk

Pine Cottage Plants
1 Fourways
Eggesford
Devon, EX18 7QZ
www.pcplants.co.uk

Urban Jungle
The Nurseries
Ringland Lane
Old Costessey
Norwich, NR8 5BG
www.urbanjungle.co.uk

United States

Aloha Tropicals
P.O. Box 6042
Oceanside, California 92052
http://alohatropicals.com

Gainesville Tree Farm
Adams Eden Nursery
15321 North State Road 121
Gainesville, Florida 32653
Tel: (904) 418-0484

Gingerwood Nursery
5855 Bayou Paul Road
St. Gabriel, Louisiana 70776
www.gingerwoodnursery.com

Glasshouse Works
Church Street
P.O. Box 97
Stewart, Ohio 45778
www.glasshouseworks.com

Harmony Gardens
5528 Aragon Avenue
DeLeon Springs, Florida 32130
www.harmonygardens.org

Natural Selections Exotics
1401 SW 1st Avenue
Fort Lauderdale, Florida 33315
http://naturalselections.safeshopper.com/

Plant Delights Nursery
9241 Sauls Road
Raleigh, North Carolina 27603
www.plantdelights.com

Plantation Gardens (Tai *Hedychium* hybrids)
112 Doris Drive
Goldsboro, North Carolina 27534
www.rose.net/~jimeds/gingers.htm

Skychild Tropicals
1371 Fayetteville Drive
Spring Hill, Florida 34609
www.skychildtropicals.com

Stokes Tropicals
4806 East Old Spanish Trail
Jeanerette, Louisiana 70544
www.stokestropicals.com

Tropical Paradise Nursery
5060 SW 76th Avenue
Fort Lauderdale, Florida 33328
www.tropicalparadisegarden.com

Appendix 3

On-line Ginger Discussion Groups

At the time of writing, two on-line ginger discussion groups are known.

1. Ginger Forum

http://forums.gardenweb.com/forums/ginger
"This forum is for the discussion of tropical gingers, plants of the family Zingiberaceae". Many major growers, breeders, and enthusiasts contribute to this lively and informative forum.

2. Zingeberales (sic)

http://groups.yahoo.com/group/zingeberales
"Ginger and ginger-related plants. Costus, kaempferias, heliconias, bananas, globba, hedychiums, curcumas, and more. A great world of tropical and subtropical interesting blooming plants that are a great addition to almost every garden. A landscape application available with every plant". A Yahoo! mailing list.

Bibliography

Arnold, T. H., and B. C. De Wet, eds. 1993. Plants of southern Africa: Names and distribution. *Memoirs of the Botanical Survey of South Africa* 62. Pretoria: National Botanical Institute.

ASEAN Regional Centre for Biodiversity Conservation. 2004. *Checklist of Medicinal Plants in Southeast Asia.* http:www.arcbc.org/arbcweb/medicinal_plants/default.htm (accessed 14 February 2004).

Baker, J. G. 1892. Scitaminaceae. *Flora of British India* 6: 198–264.

Baker, W. J. 1994. Three men and an orchid. *Bulletin of the Alpine Garden Society of Great Britain* 62 (1): 99–114; 62 (2): 181–199.

Branney, T. 2002. More than a hint of ginger. *The Garden* 127 (9): 718–723.

Carr, G. 2003. *Zingiberaceae. Vascular Plant Families.* University of Hawaii Botany Department. http://www.botany.hawaii.edu/faculty/carr/zingiber.htm (accessed 20 October 2003).

Cousens, R. 2001. Sorting *Curcuma* names. *Multilingual Multiscript Plant Names Database.* University of Melbourne. http://gmr.landfood.unimelb.edu.au/Plantnames/Sorting/Curcuma.html (accessed 12 December 2003).

Cowley, E. J. 1980. A new species of *Roscoea* (*Zingiberaceae*) from Nepal. *Kew Bulletin* 34 (4): 811–812.

Cowley, E. J. 1982. A revision of *Roscoea* (*Zingiberaceae*). *Kew Bulletin* 36 (4): 766–768.

Cowley, E. J. 1997. *Roscoea alpina* (*Zingiberaceae*). *Kew Bulletin* 14 (1): 77–81.

Cowley, E. J., and W. Baker. 1994. *Roscoea purpurea* 'Red Gurkha' (*Zingiberaceae*). *Kew Bulletin* 11 (3): 104–109.

Cowley, E. J., and W. Baker. 1996. *Roscoea ganshenensis* (*Zingiberaceae*). *Kew Bulletin* 13 (1): 8–13.

Cowley, E. J., and R. Wilford. 1998. *Roscoea capitata* (*Zingiberaceae*). *Kew Bulletin* 15 (2): 226–230.

Cowley, E. J., and R. Wilford. 2000. *Roscoea humeana* (*Zingiberaceae*). *Kew Bulletin* 17 (1): 22–28.

Dharmananda, S. 1999. *Turmeric: What's in a Herb Name? How Turmeric (Jianghuang) and Curcuma (Yujin) Became Confused.* http://www.itmonline.org/arts/turmeri3.htm (accessed 08 November 2003).

Dixit, V. K., and K. C. Varma. 1979. Effect of essential oils of rhizomes of *Hedychium coronarium* and *Hedychium spicatum* on the central nervous system. *Indian Journal of Pharmacology* 2 (2): 147–149.

Dole, J. M., and H. F. Wilkins. 1999. *Floriculture Principles and Species.* Upper Saddle River, New Jersey: Prentice Hall.

Domrachev, M., et al. 2003. NCBI *Taxonomy Browser (Zingiberales).* http://www.ncbi.nlm.nih.gov/Taxonomy/Browser/wwwtax.cgi?id=4618 (accessed 16 January 2004).

Driscoll, M. J. 2001. Jocoseria Arna-Marianiana: Seksogtyve udvalgte dels kortvillige, dels alvorlige Historier, hvorved Mariane Overgaard kan opbygges. Copenhagen. (English translation at http://www.hum.ku.dk/ami/ginger.html).

Felter, H. W., and J. U. Lloyd. 1891. *King's American Dispensatory*. 2 vols. 18th ed. 3rd rev. Cincinnati, Ohio: Ohio Valley Company.

Gagnepain, F. 1908. *Zingiberaceae*. In P. H. Lecomte, *Flore Generale de l'Indochina* 6: 22–121.

Gay, L. 2001. Gay's gingers. *Stephen F. Austin State University Mast Arboretum*. http://arboretum.sfasu.edu/gaylilies/index.htm (accessed 14 November 2003).

Grieve, M. 1995–2003. Turmeric—herb profile and information. *Botanical.com—A Modern Herbal*. http://botanical.com.botanical/mgmh/t/turmer30.html (accessed 17 February 2004).

Hara, H., L. H. J. Williams, and W. T. Stearns. 1978. *An Enumeration of the Flowering Plants of Nepal*. Vol. 1. London: British Museum (Natural History).

Hayward, K. 1999. *Gingers: The Zingiberaceae Collection of Keith Hayward Farnborough, Hampshire, England*. http://www.farnborough.u-net.com/ginger (accessed 02 January 2004).

Jackson, W. P. U. 1990. *Origins and Meanings of Names of South African Plant Genera*. Capetown: University of Capetown Ecolab.

Jaramillo, M. A., and W. J. Kress. 1997. Phylogenetic relationships of the genera of the family *Costaceae*. *Bulletin of the Heliconia Society* 9 (1/2): 5–8.

Katzer, G. 1998. *Gernot Katzer's Spice Pages*. http://www-ang.kfunigraz.ac.at/~katzer/engl (accessed 11 October 2003).

Kingdon-Ward, F. 1960. *Pilgrimage for Plants*. London: George G. Harrap and Company.

Kress, W. J. 1990. The phynology and classification of the *Zingiberales*. *American Journal of Botany* 77: 698–721.

Kress, W. J., L. M. Prince, and K. J. Williams. 2002. The phylogeny and a new classification of the gingers (*Zingiberaceae*): Evidence from molecular data. *American Journal of Botany* 89 (10): 1682–1696.

Lancaster, R. L. 1993. *Travels in China*. Woodbridge, United Kingdom: Antique Collectors' Club.

Larsen, K. 1964. Studies in *Zingiberaceae* IV. *Caulokaempferia*, a new genus. *Botanik Tidsskrifter* 60: 165–179.

Larsen, K. 1980. Annotated key to the genera of *Zingiberaceae* of Thailand. *Natural History Bulletin of the Siam Society* 28: 151–169.

Larsen, K. 1998. *Costaceae*. In K. Kubitzky, ed., *Families and Genera of Vascular Plants* 4: 128–132. Berlin: Springer Verlag.

Larsen, K. 2003. Three new species of *Caulokaempferia* (*Zingiberaceae*) from Thailand with a discussion of the generic diversity. *Nordic Journal of Botany* 22: 409–417.

Larsen, K., H. Ibrahim, S. H. Khaw, and L. G. Saw. 1999. *Gingers of Peninsular Malaysia and Singapore*. Kota Kinabalu, Malaysia: Natural History Publications.

Larsen, K., J. M. Lock, H. Maas, and P. J. M. Maas. 1998. *Zingiberaceae*. In K. Kubitzki, ed., *Families and Genera of Vascular Plants* 4: 474–495. Berlin: Springer Verlag.

Larsen, K., and J. Mood. 1997. *Cornukaempferia*, a new genus of *Zingiberaceae* from Thailand. Natural *History Bulletin of Siam Society* 45: 217–221.

Larsen, K., and J. Mood. 1999. New to cultivation: The genus *Cornukaempferia* in Thailand with description of a second species. *The New Plantsman* 6 (4): 196–205.

Lekawatana, S., and O. Pituck. 1998. New floracultural crops in Thailand. *Acta Horticulture* (ISHS) 454: 59–64.

Mangaly, J., and M. Sabu. 1993. A taxonomic revision of the South Indian species of *Curcuma* Linn. (*Zingiberaceae*). *Rheedea* 3 (2): 139–171.

Maas, P. J. M. 1972. *Costoideae* (*Zingiberaceae*). Monograph No. 8, *Organisation for Flora Neotropica* (New York Botanical Garden). New York: Hafner Press.

Maas, P. J. M. 1977. *Renealmia* (*Zingiberaceae-Zingiberoideae*). Monograph No. 18, *Organisation for Flora Neotropica* (New York Botanical Garden). New York: Hafner Press.

Maas, P. J. M. 1979. Notes on Asiatic and Australian *Costoidae*. *Blumea* 25: 543–549.

Mood, J., and K. Larsen. 2001. New curcumas from Southeast Asia. *The New Plantsman* 8: 207–217.

Nagano, T., Y. Oyama, N. Kajita, L. Chikahisa, M. Nakata, E. Okazaki, and T. Masuda. 1997. New curcuminoids isolated from *Zingiber cassumunar* protect cells suffering from oxidative stress: A flow-cytometric study using rat thymocytes and H_2O_2. *Japanese Journal of Pharmacology* 75 (4): 363–370.

Naik, V. N., and G. Panigrahi. 1961. Genus *Hedychium* in Eastern India. *Bulletin of the Botanical Survey of India* 3 (1): 67–73.

Newman, M., and M. Pullen. 2001. *Zingiberaceae Resource Centre.* http://193.62.154.38/ZRC/home.html (accessed 01 February 2003).

Nichols, G. 1989. Some notes on the cultivation of Natal ginger (*Siphonochilus aethiopicus*). *Veld and Flora* 75 (3): 92–93.

Paterson, A. 1975. Ginger up your garden. *Amateur Gardening* 92 (4716).

Perry, L. M. 1980. *Medicinal Plants of East and Southeast Asia: Attributed Properties and Uses.* London: MIT Press.

Poulsen, A. D., and J. M. Lock. 1997. New species and new records of *Zingiberaceae* and *Costaceae* from tropical East Africa. *Kew Bulletin* 52: 601–616.

Reveal, J. L. 1998. *Selected Families of Angiosperms: Zingiberidae.* http://www.inform.umd.edu/PBIO/pb450/zing02.html (accessed 16 September 2003).

Roscoe, W. 1828. *Monandrian Plants of the Order Scitaminaceae*, with 112 hand coloured plates. Liverpool.

Schilling, T. 1982. A survey of cultivated Himalayan and Sino-Himalayan *Hedychium* species. *The Plantsman* 4: 129–149.

Schilling, T. 1984. More on hedychiums. *The Plantsman* 5: 255–256.

Schilling, T. 1994. Further notes on Himalayan and Sino-Himalayan *Hedychium* species. *The New Plantsman* 1: 114–116.

Schumann, K. 1904. Monograph of the genus *Hedychium*. *Engler's Das Pflanzenreich*, Heft 20: 4; 46: 40–59.

Scoggins, J. 2002. *Exciting New Hedychium Hybrids.* http://home.rose.net/~jimeds/hybrids.htm (accessed 10 September 2002).

Searle, R. J. 1999. A new combination and new synonymy in *Kaempferia* (*Zingiberaceae*: *Hedychieae*). *Telopea* 8 (3): 375.

Sirirugsa, P. 1999. Thai *Zingiberaceae*: Species diversity and their uses. *Pure and Applied Chemistry* 70 (11): 2111–2119.

Sirirugsa, P., and K. Larsen. 1995. The genus *Hedychium* (*Zingiberaceae*) in Thailand. *Nordic Journal of Botany* 15: 301–304.

Sirirugsa, P., and M. Newman. 2000. A new species of *Curcuma* L. (*Zingiberaceae*) from SE Asia. *The New Plantsman* 7 (4): 196–199.

Skinner, D. 1997. *Le Jardin Ombragé*. http://www.nettally.com/skinnerd/ombrage.html (accessed 01 February 2003).

Specht, C. D. 2003. Research: Systematics and Evolution of *Costaceae. American Museum of Natural History*. http://research.amnh.org/users/chelsea (accessed 03 January 2004).

Specht, C. D., W. J. Kress, D. W. Stevenson, and R. DeSalle. 2001. A molecular phylogeny of *Costaceae* (*Zingiberales*). *Molecular Phylogenetics and Evolution* 21 (3): 333–345.

Spencer-Mills, L. 1996. Glorious *Hedychium. The Garden* 121 (12).

Van Wyk, B., B. Van Outdshoorn, and N. Gerike. 1997. *Medicinal Plants of South Africa*. Pretoria: Briza Publications.

Wallich, N. 1853. Initiatory attempt to define the species of *Hedychium* and settle their synonymy. *Hooker's Journal of Botany* 5.

Williams, K. J., W. J. Kress, and P. S. Manos. 2004. The phylogeny, evolution, and classification of the genus *Globba* and tribe *Globbaceae* (*Zingiberaceae*): Appendages do matter. *American Journal of Botany* 91: 100–114.

Wu, D., and K. Larsen. 2000. *Zingiberaceae*. In Z. Y. Wu and P. H. Raven, eds., *Flora of China* 24: 322–377. Beijing: Science Press; St. Louis: Missouri Botanical Garden Press.

Yang, Jeng, and Jenn Wang. 1998. In S. T. Chiu and C.-I. Peng, eds., *Proceedings of the Cross-Strait Symposium on Floristic Diversity and Conservation*, 183–197. Taichung: National Museum of Natural Science.

Index

Lightning Source UK Ltd.
Milton Keynes UK
UKOW041556031211

183086UK00002B/162/P